The American Constitution and Ayn Rand's "Inner Contradiction"

Henry Mark Holzer

A **Madison Press** Book
Highlands Ranch, Colorado

The American Constitution and Ayn Rand's "Inner Contradiction"

A Madison Press book

First Edition

Manufactured in the United States of America

ISBN 9781475237887

About the Author

Henry Mark Holzer received his B.A. degree from New York University, where he studied Russian and political science.

After graduation, he served in Korea with United States Army intelligence, holding top secret security clearance, and was Chief Order of Battle Analyst (Chinese Communist Forces) at Eighth Army Headquarters in Seoul.

Following Holzer's military service, he earned his Juris Doctor degree at New York University School of Law. Since December 7, 1959, he has practiced constitutional and appellate law. (His clients have included owners of pre-legalized gold, veterans seeking medical benefits, Soviet dissidents and defectors, and the author Ayn Rand.)

In addition to Holzer's law practice, for over two decades (1972–1993) he was a full-time tenured professor of law at Brooklyn Law School, where he is now professor emeritus. Professor Holzer's courses included Constitutional Law, First Amendment, National Security, Jurisprudence, and Appellate Advocacy.

Professor Holzer is the author of approximately three hundred articles, essays, and reviews. He frequently publishes commentary on current legal and political issues in print and electronic media. He has often been invited to provide his commentary on, and be interviewed by, broadcast media.

Several of Professor Holzer's out-of-print books—*The Gold Clause: Government's Money Monopoly; Sweet Land of Liberty? The Supreme Court and Individual Rights; The Layman's Guide to Tax Evasion; Speaking Freely: The Case*

Against Speech Codes; and Why Not Call It Treason? Korea, Vietnam, Afghanistan and Today—are available from various Internet booksellers, including Amazon.

With his wife, lawyer and novelist Erika Holzer, Professor Holzer is co-author of *Aid and Comfort*: *Jane Fonda in North Vietnam*, a book that definitively answers the question of whether Fonda's trip to Hanoi during the Vietnam War, and her activities there, constituted constitutional treason. With Erika Holzer, Professor Holzer also co-authored *Fake Warriors*: *Identifying, Exposing, and Punishing Those Who Falsify Their Military Service*. These two books are also available at Amazon

Professor Holzer's judicial biography, *The Supreme Court Opinions of Justice Clarence Thomas, 1991–2006: A Conservative's Perspective*, was published in January 2007 by McFarland & Company, a noted publisher of scholarly, reference, and academic books. The second edition, covering the years 1991–2011, was published by McFarland in 2012.

Professor Holzer's website is www.henrymarkholzer.com; he blogs at www.henrymarkholzer.blogspot.com; and can be contacted by e-mail at hank@henrymarkholzer.com.

Other Books by the Author

Best Opinions of the United States Supreme Court (Vol. I: Race) (eBook edition.).

The Supreme Court Opinions of Clarence Thomas, 1991–2011 (2d ed.)

The Supreme Court Opinions of Clarence Thomas, 1991–2006

The Keeper of the Flame

Aid and Comfort: Jane Fonda in North Vietnam (with Erika Holzer)

Fake Warriors: Identifying, Exposing, and Punishing Those Who Falsify Their Military Service (with Erika Holzer)

Why Not Call It Treason? Korea, Vietnam, Afghanistan and Today

The Layman's Guide to Tax Evasion

Speaking Freely: The Case Against Speech Codes (ed.)

Sweet Land of Liberty? The Supreme Court and Individual Rights

Government's Money Monopoly: Its origin and scope and how to fight It (ed.)

The Gold Clause: What it is and how to use it profitably (ed.)

To those who continue the good fight,
despite facing considerable apathy,
inexcusable stupidity, and
sometimes even evil.

Acknowledgments

Ayn Rand is best known for her four novels: *We the Living, Anthem, The Fountainhead,* and her magnum opus, *Atlas Shrugged.* Her brilliant *nonfiction*, however, contains essays ranging across a broad spectrum of thought, among them ethics and political philosophy. From my perspective as a constitutional lawyer, no American political philosopher has written more illuminating essays than Rand's "Man's Rights," "Collectivized Rights," and "The Nature of Government."

Ayn Rand was a friend and client of the Holzers, and we were fortunate to have spent many hours in her company. Apart from conducting legal business, much of our time together was spent discussing political philosophy in general, and constitutional law in particular. Ayn Rand's influence on my thinking is evident in this book, and I thank her for it.

I have practiced constitutional law from my admission to the New York bar in 1959 to the present. From 1972 to 1992, I not only practiced constitutional law, I also taught that subject and related courses at Brooklyn Law School. It was in the crucible of those countless hours of intellectual engagement in Socratic dialogue with students that my own constitutional jurisprudence crystallized. I am indebted to many of them, especially to those who disagreed with me. I may have been the hammer, but they were the (mostly) willing anvil.

Erika Holzer, lawyer and writer (www.erikaholzer.com), has made a major contribution to *The American Constitution and Ayn Rand's "Inner Contradiction,"* as she has done with my previous books.

Rita Samols (jejeune@mail.com) has made a substantial contribution to the clarity of this book, written by a lawyer and former law professor who sometimes suffers from the assumption that laypersons know the jargon and context of our profession. Rita is the perfect intelligent lay reader, possessing a keen sense for objective meaning and a deft ability to make necessary corrections. Without reservation, I strongly recommend her general and copy editing skills to all authors unwilling to accept anything less than a manuscript of which they can be proud.

Judith Sansweet (www.proofreadnz.co.nz and www.santele-publishing.com) put the text through the final fires of professional proofreading as she polished and formatted the manuscript for digital publishing as a paperback book on Amazon. Her thoughtful reading also caused me to take another look at the book's title and rename it. On a more personal note, like Rita Samols, Judith was a pleasure to work with in the always delicate matter of editing an author's writing.

Val Edward Simone (www.morningsidepublishing.com) is not merely an e-book maven; he is also a fellow author who generously initiated me into the wonders of this new form of publishing. I am especially grateful, because his tutelage has made it possible for *The American Constitution and Ayn Rand's "Inner Contradiction"* to be published much faster than through conventional means, to a far greater readership, and well in advance of the forthcoming presidential election.

Introduction

I've written this book for two reasons. First, to provide patriotic Americans with an overview of the Constitution's most important provisions as interpreted by the Supreme Court of the United States.[1] At the same time, I want to demonstrate something unknown to virtually all Americans: that foundational to every political, social, economic, and legal system are ethical principles; and that from our nation's earliest days to the present there has been an ethical leitmotif running through the Court's most important decisions affecting individual rights and limited government. Not all their decisions, but many—and some of the most important ones.

As to that leitmotif, that recurring theme, a short version of my personal journey to its discovery will be useful.

In law school, I studied English common law and its influence on the American legal system. What I learned was a revelation. I came to realize that from the days of the common law to my days in law school in the late 1950s, the principles of individual rights and limited government had consistently been sacrificed to what was perceived as "the common good." I learned, as we shall see in Chapter 1, that the ink was barely dry on the Bill of Rights when the new federal government began to violate individual rights and renege on the constitutional promise of limited government. (The states had done so even before the Bill of Rights was enacted.)

In almost every law school course (especially Constitutional Law) dealing with the power of the government and its delicate (and usually adverse) relationship to individuals (especially constitutional law,[2]), it quickly became apparent to me that much of the blame for violating those rights and repudiating that promise fell on state and federal courts in general and the Supreme Court of the United States in particular—the latter, ironically, the supposed guardian of the Constitution.

The problem wasn't with any particular court at any particular time, or even with whether particular judges were "liberals" or "conservatives." The problem was that the state and federal judiciaries consistently upheld the constitutionality of laws enacted by legislatures and approved by executive branches that violated the principles of individual rights and limited government.

From the time I graduated in 1959 until 1972, I practiced privately, specializing in constitutional law. I represented, among others: defectors fleeing communism for freedom in the West; physicians choking on government over-regulation, who couldn't properly serve their patients; young men resisting the draft and the nightmare of Vietnam; "gold bugs" seeking to protect their assets from government-induced inflation and other schemes to destroy wealth; political candidates struggling against First Amendment-strangling campaign finance laws; publishers defying censorship; asylum-seekers battling the then-INS; homeowners trying to preserve their neighborhoods from do-gooder housing-integration federal judges; and students on the wrong end of affirmative action programs.

In general, I represented constitutionalists challenging, and defending themselves against, the explosion of government power that violated the principles of individual rights and limited government.

In 1972, while continuing my full-time law practice, I became a full-time law professor.

For many of those years of practicing, teaching, and writing, a recurring question bedeviled me: *What had subverted America's founding principles of individual rights and their necessary corollary, limited government?*

I found the answer to that question—and the leitmotif of this book—in an eight-word sentence written by the late Ayn Rand: ***"America's 'inner contradiction' was the altruist-collectivist ethics."*** [3]

TABLE OF CONTENTS

1

Expanded Table of Contents

1. Formation of the American Republic

2. The American Constitutional System: Judicial Review, Federalism, Separation of Powers

Marbury v. Madison, where Chief Justice John Marshall established the principle of judicial review, and the Supreme Court of the United States came to be the Constitution's final arbiter and the "more equal" branch of government

"Originalism" and other methods of constitutional interpretation: pragmatic and otherwise

The "Living Constitution"

Federalism: The relationship and tensions between the federal and state governments, showing federal legislation affecting matters that should be within the Tenth Amendment powers of the states. How the Court thwarted Arkansas voters, and how the Court's conservatives thwarted Congress in the Brady Law gun case of *Printz* v. *United States.*

Separation of powers: The relationship and tensions between the three supposedly co-equal branches of government—legislative, executive and judicial—showing how the "more equal" Supreme Court refereed battles between the president and Congress and, in the bargain, expanded its own powers. For example, President Truman's seizure of the steel mills during the Korean War, and the House of Representatives' refusal to seat a playboy congressman.

Griswold v. *Connecticut*, illustrating ignored federalism, violation of separation of powers, and run-amok judicial review

United States senator's attempt to prevent the U.S. from becoming just another "state" on a planet with no individual countries, and the Supreme Court's "reassurance" that treaties and the dangerous "executive agreements" don't override domestic United States law

The president, as commander-in-chief, is undercut by the Supreme Court in its four twenty-first-century terrorism cases. These have nearly emasculated his war-fighting powers by treating al-Qaeda terrorists like common criminals, granting them constitutional rights in defiance of controlling precedent and remaking the judiciary into America's ultimate generalissimo.

5. The Judiciary and Its Powers

The source, nature, and scope of judicial power, as provided in the Constitution and federal statutes

Limitations, if any, on judicial power. For example, are courts able to render opinions that are only advisory; may they simply decide not to decide; are there questions too "political" to be decided; can just anyone sue; and what do tomatoes have to do with the federal judicial power?

6. Intergovernmental Relations

The "horizontal" relationship between the states
State compacts

The requirement of "full faith and credit" in our constitutional system of "joint sovereignty"

Extradition

Constitutional Limitations on Congressional Power

Textual limitations on the power of Congress, including suspension of the writ of *habeas corpus* to which alien terrorists, now captured on the field of battle, are apparently entitled.

Constitutional Limitations on the Power of the States

The few textual constitutional limitations on the power of the states, including the prohibition against impairment of contracts—which didn't prevent the Supreme Court from upholding the Minnesota Mortgage Death Act in the heyday of the New Deal.

Racially restrictive realty covenants

7. Prohibitions on Congress and the States: The Bill of Rights and the Fourteenth Amendment

Introduction to the Bill of Rights

By what trick of judicial legerdemain did the Bill of Rights—of which the First Amendment begins: "*Congress shall make no law...*"—come to limit the powers reserved to the states under the Tenth Amendment?

The "Incorporation Doctrine"

The myth of "Substantive" Due Process, and its impact on laundresses, anarchists, killers; and also on contraception and abortion.

8. The First Amendment

Religion. Who's correct about "establishment of religion," the Founders, or the ACLU and the Supreme Court? And to know whether the "free exercise" of religion is really free, ask the Mormons.

Speech. Of the various categories of speech—political, obscene, threatening, commercial, symbolic, employee, defamatory, and indecent—which are more, and which less, protected— and why? What about subversive advocacy, and political campaigns?

9. The Eighth Amendment

Cruel *and* Unusual Punishment, including why drawing and quartering is no longer acceptable but vegetarian meals for murderous prisoners might be required.

10. Equal Protection of the Law

The Emancipation Proclamation to the Fifteenth Amendment, including various Civil Rights Acts

Racial discrimination, white juries, and interracial marriages

The racism euphemistically called "affirmative action"

Racial segregation, including *Brown* v. *Board of Education* (I), desegregation with "all deliberate speed," and the dozen-year school desegregation case

Does desegregating a school mean that it must then be forcibly integrated?

Conclusion

Notes

Foreword

The dominant ethics of mankind's history were variants of the altruist-collectivist doctrine which subordinated the individual to some higher authority, either mystical or social. Consequently, most political systems were variants of the same statist tyranny, differing only in degree, not in basic principle, limited only by the accidents of tradition, of chaos, of bloody strife, and periodic collapse. Under all such systems, morality was a code applicable to the individual, but not to society. Society was placed *outside* the moral law, as its embodiment or source or exclusive interpreter— and the inculcation of self-sacrificial devotion to social duty was regarded as the main purpose of ethics in man's earthly existence

Since there is no such entity as "society"—as society is only a number of individual men—this meant, in practice, that the rulers of society were exempt from moral law; subject only to traditional rituals, they held total power and extracted blind obedience—on the implicit principle of: "The good is that which is good for society (or for the tribe, the race, the nation), and the ruler's edicts are its voice on earth."

This was true of all statist systems, under all variants of the altruist-collectivist ethics, mystical or social. "The Divine Right of Kings" summarizes the political theory of the first— "*vox populi vox dei*" of the second. As witness: the theocracy of Egypt, with the Pharaoh as an embodied god—the unlimited majority rule or *democracy* of Athens—the welfare state run by the Emperors of Rome—the Inquisition of the late Middle Ages—the absolute monarchy of France—the welfare state of Bismark's Prussia—the gas chambers of Nazi Germany—and the slaughterhouse of the Soviet Union. (Ayn Rand, "Man's Rights," *The Virtue of Selfishness*, 123.)

Preface

Like many other Americans, for years I've been deeply concerned about our nation's future. My fears have been exacerbated in the past three years because of the often lawless, anti-American, recklessly incompetent reign of Barack Obama. Worse, his presidency will continue for another year. Even worse, he might be reelected.

In light of that possibility, consider a recent report in *The Weekly Standard* of a survey commissioned by the American Revolution Center, which found that nearly 83 percent of Americans failed a simple test of knowledge about the founding of the United States of America.

Many of our fellow citizens believe that the founding principles of this nation are passé, that the Declaration of Independence's ringing endorsement of republican institutions,[4] individual rights[5] and limited government[6] is outdated, that the Constitution's creation of a representative republic belongs to a time gone by, and that the Bill of Rights is not a restraint on government but rather a source of newly found, invented "rights."

Along with this woeful ignorance, and largely because of it, the Constitution of the United States of America and the Bill of Rights—rooted in republican institutions, individual rights, and limited government—are under an unprecedented attack by Barack Obama and his far left Democratic Party, aided and abetted by the complicit mainstream media, unions, academia, and entertainment industry . . . to say nothing of many courts, including the Supreme Court of the United States in more than a few cases.

Employing and legitimizing the exercise of statist power, the Supreme Court of the United States has facilitated state legislatures and Congress in their sacrifice of individual rights to the common good, and made a mockery of the Founders' creation of a limited government.

But, with a few notable exceptions, there is hardly any knowledgeable, explicit and principled defense of our Constitution and Bill of Rights to be found anywhere.

Not on radio, television, nor in Hollywood. Not in the press. Not at the grassroots. Certainly not in academia, nor, sadly, emanating from many Republicans, Conservatives, and Libertarians. Most of the media's pontificating so-called constitutional experts—especially those on national television—usually do more harm than good because they spread disinformation that is neither knowledgeable nor principled. And note, for example, the Republican presidential candidates' pitiful and embarrassing "debates."

While many Tea Party activists and other patriots have been valiantly fighting for core constitutional values, many of them are disarmed because they've been taught little about American constitutional law. In order to defend the Constitution and the Bill of Rights, everyone fighting for America today needs to know much more about these two documents than most of them do.

Those who are committed to fighting for America's future are obligated to acquire at least a basic understanding of the Constitution's origins and birth, its written text, the manner in which it has been deliberately violated, and the consequences of how it has been deliberately misinterpreted by its enemies.

Because of the importance of our struggle, about eighteen months ago I put aside most of my writing and legal work to offer a twenty-hour, ten-lecture Internet course on American constitutional law.[7] (Those unfamiliar with my credentials and my commentaries on legal and political issues can peruse my blog at www.henrymarkholzer.blogspot.com, and my website, www.henrymarkholzer.com)

The Internet course was successful, but some of the listeners expressed disappointment that the lectures weren't available in a permanent text form.

They are now.

The entire twenty hours of lectures have been transcribed, and I have edited them for a less extemporaneous, more polished presentation, and added new material.

The result of my labors is this book: *The American Constitution and Ayn Rand's "Inner Contradiction"* published by Madison Press.

Because my goal is to maximize readership—especially during the months before the November 2012 election—*The American Constitution and Ayn Rand's "Inner Contradiction"* is priced at a low point. It is also now available on most digital readers, including Amazon's Kindle.

If you find *The American Constitution and Ayn Rand's "Inner Contradiction"* worthwhile, I have two requests. One is that you inform everyone you know about this project, and ask them to do the same. This goes double for all Tea Partiers, because most of them have their own lists containing the names of like-minded folks. Second, please write a positive review on Amazon and as many other places as possible.

1.
Formation of the American Republic

Most people think that "altruism" means nothing more than being nice to people. Contributing to Haitian relief, or medical research. Helping the poor, supporting the arts.

But the meaning of altruism in an ethical/political context is significantly different. *Webster's New World Dictionary of the American Language* defines altruism as "the doctrine that the general welfare of society[8] is the proper goal of an individual's action"[9]—the antithesis of acting in pursuit of one's own interests. Others, anyone, everyone—before myself.

Ayn Rand defined altruism in this context more fully: "the ethical theory which regards man as a sacrificial animal, which holds that man has no right to exist for his own sake, that service to others is the only justification of his existence, and that self-sacrifice is his highest moral duty, virtue and value."[10] She elaborated:

> Do not hide behind such superficialities as whether you should or should not give a dime to a beggar. That is not the issue. The issue is whether you *do* or do *not* have the right to exist *without* giving him that dime. The issue is whether you must continue buying your life, dime by dime, from any beggar who might choose to approach you. *The issue is whether the need of others* ["society"?] *is the first mortgage on your life and the moral purpose of your existence.*[11] (Emphasis in original.)

Think slavery. Think the draft.

15

Because altruism, properly defined, has been pervasively institutionalized throughout this nation's political/legal system, especially by the Supreme Court of the United States, the consequences for individual rights and limited government have been devastating, as we shall see.

Closely related to altruism is the concept of *collectivism*.

Contrary to popular belief, *collectivism* has nothing to do with people sharing common interests voluntarily coming together, as in a bowling league. On the contrary, and antithetical to the principles of individual rights and limited government, collectivism means "that the individual has no rights, that his life and work belong to the group (to 'society,' to the tribe, the state, the nation), and that the group may sacrifice him at its own whim to its own interests."[12] It means

> . . . the subjugation of the individual to a group— whether to a race, class or state does not matter. Collectivism holds that man must be chained to collective action and collective thought for the sake of what is called the 'common good.'[13]

Think slavery. Think the draft.

Regarding that 'common good,' as I discuss one Supreme Court case after another it will be obvious to the reader that this criterion has been used as the principal justification for courts to approve unconstitutional laws made by legislatures and, legislating from the bench, even to invent their own laws.

The reader will see in case after case, many of them among the most important ever decided by the Supreme Court, elements of altruism-collectivism—meaning sacrifice of the individual for the collective's 'common good'—as you witness the Court's destruction of individual rights and violation of the principle of limited government.

16

As to the political aspect of collectivism, in order to enhance the reader's understanding of this book's subject and its theme, there's one more definition I need to include.

Because altruism and collectivism are ethical doctrines, not political/legal ones, the only way to implement them is by brute force, on which the government has a monopoly.

Think local police and the FBI.

Necessarily, altruism and collectivism have a political/legal corollary, *statism*: "the principle or policy of concentrating extensive economic, political, and related controls in the state at the cost of individual liberty."[14] And of limited government.

Think the 2009–2012 Obama Administration.

Rand's "inner contradiction"—these doctrines of altruism, collectivism and statism—have been the leitmotif running through American constitutional law from the beginning.

To understand how this nation has gone from the individual-rights principle of the Declaration of Independence and the Bill of Rights, and the limited-government philosophy of the Constitution, to today's entitlement-ridden, wealth-distributing, egalitarian democracy, it is first necessary to understand the context in which the founding of the United States of America occurred.

In 1492, King Ferdinand and Queen Isabella granted Christopher Columbus a commission to explore the New World and seize it in the name of Spain. He did.

Nearly a century later, the English Crown granted letters patent—sort of a franchise—to Sir Humphrey Gilbert and tasked him with establishing colonies in America. He tried twice. The second time, he died.

Some years later, his half-brother, Walter Raleigh, who had been on both of Gilbert's voyages, received the identical patent. Raleigh launched five expeditions, actually establishing a colony on Roanoke Island, off the coast of present-day North Carolina in 1585.

In 1606, came the first charter of Virginia and 120 settlers. A toehold at Jamestown in 1607 became the first permanent English colony in America. But it was not in any sense a government. Not yet.

Twelve years later, a British governor convened an assembly in Virginia. Although it lacked much power, this assembly can be considered to be the beginning of representative government in America.

In 1620, came the pilgrims, without a royal charter but with their Mayflower Compact, a typical church covenant applied to civil circumstances. Not any kind of a constitution. Not by a long shot.

Nine years later, the survivors of the Mayflower obtained a royal charter for Massachusetts. Dutch colonists received a charter the same year, calling their colony New Netherland.

European nations were sending colonists to the New World to establish footholds in the name of, and for the benefit of, their patron countries.

In the same period, about 1639, colonists from Massachusetts formed enclaves in Connecticut. They promulgated a document called the "Fundamental Orders." These, too, were not a constitution. Like the Mayflower Compact, the Fundamental Orders were in the nature of a church covenant, an agreement without political significance.[15] The Fundamental Orders related man to God in a religious compact, not to a civil government—nothing more, nothing less.

18

Real representative government in the New World came closer with the Massachusetts Declaration of Rights in 1661. It held that the colony of Massachusetts was bound only by laws passed by its own legal representatives, not by the overseas British Parliament.

More colonies sprouted. There were more colonists arriving, more colonies spreading out from the Atlantic coast, more growth in farming and animal husbandry.

Now, let's jump ahead about 100 years, to 1754, and look at some of the political bubbles rising to the surface.

Benjamin Franklin of Philadelphia proposed a plan to ask Parliament to create a central government for the American colonies.

In 1761, James Otis, a lawyer, openly argued in court against the Writs of Assistance, probably the first legal argument for what became the Fourth Amendment of the Bill of Rights. The British tax court, the Court of Exchequer, had issued these writs allowing colonial tax collectors to enter private premises and seize, in money and goods, whatever they thought was owed to the British Crown.

Otis's argument was one of the earliest statements that before Crown officials could search or seize private property they needed a search warrant and, even more importantly, that *a law against natural law is void.*

In 1765, the Stamp Act was passed to raise revenue from the colonies for England. The same year, the Virginia House of Burgesses, led by Patrick Henry, passed a resolution that only *it* had the power to tax Virginians. The protest of Braintree, Massachusetts against the Stamp Act was written by John Adams. In October, at Otis's urging, the Massachusetts House of Representatives organized a meeting of representatives from all the colonies to be held in New York: the Stamp Act Congress. The purpose of this congress was to "consult together on the present circumstances of the colonies." Twenty-eight delegates from nine of the thirteen American colonies showed up.

The Stamp Act Congress told the English monarch, the House of Lords and, for good measure, the House of Commons that only the colonial legislatures could levy taxes on Americans.

The same year, Parliament passed the Quartering Act, permitting the quartering of troops in private homes.[16] In 1768, Massachusetts protested the Quartering Act. The importance of that protest is that it was based on the proposition that the British Parliament could not pass laws *contrary to fundamental law*. The idea was pure John Locke, James Otis, Patrick Henry, and John Adams. This is the concept of natural rights—the explicit premise upon which the foundation of American constitutional law was laid.

It was apparent that the friction between the colonies and the mother country was becoming heated. Concerns over individual rights and limited government (and their corollary, free markets and sovereignty) were in the forefront of many colonists' thinking. The pot was boiling.

Early Americans had gone from settlements to colonial legislatures, from local revenue act protests to the Stamp Act Congress, from acting as individual colonies to small steps toward concerted action.

The concept of natural rights was abroad in the land.

At the end of December 1773, the Boston Tea Party was held.

In reaction, the next year Parliament passed the so-called Intolerable Acts.

The most notorious of these was the Boston Port Act, punishing the colonists for the Boston Tea Party. The Act imposed damages for the ruined tea, payment of which was a condition of reopening the port, an essential commercial lifeline to and from abroad.

Action and reaction.

In May of 1774, eighty-one members of the Virginia House of Burgesses met in Williamsburg. They recommended a meeting of delegates from all the colonies, a "Continental Congress."

In June, Boston's Sam Adams submitted a similar resolution to the Massachusetts House. It was adopted. Among the delegates was Adams himself, the firebrand "father of the American revolution," and his cousin John Adams.

In August, the Virginians met and chose delegates, among them Richard Henry Lee, George Washington, and Patrick Henry. The meeting declared that it was legitimate, *under principles of natural law*, to oppose the lawless acts of General Thomas Gage, Commander of British Forces in North America. That it was lawful to meet Gage's actions with force. In England, this declaration was seen as an act of rebellion, even treason.

The First Continental Congress met in September 1774 in Philadelphia.

This was not the convention that later framed the Constitution of the United States of America, but the seeds of both that document and the Bill of Rights were sown here.

Eventually, fifty-five delegates attended the First Continental Congress, from twelve of the thirteen colonies.[17]
In October, the Congress adopted the "Declaration and

Resolves" of the First Continental Congress. Promulgated some eighteen months before the Declaration of Independence, thirteen years before the Constitution, and seventeen years before the Bill of Rights, the Declaration and Resolves embodied an unambiguous statement of rights and founding principles.

Some quoted excerpts:

That the English Colonists in North America, by the *immutable laws of nature*, the principles of the English constitution, and the several charters or compacts, have the following Rights:

1. That they are entitled to *life, liberty, and property*, & they have never ceded to any sovereign power whatever, a right to dispose of either without their *consent*.

4. That the foundation of English *liberty*, and of all free *government*, is a right in the people to participate in their legislative council. . . .

5. That the respective colonies are entitled to the *common law of England*, and more especially to the great and inestimable privilege of being tried by their peers of the vicinage, according to the course of that law.

8. That they have a right to *peaceably assemble, consider of their grievances*, and *petition the King*; and that all prosecutions, prohibitory proclamations, and commitments for the same, are illegal.

10. It is indispensable to good government, and rendered essential by the English Constitution, that *the constituent branches of the legislature be*

independent of each other; that, therefore, the exercise of legislative power in several colonies, by a council appointed during pleasure, by the crown, is *unconstitutional,* dangerous, and destructive to the freedom of American legislation. (My emphasis.)

Note some of the precursor ideas and words I've emphasized, written some eighteen months before the Declaration of Independence: natural law; entitled; life, liberty, and property; right in the people; free government; common law; assembly, grievances, petition; separation of powers—and perhaps the most important word of all, *unconstitutional,* meaning against foundational principles to be embodied in the Declaration of Independence, Constitution and Bill of Rights yet to come.

The First Continental Congress adjourned in October 1774.[18]

The following month, an Englishman who would later be prominent in the American Revolution arrived in America: Tom Paine.

"On the eighteenth of April, in 'Seventy-five"[19] Paul Revere warned that the British were coming. The next day, at Lexington and Concord, American minutemen fought British redcoats for the first time and—as Ralph Waldo Emerson said in his "Concord Hymn"—embattled farmers "fired the shot heard round the world." Then and there, they lit the fuse for the explosion that would come a year later, changing the world forever.

In May 1775, the Second Continental Congress met in Philadelphia. Massachusetts had already organized its own government in defiance of England. The Second Continental Congress became the *de facto* (i.e., actual) government of the thirteen colonies. The Congress asked the other colonies to help defend Massachusetts. It appointed George Washington commander in chief.

23

In June 1775, the Battle of Bunker Hill was fought.

Washington took command of the Continental Army.

On July 6, 1775, a year before the Declaration of Independence, the Second Continental Congress adopted the "Declaration of the Causes and Necessity of Taking Up Arms," prepared by John Dickinson and Thomas Jefferson.

Action and reaction.

The next month, King George III issued a proclamation of rebellion.

The fuse to an explosive rebellion was burning faster and faster, shorter and shorter.

December 1775, Parliament prohibited trade and intercourse with the colonies in an effort to isolate them. Parliament approved the impressing of American seamen into the British navy.

Early in the transformative year of 1776, an English Quaker published a pamphlet in Philadelphia, converting countless thousands of Americans to the cause of independence. The author of "Common Sense" was English immigrant, Tom Paine.

In May of 1776, Virginia instructed her delegates to the Continental Congress to "declare the United Colonies free and independent states." Other colonies had already done the same. Accordingly, on June 7, Virginian Richard Henry Lee introduced a resolution that "these United Colonies are, and of *right* ought to be, free and independent States, that they are absolved of all allegiance to the British Crown, and that all political connection between them and the state of Great Britain is, and ought to be totally dissolved." (My emphasis.)

Note Lee's use of the word "right," an unmistakable reference to the concept of "natural rights" that so strongly influenced the Founders' thinking.

The relentlessly burning fuse had very nearly reached the powder keg.

On June 10, 1776, a committee was appointed to prepare the Declaration of Independence: Thomas Jefferson, John Adams, Benjamin Franklin, Roger Sherman, and Robert Livingston. Jefferson was the principal draftsman.

Then, on the evening of July 4, 1776, there occurred the most profoundly moral and political explosion in the history of mankind.

The delegates to the Continental Congress adopted the Declaration of Independence of the United States of America. The rights of Americans (some, at least) had been given a dramatic and principled voice.

In the Introduction to the Cato Institute's pocket version of the Declaration of Independence and the Constitution, Dr. Roger Pilon writes that the Constitution of 1787 is illuminated by the principles of the Declaration of Independence. Look in the Declaration of Independence, Pilon urges, for the moral vision and the kind of government it implied. While the ostensible purpose of the Declaration was to make the case for independence, fundamentally it was to set forth a philosophy of individual rights and limited government. Dr. Pilon writes that the Declaration invokes natural law, moral reasoning, and the common-law tradition of liberty, property, and contract, all hallmarks of a free country.

Dr. Pilon is correct, because in one short paragraph, the Declaration of Independence articulated a truly revolutionary view of man and his relation to government.

We hold these truths to be self-evident, that all Men are created equal, that they are endowed by their Creator with certain unalienable Rights; that among these are Life, Liberty, and the Pursuit of Happiness—That to secure these Rights, Governments are instituted among Men, deriving their just Powers from the consent of the Governed . . . .[20]

Jefferson—who would later characterize the Constitution as "a mere thing of wax in the hands of the judiciary, which they may twist and shape into any form they please"[21]— not only spoke in the Declaration of "truths," but also regarded them as "self-evident." He invoked the idea of "equality" (as imperfect as it then was).

The centerpiece of the Declaration was the core moral/political concept of "rights," upon which no system of free government had ever before been founded. Jefferson enumerated three of the basic rights—"life, liberty, and the pursuit of happiness"— from which another basic right, *property*, must be logically inferred. He understood the necessity of protecting those rights through government, but only by a political institution "created" by men, not arising mystically by divine right or raw sovereign power. And, too, that government's powers must be "just," and derived only from "consent" of the governed.

Revolutionary, indeed!

Next, the Declaration's statement of philosophical/ moral/political principles had to be implemented by a charter for the actual organization and operation of a functioning republic.

In November 1777, the Continental Congress approved Articles of Confederation and submitted them to the states for their approval; by July 1778, they were approved by enough states to become effective.

But the Articles of Confederation didn't work. One major problem was the lack of a chief executive. Also, some states had erected trade barriers against other states, a problem later sought to be cured by the Constitution's Commerce Clause (about which, more later). The Articles of Confederation may have solved one problem, but they created a host of others.

After the Revolutionary War, ostensibly to cure the deficiencies in the Articles of Confederation, the Continental Congress approved the convening of a convention in Philadelphia "for the sole and express purpose of revising the Articles of Confederation and reporting to Congress and the several legislatures such alterations and provisions therein, as shall, when agreed to in congress, and approved by the states, render the federal constitution adequate to the exigencies of government and the preservation of the union."

Who were to be the delegates?

As Jefferson would later observe, an assembly of "demigods."

Of the approximately seventy men named by the various state legislatures as delegates to the Constitutional Convention, only about fifty-six attended, and fewer did the real work.

Among the more prominent delegates was George Washington, who led the Virginia delegation. Also from Virginia was Edmund Randolph, thirty-four years old and governor of the state. John Blair was a judge in Virginia's highest court. James Madison, universally regarded as the father of the Constitution, at thirty-six years of age had already served twice in the Continental Congress. George Wyeth, a signer of the Declaration of Independence, had been for ten years chancellor of Virginia. George Mason was author of the Virginia Bill of Rights.

New Jersey sent David Brearley, forty-one years old and chief justice of the state. William Paterson, a member of the Continental Congress, had been attorney general of New Jersey for eleven years and later become a justice of the Supreme Court of the United States. William Livingston was governor of New Jersey. Jonathan Dayton, twenty-seven years old, had served with distinction in the revolution.

Pennsylvania's delegation included James Wilson, forty-five years old, a signer of the Declaration of Independence who had served several times in Congress and would later become a justice of the Supreme Court of the United States. Wilson was considered by Washington to be one of the strongest men at the convention. At the last minute, Pennsylvania's Benjamin Franklin was added as a delegate.

North Carolina's delegation was headed by a former governor, accompanied by two other delegates who were not yet thirty years old.

The most noted member of the Delaware delegation was John Dickinson, chairman of the committee of Congress that had framed the Articles of Confederation.

South Carolina sent John Rutledge, another future Supreme Court justice, who had been a member of Congress and governor of the state. Two Pinckney cousins were lawyers and had served with distinction in the revolution, one as a brigadier general.

Connecticut's Roger Sherman was mayor of New Haven and, at age sixty-six, one of the oldest delegates. He had been a signer of the Declaration of Independence and a member of Congress. Another delegate was Oliver Ellsworth, judge of the Connecticut Supreme Court.

From Maryland came Dr. James McHenry, secretary to Commander in Chief George Washington, member of the state Senate, and Washington's friend and adviser.

Luther Martin was attorney general of New York. Alexander Hamilton, then thirty years old, had been an aide to Washington during the revolution.

These men were a new breed. They were free men. Some had put their names to the treasonable Declaration of Independence. They had branded their sovereign a tyrant. They had fought the British, and some had been captured and held as prisoners of war.

Most important, they had dared what nobody before them ever had. President Abraham Lincoln put it very well a century later: they "brought forth on this continent a new nation, conceived in Liberty and dedicated to the proposition that all men are created equal." Yet the Constitution was not without faults arising from historical influences and contemporary culture, the major one of which, acceptance of slavery, would decades later tear this nation asunder.

Recall that the convention's assignment was to revise the Articles of Confederation. However, on behalf of Virginia, delegate Randolph submitted fifteen proposals as the plan for a brand new form of government. The federal government would consist of three branches—legislative, executive, judicial— whereas under the Articles of Confederation, Congress had all the power. There would be a two-house legislature instead of one, with proportional representation in each.

Naturally, the small states were dissatisfied with the idea of proportional representation in both the House of Representatives and the Senate. Hence, there were compromises. Each state would have two senators, but House membership would be based on population. Money bills would originate in the House. There were other compromises, and flaws—the major constitutional contradictions being slavery and limited suffrage.

But if one considers the essentials of the Constitution—without, for example, provisions such as the Electoral College and organization of the House of Representatives—it is immediately apparent that the document masterfully reduces the very complex machinery of a representative government to its fundamentals.

These fundamentals begin with the Preamble, and it is not without reason that the Constitution's first words are "We the people of the United States." Remember the words of the Declaration of Independence: "Governments are instituted among Men, deriving their just Powers from the consent of the Governed."

It is also not without reason that the stated objectives of that government-in-creation were "to form a more perfect Union, establish Justice, ensure domestic Tranquility, provide for the common defence [*sic*], promote the general Welfare, and secure the Blessings of Liberty to ourselves and our Posterity."

Recall the words of the Declaration of Independence that "all Men are created equal, that they are endowed by their Creator with certain unalienable Rights, that among these are Life, Liberty and the Pursuit of Happiness."

It is obvious that the Declaration of Independence was the inspiration not only for what the Preamble defined as the Constitution's goal, but also for many of the specifics in the Constitution itself.

To accomplish that goal by creating a national government possessing only delegated powers, the Constitution consists of only six articles.

Articles I, II and III—legislative, executive, and judicial—delegate specific, enumerated power to the three branches of the federal government and establish their working machinery.

Article IV expresses, through the principle of federalism, the relationship of the federal government to the states.

Article V provides the process for amending the Constitution (a process that does not include the Supreme Court).

Article VI establishes federal supremacy over the states.

No one can reasonably read the Constitution as accomplishing anything other than creating a federal system, establishing a national government and constituent states, delegating power to the national government, making it supreme in its sphere, and providing the machinery for its amendment.

When the Constitutional Convention finished its work, the Second Continental Congress submitted the proposed Constitution to the states for ratification.

Battle was immediately joined.

The colonists so cherished and jealously guarded their hard-won freedom from England that many of them opposed ratification. They had suffered George III. They had been oppressed by Parliament. They had felt the yoke of centralized, arbitrary power.

Recall that under the Articles of Confederation there was no central government, yet the proposed Constitution had created one—albeit one with only enumerated, delegated powers. But even as intended and written, those powers were far greater than the colonists had ever experienced.

Then, too, was the absence of a Bill of Rights.

Even though nowhere in the Constitution were individual *rights* being *surrendered*, opposition to the Constitution was fierce. Fear of a strong central government coupled with the absence of explicit guarantees of individual rights gave pause to many American patriots—citizens who had fought against England in the name of independence, freedom, individual rights, and limited government.

The ratification period was, many believe, the most intellectually stimulating period in American history. For example, Governor George Clinton of New York (a crucial state in the ratification battle) engaged in a war of letters with Alexander Hamilton. Most of the ablest men in America exchanged countless letters attacking and defending the proposed Constitution.

It was Hamilton, one of the strongest voices in the country for ratification, who soon after the convention conceived the idea for a series of essays analyzing the Constitution systematically in support of its approval by the states.

The essays were *The Federalist.*

For the next seven months, Hamilton and James Madison (assisted at the beginning by John Jay) wrote the most important political commentary in American history. Nothing has ever equaled it.

Close to the end of this Herculean task, Hamilton produced *Federalist* 84, the classic argument not *for* a Bill of Rights, but *against* one. His essay foretells the cleavage in later constitutional thought between proponents and opponents of individual rights and limited government, and implicitly suggests the existence of Ayn Rand's "inner contradiction."

For this reason, and because of *Federalist* 84's considerable impact on ratification of the Constitution, and also because of Madison's later accommodation of Hamilton's argument in the First Congress when the Bill of Rights was introduced, I quote at length the essence of *Federalist* 84:

> It has been several times truly remarked that bills of rights are, in their origin, stipulations between kings and their subjects, abridgments of prerogative in favor of privilege, reservations of rights not surrendered to the prince. Such was Magna Carta obtained by the barons, sword in hand, from King John. * * *22

The barons were subjects of the king, therefore suppliants seeking mere privileges, such as due process of law. Americans were free men and women, entitled to life, liberty and the pursuit of happiness as a matter of right.[23]

> It is evident, therefore, that, according to their primitive signification, they have no application to constitutions, professedly founded upon the power of the people, and executed by their immediate representatives and servants. Here, in strictness, the people surrender nothing [i.e., their rights]; and as they retain every thing [i.e., their rights] they have no need of particular reservations. "We, the People of the United States, to secure the blessings of liberty to ourselves and our posterity, do *ordain* and *establish* this constitution for the United States of America."

> Here is a better recognition of popular rights than volumes of the aphorisms which make the principal figure in several of our State bill of rights, and which

would sound much better in a treatise of ethics than in the constitution of government. (Emphasis in original.)

The Constitution's genesis—unlike monarchical power, supposedly a gift from God to kings and queens, who may or may not grant dispensations such as due process—is in the people, and it is they through that Document who create government.

Then Hamilton, the consummate lawyer, put a spin on his argument, reinforcing it.

I go further, and affirm that bills of rights, in the sense and to the extent in which they are contended for, are not only unnecessary in the proposed Constitution, but would even be dangerous. They would contain various exceptions to powers not granted; and, on this very account, would afford a colorable pretext to claim more than were granted. For why declare that things shall not be done for which there is no power granted to do? Why, for instance, should it be said that the liberty of the press shall not be restrained, when no power is given by which restrictions may be imposed? I will not contend that such a provision would confer a regulating power; but it is evident that it would furnish, to men disposed to usurp, a plausible pretense for claiming that power. They might urge with a semblance of reason, that the Constitution ought not to be charged with the absurdity of providing against the abuse of an authority which was not given, and that the provision against restraining the liberty of the press afforded a clear implication, that a power to prescribe proper regulations concerning it was intended to be vested in the national government."

There are three very telling points in *Federalist* 84.

First, bills of rights were traditionally restrictions on sovereign prerogatives. The restrictions were obtained from a monarch not by free men, but by the monarch's *subjects*. The monarchs concededly possessed all power, except that which they voluntarily relinquished. But in the United States of America, where there was no sovereign, no royal prerogative, no power anywhere except in the people or their chosen representatives, there was no need to reserve from our government, in a Bill of Rights, powers which it never possessed.

Second, since the Constitution did not delegate to the federal government any power to violate the rights of its citizens, a Bill of Rights would make "exceptions to powers not granted." More specifically, since the Constitution had delegated no power to the federal government to abridge free speech, press, or religion, no power to compel self-incrimination or make unreasonable warrantless searches and seizures, no power to violate any of the other rights possessed by a free people, it was unnecessary for a Bill of Rights to expressly prohibit the government from doing so.

And three, it was dangerous.

Because once a specific enumeration of certain rights was provided, as Hamilton correctly observed, what would become the status of other rights that, either deliberately or inadvertently, were not in the enumeration?

Hamilton lost the argument.

Delaware's ratifying convention approved first, 30 unanimous votes.

Pennsylvania's vote was 46 to 23 in favor, after a very hard struggle.

35

New Jersey and Georgia approved unanimously, 38 and 26 votes, respectively.

Connecticut overwhelmingly supported the new Constitution, 128 to 40.

Massachusetts approved, 187 to 168—by 19 votes in a convention with a membership of 355, and recommended the addition of a bill of rights to protect the *states*, not necessarily individuals, from federal encroachment on their liberties.

Maryland approved, 63 to 11.

South Carolina, 149 to 73.

New Hampshire voted 57 to 47 to ratify, and also suggested a bill of rights.

These nine state approvals satisfied the express terms of the Constitution to constitute ratification, but its proponents understood that the new government could not succeed without New York and Virginia as integral parts of it.

In Virginia, the struggle for ratification was led by Edmund Randolph, James Madison, and John Marshall. Washington threw his weight behind ratification, virtually promising that Congress would early address the bill of rights issue. Ratification was finally achieved in June 1788 by 10 votes, 89 to 79. The approval came over the objections of founding giants George Mason and Patrick Henry, who strongly feared the absence of a bill of rights.

New York attempted to attach conditions to its ratification, but failed. Despite Hamilton's efforts and his and Madison's essays, the approval vote on July 26 was close: 30 to 27. As other states had done, New York recommended a bill of rights.

With these two key states having now ratified, the Second Continental Congress, which had been meeting at irregular intervals during the Constitutional Convention and the ratification battle, resolved in September of 1788 to put the new Constitution into operation.

In 1789, North Carolina came aboard, by a vote of 194 to 77.

Rhode Island was the last of the thirteen colonies to ratify, in 1790, 34 to 32.

With a bill of rights imminent, it is useful to step back to 1787, when there already existed a template for provisions that would later surface in the First Congress of the new government.

While the Constitutional Convention drafted the Constitution, the Second Continental Congress was not entirely idle. On July 13, 1787, it had adopted an ordinance for the governance of the Northwest Territory. That vast area was not a state, but the fledgling United States had acquired the Territory during the Revolutionary War and in mid-1887, exercised dominion over it.

The Northwest Ordinance included provisions regarding religious liberty, trial by jury, use of the English common law, bail, cruel or unusual punishments, due process, government interference with private contracts, and slavery and involuntary servitude.

Yet, two months after the Second Continental Congress adopted the Northwest Ordinance—with its groundbreaking provisions institutionalizing the individual rights and limited government that echoed the Declaration of Independence—it rejected, with hardly any consideration at all, a proposal by Oliver Ellsworth, Elbridge Gerry, and George Mason to prepare a bill of rights.

Why?

Because, just as Hamilton would later argue in *Federalist* 84, the Convention delegates were only *delegating enumerated power, not relinquishing rights.* This crucial distinction— between delegating power and relinquishing rights—pervades Madison's and others' reports of the Constitutional Convention and has great significance in constitutional jurisprudence, particularly in the decisions of the Supreme Court, from that day to the present.

But, during the ratification fight, many Americans—the prominent and the average alike—insisted on a bill of rights. It is no surprise that some 124 amendments were proposed by the states.

I now turn to the First Congress of the United States and the Bill of Rights.

James Madison, who having made enormous contributions to the Constitution itself, would now add a colossally impressive achievement to his record. Madison introduced a set of amendments, a bill of rights, at the first session of the new Congress. Later, the Supreme Court would observe that Madison's purpose in submitting the amendments was "to quiet the apprehension of many that without some such declaration of rights, the government would assume and might be held to possess the power to trespass upon those rights of persons and property which by the Declaration of Independence were affirmed to be unalienable rights."[24]

Madison's proposed amendments had been inspired by the Declaration of Independence, influenced by the Northwest Ordinance, culled from suggestions by states' ratifying conventions and their own bills of rights, and informed by the writings of John Locke and Adam Smith.

The heart of Madison's proposals was a ten-clause resolution designed to protect the individual rights of the American people against violation by *Congress*.

I emphasize *Congress* because what became the first nine amendments were not designed to constrain the *states*, and they do not. Note that the first word of the First Amendment is "Congress," which "shall make no law . . . ." Note also that one of Madison's proposed amendments—one that he considered the most valuable of all, but which died in the Senate—*did* prohibit the rights of conscience, speech, press, and jury trial from being violated *by any state*. Madison, and everyone else, knew that without the latter proposed amendment, the Bill of Rights would check only *Congress*, not the states.

This Congress/state distinction regarding violation of individual rights and the principle of limited government is crucial to later constitutional jurisprudence in the Supreme Court of the United States.

But wait! What about Hamilton's *Federalist* 84 argument about the danger of a bill of rights? Hamilton's co-author had been James Madison. Hadn't Madison, before he submitted his proposed bill of rights to the First Congress, read what Hamilton had written in *Federalist* 84? Or, perhaps, he wasn't persuaded by it? To paraphrase Hamilton, "don't make a list of rights because if, for whatever reason you omit one (e.g., the right to bear arms), a plausible argument can be made that it doesn't exist.

Madison had a brilliant answer:

> It has been objected also against a Bill of Rights, that, by *enumerating* particular exceptions to the grant of power, it would *disparage* those rights which were not

39

placed in that *enumeration*; and it might follow, by implication, that those rights which were not singled out, were intended to be assigned into the hands of the General Government, and were consequently insecure. This is one of the most plausible arguments I have ever heard urged against the admission of a bill of rights into the system; but, I conceive, that it may be guarded against. I have attempted it.

His solution reflected his perfect grasp of the problem: how to enumerate, and thus assure, certain rights—speech, press, religion, assembly, reasonable searches and seizures, compulsory process, no self-incrimination, and the rest—without allowing a plausible argument to be made that their enumeration was exhaustive.

The solution was elegantly (and lawyerly) simple. Enumerate *some* rights and, at the same time and in the same place, *expressly reserve all rights not enumerated.* To accomplish this end, he proposed the following amendment:

The exceptions here or elsewhere in the Constitution, made in favor of particular rights, shall not be so construed as to diminish the just importance of other rights retained by the people; or as to enlarge the powers delegated by the Constitution; but [the inclusion of particular rights should be understood] either as actual limitations of such powers or as inserted merely for greater caution.

In other words, a list of *enumerated* rights doesn't mean that there aren't *non-enumerated* rights.

A House Committee on Style foreshortened Madison's proposed amendment into a form that passed the House and Senate with virtually no debate:

The enumeration in the Constitution of certain rights shall not be construed to deny or disparage others, of their rights, retained by the people.

This one sentence is the Ninth Amendment to the Constitution of the United States of America. It has been called, rightly, the "forgotten" Ninth Amendment.

What, then, were those enumerated rights the First Congress was so eager to secure?

The First Amendment guaranteed freedom of religion, speech, press, assembly, and petition.

The Second and Third, derived from experience with the British, protected the right to bear arms and prohibited quartering of soldiers.

The Fourth, Fifth, and Sixth Amendments, except for circumscribing the government's power of eminent domain in the Fifth, provided criminal procedure protections, including due process of law.

The Seventh Amendment guaranteed jury trials in federal civil cases.

The Eighth Amendment protected against excessive bail or fines, and prohibited cruel and unusual punishments.

The Ninth Amendment has already been discussed. It was James Madison's special accomplishment. He had conceived of it as the solution to the problem raised by his federalist co-pamphleteer, Alexander Hamilton. Yet, the Ninth Amendment has never been the deciding factor in any case in any court in America.

This brings us to the Tenth Amendment, which does not deal with *rights* but rather with the recognition of reserved *power*.

In the Tenth Amendment, we find the Constitution's *express* acknowledgment of the reserved powers not just of the states but of the *people* of those states as well.

> The powers not delegated to the United States by the Constitution, nor prohibited by it to the States, are reserved to the States respectively, or to the people.

In the closing days of 1791, the first ten amendments were officially ratified, guaranteeing among other things the *right* recognized in the Declaration of Independence to "life, liberty, and the pursuit of happiness"—and, necessarily, property.

In sum, the Constitution itself gave us democratic institutions in a republican form of limited government, and the Bill of Rights protected individual rights.

Or so the Founders thought.

They would be appalled by what the Supreme Court of the United States has done to Jefferson's "thing of wax."

Some Supreme Court decisions have enlarged the power of the federal government at the expense of the states probably far more than the Founders imagined (violation of federalism). Other decisions have moved the demarcation line the Founders drew between the three branches of government (violation of separation of powers). Still other decisions have anointed the courts as arbiters of every imaginable dispute between individuals (violation of judicial restraint). Too many decisions have curtailed rights enumerated in the Bill of Rights, while engorging the intent and meaning of the post–Civil War Fourteenth Amendment by creating "rights" its proponents never dreamed of (the "Living Constitution" phenomenon).

In the Supreme Court's vitiation of the Founders' vision of individual rights and limited government, we shall see in the

42

following chapters the leitmotif that I discussed earlier: Ayn Rand's "inner contradiction" of altruism and collectivism. Lest anyone doubt that the contradiction has been present from virtually the Court's first days, carefully absorb the words of two Supreme Court justices in *Calder* v. *Bull*, a 1798 case decided only *seven years* after ratification of the Bill of Rights:

> It seems to me, that the right of property, in its origin, could only arise from compact express, or implied, and I think it the better opinion, that the right, as well as the mode or manner, of acquiring property, and of alienating or transferring, inheriting, or transmitting it, *is conferred by society . . .*
>
> * * *
>
> Some of the most necessary and important acts of Legislation are . . . founded upon the principle, that *private rights must yield to public exigencies.* Highways are run through private grounds.
>
> Fortifications, light-houses, and other public edifices, are necessarily sometimes built upon the soil owned by individuals. In such, and similar cases, if the owners should refuse voluntarily to accommodate the public, *they must be constrained, as far as the public necessities require*; and justice is done, by allowing them a reasonable equivalent. Without the possession of this power, the operations of Government would often be obstructed, and *society itself would be endangered.* (My emphasis throughout.)[25]

The altruist/collectivist virus was already loose in the Supreme Court of the United States—and the ink was not yet dry on the Bill of Rights.

2.
The American Constitutional System: Judicial Review, Federalism, Separation of Powers

In the twenty-two years before the Supreme Court's decision in *Calder* v. *Bull*, independence had been declared, the Revolutionary War had been won, the Constitution had been hammered out and ratified, a president and vice president elected, Jefferson and Hamilton appointed to the cabinet, and the Bill of Rights introduced at the First Congress and later ratified by the states.

The First Congress was noteworthy for another important reason as well: it enacted the Judiciary Act of 1789, one provision of which was that the Supreme Court of the United States "shall . . . have power to issue writs . . . of *mandamus* . . . ."[26] (Emphasis in original.) In other words, under the Judiciary Act of 1789, a litigant seeking a writ of mandamus could bypass the lower federal courts and sue directly in the Supreme Court of the United States.

The Judiciary Act of 1789, and what became of it, would teach much about the three fundamental pillars of American constitutionalism: judicial review, federalism, and separation of powers.

On its face, enactment of the Judiciary Act would seem within the power of Congress. After all, Article III, section 1, paragraph 1 of the Constitution not only vests "judicial Power of the United States . . . in one supreme Court," it also vests it "in such inferior Courts as the Congress may from time to time

45

ordain and establish." Thus, under Article III *everything* concerning the nature, structure, and jurisdiction of the federal judicial system was left to the sole discretion of Congress.[27] And in the Judiciary Act of 1789, Congress authorized the Supreme Court of the United States to issue writs of mandamus.

On the other hand, Article III, section 2, paragraph 2 of the Constitution of the United States of America provides that:

> In all Cases affecting Ambassadors, other public Ministers and Consuls, and those in which a State shall be Party, the Supreme Court shall have *original* Jurisdiction.[28] (My emphasis.)

Note the apparent inconsistency. In the Constitution, the Founders vested the Supreme Court with original jurisdiction in only *four kinds of cases*, none of which dealt with mandamus. But in the Judiciary Act of 1789, Congress purported to vest the Supreme Court with original jurisdiction to hear applications for writs of mandamus.

Resolution of this inconsistency, in one of the most constitutionally seminal Supreme Court decisions in American history, *Marbury* v. *Madison*, would set the table for over two centuries of other decisions, and contribute largely to the violation of individual rights and the principle of limited government. Those decisions would institutionalize the ethics of altruism and collectivism, making them the litmus paper by which to measure countless Supreme Court decisions.

Due to the common-law understanding of what "judicial power" meant historically, the express provisions of the Constitution's Article III, and the additional grant of power to the Court in the Judiciary Act of 1789, the Supreme Court of the United States had become a powerful force. It was the only branch of government that could carry out its business behind

46

closed doors in utter secrecy, without having to keep records of its deliberations. The Court was responsible to no one, and justices couldn't be disciplined (except by impeachment and conviction). Yet, the Court could render decisions affecting everyone from the president of the United States to a local sheriff. As the illustrious Charles Evans Hughes observed, "We are under a Constitution, but the Constitution is what the judges say it is. . . ."[29]

Thomas Jefferson's fear about the federal judiciary was a tad more colorful:

> The constitution . . . is a mere thing of wax in the hands of the judiciary, which they may twist, and shape into any form they please.

Some may wonder why, with congressional enactment and presidential approval of the Judiciary Act of 1789, those two branches of the federal government had willingly made their actions subordinate to, and even potentially reversible by, the courts—the third, supposedly co-equal, branch of the federal government.

Enter the omnipresent political considerations.

Recall that George Washington was president; John Adams was vice president. They were the most important federalists in the United States, and the House of Representatives and Senate were controlled by federalists.

The federalists' major political concern was not to forestall a clash between the *branches* of the federal government— executive, legislative, and judicial—because they controlled all three. The clash they feared, and desperately tried to guard against, was between the federalists and their vociferous anti-federalist opposition. The federalists knew that members of the House of Representatives were elected every two years, *by the people;* senators were elected every six years by the state legislatures, members of which were elected *by the people;* and the president was elected every four years by the Electoral College, which was elected *by the people.*

The federalists understood all too clearly that if the problems they had encountered in achieving ratification of the Constitution were any indication of the strong popular opposition to the new, powerful centralized federal government, the Federalist Party might not be in power much longer.[30] Thus, for the federalists, the Judiciary Act of 1789 was tailor-made: the broad powers of the federal judiciary were going to be administered by federal—read "federalist"— judges. All federal judges were appointed, their tenure was for life, and it was not unreasonable to believe that federalist judges would remain loyal to the party and president that appointed them, and to the Senate that confirmed them.

That's why President Washington appointed federalists to virtually every judgeship in the newly created federal judiciary.

What, then, would be the resolution in the federalist courts of the inconsistency between the Constitution's Article III and the Judiciary Act of 1789 concerning original jurisdiction and mandamus?

Here, chronology becomes important.

In the presidential election of 1800, Thomas Jefferson won the popular vote but tied with Aaron Burr in the Electoral College. The House of Representatives chose Jefferson.

In December 1800, Chief Justice Oliver Ellsworth resigned.

John Adams, still president until March 4, 1801, when Jefferson would take over, appointed Secretary of State John Marshall as Chief Justice. Marshall took office on February 4 and remained as secretary of state, wearing two hats until Adams left office a month later.

During that month, the federalists went even further to solidify their control over the federal/federalist judiciary. One gambit was for Congress to create additional federal judgeships, which Adams filled with federalist appointees.

In February 1801—less than one week before Jefferson was to assume the presidency—the lame-duck federalist Congress had created various new judgeships, including forty-two new justice of the peace positions, with five-year terms, for the District of Columbia and Alexandria, Virginia courts. Unsurprisingly, President Adams filled the judgeships with federalists, whom the Senate confirmed on March 3, 1801, one day before Jefferson's inauguration.

To make the appointments official, Adams signed the new justices' commissions, diploma-like certificates attesting to their status and, some believed, a prerequisite to making the appointment process complete.

When Jefferson and his Republicans took office, they were not happy about the federalists' court-packing maneuver, so they struck back in two ways.

First, they discovered that some of the commissions had not yet been delivered—by Adams's secretary of state, John Marshall!—to the newly appointed justices of the peace. So Jefferson's secretary of state, James Madison, withheld the commissions.

Second, in 1802, the Republican Congress repealed the 1801 law creating the additional justice of the peace provisions.

Thus was the stage set for *Marbury* v. *Madison.*
It was with that case and with arch-federalist John Marshall,
Chief Justice of the United States that American constitutional
law began.

Some statistics put in perspective what a judicial giant
Marshall was, and make it easier to understand what he
accomplished in his *Marbury* v. *Madison* decision.

He was chief justice for thirty-four years, his tenure spanning
the terms of six presidents: John Adams, Thomas Jefferson,
James Madison, James Monroe, John Quincy Adams, and
Andrew Jackson.

In Marshall's first four years as chief justice, the Supreme
Court delivered formal opinions in twenty-six cases. Marshall
wrote twenty-four of the twenty-six, and there were no
dissents; he didn't sit on the other two cases.

The Court rendered 1,106 opinions during Marshall's tenure;
he wrote 519, nearly half of them. Sixty-two dealt with the
meaning of the Constitution, and of these he wrote thirty-six.
Even when Marshall didn't write the majority opinion, he led
his colleagues, because in all of the 1,106, he deemed it
necessary to dissent only nine times—less than one percent of
the total number of cases. Marshall was extraordinarily adept
at getting what he wanted. His influence on the other justices
was particularly impressive because for most of his chief
justiceship the Supreme Court was weighted with *Republican*
appointees of Jefferson and Jefferson's successor, James
Madison.

It didn't take long for Jefferson and the Republicans to realize
that federalists had "retired into the Judiciary as a stronghold,
and there the remains of Federalism are to be preserved and fed
from the Treasury, and from that battery all the works of
Republicanism are to be beaten down and erased."[31]

Instead of waiting for an attack to be launched from the federalist judiciary, the Republicans made a preemptive strike. The target was the federal bench itself. The Republicans proposed to undermine it by repealing the federalists' court-packing Judiciary Act of 1801.

From the perspective of the federalists, the Republicans' repeal of the Act was not only a means through which the latter could eliminate Adams's newly appointed federalist judges, but also a serious attack on the independence of the judiciary.

Indeed, an attack on the 1801 Act was potentially an attack against the original Judiciary Act of 1789, which had organized the entire federal judiciary.

The federalists were also deeply concerned about whether the Republicans—if they were powerful enough and could get away with repeal—could pass a new act and then fill every federal judgeship in America with Republicans. The high-stakes battle over the repeal act raged in Congress with vociferous debate. The federalists, of course, voted against repeal, but they were outnumbered. The Republicans not only repealed the 1801 Act, but also enacted a new judiciary law.

Implicit in the enactment of that statute was the profoundly important constitutional question of whether the Supreme Court could declare the Repeal Act—or, for that matter, any other act of Congress—"unconstitutional." It is necessary to understand that the political/judicial situation at that time was not as it is today when it is taken as a given that the Supreme Court routinely exercises the power to hold statutes, federal and state alike, unconstitutional.

The battle over the Repeal Act was no abstract speculation. The Supreme Court was still solidly federalist, and a Republican Congress and Republican president were determined to obliterate a considerable part of the federalist judiciary.

In Congress, the federalist opposition had made it unequivocally clear that they believed the Repeal Act was unconstitutional, and that they expected "their" Supreme Court, led by Chief Justice John Marshall, to erase it from the books.

Now, consider a fellow named William Marbury, whom President Adams had appointed a justice of the peace but who hadn't received his physical commission. Marbury wanted that document and the judgeship that went with it.

How to obtain it? Well, didn't the Judiciary Act of 1789—now perhaps about to be repealed—point the way? Didn't section 13 of the Act provide that Mr. Marbury could go directly to the Supreme Court of the United States and there seek a writ of mandamus against Secretary of State Madison ordering him to deliver the commission, the strictly formal administrative act that would finalize the process of making Marbury a justice of the peace?

Yes, but there was still that pesky problem of the Constitution's Article III, limiting the Supreme Court's *original* jurisdiction to the four enumerated types of cases, which did not include issuing writs of mandamus.

And there was that other problem of the Repeal Act's enactment.

No matter. Marbury, who himself was unimportant in the bigger picture of large-stakes judicial power, sued directly in the federalist-dominated Supreme Court. His case provided the Court with the opportunity to strike a blow simultaneously for the federalists and for their Judiciary Act of 1789.

All John Marshall had to do was convince four of his fellow

federalist justices to order President Jefferson and Secretary of State Madison to formally recognize Marbury's appointment by delivering the commission. But that was a tall order. Among other pitfalls, the order would have dictated terms to Jefferson's executive branch at a time when the Republicans were very popular.

The federalists feared that Jefferson and the Republicans would simply ignore whatever the Court ordered.

In his Supreme Court case, Marbury named Madison as the defendant. Most likely on Jefferson's instructions, Madison ignored the Court's order to appear before it.

Chief Justice John Marshall was now in a "damned-if-he-did-damned-if-he-didn't" position.

On the one hand, he was a federalist. He didn't want to let his party down by denying Marbury's claim to the judgeship with all that would imply about the plausible *invalidity* of the federalists' Judiciary Acts, and about the arguable *validity* of the Republicans' Repeal Act. A legal capitulation to Jefferson and his party, with the serious political consequences that would follow, was unthinkable.

Equally unthinkable was the potential effect on the fledgling Supreme Court and the federalists if Marshall *did* rule for Marbury, but Jefferson and Madison simply ignored the ruling. Recall that Jefferson refused to have Marbury's commission delivered, and that Marshall's order for Madison to appear in court was ignored by the Secretary of State. Likely, they would ignore any order from the Supreme Court, especially one ruling in Marbury's favor.

On the other hand, in strictly legal terms, the facts of the case were on Marbury's side. His commission had been signed and sealed by the president and by Marshall as secretary of state; the only arguable irregularity was the document had not been formally delivered to Marbury. Surely, the mere technicality of non-delivery should not be allowed to affect the appointment's validity.

Given that, how could Marshall avoid enforcing Marbury's claim, with all its unpalatable consequences?

Marshall was on the horns of a dilemma.

On the other hand, maybe not.

The Chief Justice's salvation lay in the relationship between the Constitution's Article III and the Judiciary Act of 1789's section 13. The former *limited* the Supreme Court's original jurisdiction to four types of cases, which did not include issuing writs of mandamus. The Judiciary Act, however, *granted* mandamus jurisdiction to the Court. In effect, the Constitution's Article III had been amended by a mere statute—even though Article V provides the exclusive process for amending the Constitution.

This conflict was Marshall's way out. Despite section 13's purported grant of the mandamus power to the Supreme Court, under Article III, a mere statute could not trump the Constitution. Marshall lacked the constitutional jurisdiction to issue a writ of mandamus.

Of his two choices—the Constitution controls the Supreme Court's original jurisdiction, or a statute does—the Constitution prevailed. The decision would have profound reverberations far beyond the *Marbury* case. The Supreme Court ruled that Marbury had a right to the commission; the appointment's validity was not contingent on delivery of the commission certificate/document. (Score one for the federalists.)

Next, and most importantly, the Court ruled that the refusal of Jefferson's executive branch to deliver the commission was appropriate "judicial business." As such, the refusal was suitable for review by the Supreme Court, which could also order enforcement, if necessary, of Marbury's right to the commission document.

Thus did Marshall set on a constitutional foundation the principle of judicial review. Henceforth, the Supreme Court of the United States would possess power under Article III to rule on the constitutionality of Acts of Congress. (Score one for the Court itself.)

One would think that having come this far, Marshall was going to rule for Marbury, and thereby risk non-compliance by Jefferson and Madison at a costly political price to the federalists, the Supreme Court, and to Marshall himself.

Not so.

Marshall posited the following question. Given that the Supreme Court had just established that it possesses the power of judicial review, is a federal statute (Section 13) that conflicts with the Constitution (Article III) valid, and if it is not, does the Supreme Court have to power to *invalidate* that law? The Chief Justice's answer would establish from that day to this a bedrock principle of American constitutional law: *a statute conflicting with the Constitution is not valid, and the Court possesses the power to declare it unconstitutional*. As Professors Nowak and Rotunda have written:

> Marshall's argument for judicial review—the power of courts to invalidate laws as unconstitutional—is deceptively simple. The essence of the argument is his first point, that "it is emphatically the province and duty of the judicial department to say what the law

is." Having previously recognized the Constitution as being the superior "law" in the nation, Marshall, with this statement, lays claim to the judiciary's final authority on matters of constitutional interpretation. It is this concept of the Constitution as law, and the judiciary as the institution with the *final* responsibility to interpret that law, that is the cornerstone of judicial review today.[32] (Emphasis in original.)

After the Supreme Court's decision in *Marbury* v. *Madison*, with judicial supremacy established and Jefferson in his second term, with agrarian democracy about to yield to the invention of the steam engine and the surge of capitalist expansion to which that machine and other inventions gave birth, John Marshall had a free hand to mold the Constitution of the United States—what Jefferson had called "that thing of wax." And that's exactly what he did.[33]

It is one thing for the virtually unchecked power of judicial review to be vested in the courts. It is quite another to know by what *criteria* that power is to be exercised. Which brings us to the important subject of what methodology is to govern constitutional interpretation.[34]

In one sense, the interpretation question was easy to answer in *Marbury* v. *Madison*. Article III of the Constitution, the supreme law of the land, vested the Supreme Court with original jurisdiction in only four types of cases. Section 13 of the Judiciary Act of 1789, a mere statute, sought to add a fifth. The Article III "original jurisdiction" language was clear on its face (as was the language of section 13), so the Constitution trumped the statute.

Let's look at a more difficult problem of constitutional interpretation, as an introduction to where I'm going next.

Article II, section 1, paragraph 5 provides that:

> No Person except a *natural born Citizen*, or a Citizen
> of the United States, at the time of the Adoption of
> this Constitution, shall be eligible to the Office of
> President; neither shall any Person be eligible to that
> Office who shall not have attained to the Age of *thirty
> five Years*, and been fourteen Years a *Resident* within
> the United States.[35] (My emphasis.)

Thus, there are three constitutional requirements for the presidency: being natural born, being thirty-five years old, and having residency for fourteen years.

For argument's sake, let's say that during the Democratic Party primaries in 2008, a federal district court challenge was made to a twenty-two-year-old congressman's eligibility for the presidency, on all three grounds: (1) that he wasn't a "natural born citizen" because of his parentage, place of birth, and other reasons; (2) that the requirement to be thirty-five years old may have been understandable in 1787, when younger people were less mature than today; and (3) that the congressman's sojourn in England for four years on a Fulbright scholarship disqualified him from satisfying the "resident" requirement.

As for the age requirement, no judicial interpretation would have been necessary. Thirty-five means thirty-five, and even former Supreme Court justice Sandra Day O'Connor couldn't contort another "interpretation" out of that fixed number.

But how are the courts, especially the Supreme Court of the United States, to ascertain the meaning of the Constitution's "natural born citizen" and "resident" requirements?

They could take a poll, asking Mr. Rasmussen to find out what most Americans think these terms mean. Or they could ask a rabbi or priest whether divine guidance could define the terms: what saith the Bible, Talmud, or Dead Sea Scrolls about Article II of the Constitution? They could ask experts, maybe Harvard's Alan Dershowitz or Fox News' "Judge" Napolitano; or TV's "Judge" Judy. They could consult former judges and justices, or philosopher kings. If they tried to ascertain the Founders' "intent," they could try to examine the minds of every delegate to the Constitutional Convention and member of state ratifying conventions. They could ask law professors and political scientists, or the man on the street, what they thought.

But surely, there must be a better methodology—one comporting with reason and rooted in the nature of the Constitution of the United States of America.

There is. That methodology is called "originalism."

Although originalist methodology had existed around the edges of American jurisprudence for decades, not until 1985 was it formally introduced to the organized legal profession of the United States. That year, Edwin Meese III, then attorney general of the United States, delivered an historic speech to the American Bar Association. His remarks caused a constitutional explosion whose reverberations continue to be felt in the courts and law schools of the United States, especially at the Supreme Court.[36]

After Meese delivered his speech introducing the originalist methodology to the organized bar from his pulpit as attorney general, he elaborated:

> In recent decades many have come to view the Constitution, more accurately part of the Constitution, provisions of the Bill of Rights, the 14th Amendment, as a charter for judicial activism on behalf of various constituencies. Those who hold this view often have

lacked demonstrable, textual, or historical support for their conclusions. Instead they have "grounded" their rulings in appeals to social theories, to model philosophies or personal notions of human dignity, or to "penumbras" (which we'll revisit in a few minutes) somehow emanating ghostlike from various provisions identified—and not identified—in the Bill of Rights.

Meese was of course referring to the liberal justices on the Supreme Court and their cohorts in academia and the legal profession, all of whom worship at the altar of the "Living Constitution," the High Priest of which was the late, unlamented by Conservatives and Libertarians, Associate Justice William J. Brennan Jr.

The Constitution, according to Brennan,

> . . . embodies the aspiration to social justice, brotherhood, and human dignity that brought this nation into being." * * * Our amended Constitution is the lodestar for our aspirations, like every text worth reading, it is not crystalline. The phrasing is broad and the limitations of its provisions are not clearly marked. Its majestic generalities and ennobling pronouncement are both luminous and obscure. * * * When justices interpret the Constitution they speak for their *community*, not for themselves alone. The act of interpretation must be undertaken with full consciousness that it is . . . the *community's interpretation* that is sought.[37] (My emphasis.)

Putting aside Brennan's flowery, meaningless prose—e.g., "social justice, brotherhood, and human dignity," "crystalline"—his statement is a naked paean to collectivism. Brennan sees judges of lower courts and justices of the

59

Supreme Court somehow channeling the "community"—meaning some unidentified and unidentifiable "others"—in ruling on fundamental questions of individual rights and limited government. According to Brennan, judges and justices don't decide what the Constitution means, his friends and neighbors do!

He continued: "But the ultimate question must be, what do the words or the text mean in our time?"

This revealing sentence by Brennan is a flat-out repudiation of the truism that words have objective meaning. If they don't, words are susceptible to subjective use by any Tom, Dick, or Harry (or Bill) who wants to distort them to serve his own purposes. Brennan's statement is an utter betrayal of the principle that the Constitution reflects what the Founders wanted it to mean.

He concluded with this:

> For the genius of the Constitution rests not in any static meaning it might have had in a world that is dead and gone, but in the adaptability of its great principles to cope with current problems and current *needs*. * * * Our constitution was not intended to preserve a preexisting society, but to make a new one, to put in place new principles that the prior political community have [*sic*] not sufficiently recognized. (My emphasis.)

The "world that is dead and gone," according to Brennan, was the America that proudly declared that "all men are created equal, that they are endowed by their Creator with certain unalienable Rights, that among these are Life, Liberty and the Pursuit of Happiness—That to secure these rights, Governments are instituted among Men, deriving their just powers from the consent of the governed."

60

Brennan's dead world was the one in which American patriots stood at Bunker Hill, at Lexington, Concord, and at Valley Forge; and at immeasurable cost in blood and treasure, eventually threw off the yoke of British tyranny. A dead world whose Constitution promised to "establish Justice" and "secure the Blessings of Liberty." A dead world where a Bill of Rights explicitly rejected the sacrifice of the one to the many, and protected individual rights against the collective and its enforcer, a statist government.

All this was Brennan's "world that is dead and gone," to be replaced by a world conceived by altruists, collectivists, and statists, born in legislatures, and nurtured by courts—one where "current problems and current needs" are to be satisfied by the power of government. One that used the Constitution to eschew our "preexisting society . . . [and] make a new one, to put in place new principles that the prior political community have [*sic*] not sufficiently recognized." Brennan meant that the dead hand of the Founders cannot be allowed to leave today's problems and needs unsatisfied—no matter how twisted and irrational the judicial decisions had to be to further that goal.

That is the constitutional methodology of the altruists-collectivists-statists, producing the religion of the Living Constitution.

That Living Constitution, central to liberal/progressive jurisprudence and evident in Supreme Court adjudication, in reality means no Constitution at all. Because, if that methodology is what judges can use in doing their job, the Constitution is no different from any piece of legislation, which can be constantly amended or repealed.

A Living Constitution is anti-democratic. It removes from the public forum and from those who are politically accountable—presidents, governors, legislators—and thus from the people

61

themselves, the important issues they are responsible for: social, economic, financial, and cultural issues. Indeed, policy issues of all kinds. And now, thanks to the series of terrorism cases decided by the Supreme Court, the Living Constitution has removed from the president of the United States the power over considerable military policy.

Is there another way?

In 2005, Robert H. Bork, former Yale law professor, judge of the United States Court of Appeals for the District of Columbia Circuit, and cruelly defeated nominee for a seat on the Supreme Court of the United States, observed that:

> For the past 20 years, conservatives have been articulating the philosophy of originalism, the only approach that can make judicial review democratically legitimate. Originalism simply means that the judge must discern from the relevant materials—debates at the Constitutional Convention, the Federalist Papers and Anti-Federalist Papers, newspaper accounts of the time, debates in the state ratifying conventions, and the like—the principles the ratifiers understood themselves to be enacting. The remainder of the task is to apply those principles to unforeseen circumstances, a task that law performs all the time. *Any philosophy that does not confine judges to the original understanding inevitably makes the Constitution the plaything of willful judges.*[38] (My emphasis.)

If there is any area of constitutional jurisprudence where "willful judges" have indulged in orgies of non-originalist, Living Constitution decision-making, it is in cases raising issues of federalism.

In *Gonzales* v. *Raich,* the Supreme Court ruled in 2005 that federal law prohibiting the use of marijuana (the Controlled Substances Act) trumped the California law allowing the substance to be used for medical purposes: federal versus state. The Constitution's Article I congressional power versus the California statute enacted pursuant to the Tenth Amendment's reserved-state power.[39]

Justice Clarence Thomas dissented, and had a lot to say about federalism and its importance in the constitutional system:

> Federal power expands, but never contracts, with each new locution. The majority is not interpreting the Commerce Clause, but rewriting it.

> The majority's rewriting of the Commerce Clause seems to be rooted in the belief that unless the Commerce Clause covers the entire web of human activity, Congress will be left powerless to regulate the national economy effectively.

> The Framers understood what the majority does not appear to fully appreciate: There is a danger to concentrating too much, as well as too little, power in the Federal Government.

> This Court has carefully avoided stripping Congress of its ability to regulate *inter*state commerce, but it has casually allowed the Federal Government to strip States of their ability to regulate *intra*state commerce—not to mention a host of local activities, like mere drug possession, that are not commercial.

> One searches the Court's opinion in vain for any hint of what aspect of American life is reserved to the States. Yet this Court knows that "[t]he Constitution

created a Federal Government of limited powers." That is why today's decision will add no measure of stability to our Commerce Clause jurisprudence: This Court is willing neither to enforce limits on federal power, nor to declare the Tenth Amendment a dead letter.

The majority's rush to embrace federal power "is especially unfortunate given the importance of showing respect for the sovereign States that comprise our Federal Union."

Another fine discussion of federalism is found in Justice Thomas's dissent in *U.S. Term Limits, Inc.* v. *Thornton*, a 1995 case. Sixty percent of the voters of Arkansas in 1992 had approved an amendment to the state constitution. The amendment was not the enactment of a statute by the Arkansas legislature; it was the decision of the voters themselves—the very same "people" referred to in the Tenth Amendment. They imposed term limits on members of Congress from Arkansas.

By a 5–4 vote, the Supreme Court ruled that the Arkansas voters' amendment to their own state constitution was unconstitutional under the federal constitution. Why? Because, said the majority, the state of Arkansas, even though acting directly through its citizens, lacked the power under the Tenth Amendment to impose qualifications for election to Congress beyond those expressly provided for in the United States Constitution.

The explanation of federalism is found in Justice Thomas's dissent. He emphasizes that because the people of the several states are the only true source of power, the federal government enjoys no authority beyond that which the Constitution expressly delegates. All other power is vested in the states and its citizens. In Arkansas, voters decided to amend their state constitution and impose term limits. The dissent explained that while the Tenth Amendment takes sides between the federal government and the states, it doesn't take sides between the state and its own citizens. The appropriate division of that power—between the state and its citizens—is for the people of each state to sort out for themselves. The people of Arkansas did that, and federalism requires that they be allowed to amend their own constitution.

Despite the Constitution's unambiguous design of a federal system—contrast the express delegations of federal legislative, executive, and judicial power in Articles I, II, and III with the Tenth Amendment; note the Full Faith and Credit Clause of Article IV, the Supremacy Clause of Article VI, and the Bill of Rights' original purpose—the Framers' efforts to institutionalize the federalism principle, with all its attendant benefits, has largely been frustrated.

So, too, has been the Founders' attempt to compartmentalize the power of the federal government's three branches through the constitutional architecture of separation of powers.

Recall that in *Marbury* v. *Madison* the Supreme Court nullified a law enacted by *Congress*, and in *Gonzales* v. *Raich* the Supreme Court nullified a law enacted by the *California Legislature*. In both these cases, it was the *Court* exercising judicial review to override *legislatures*. This phenomenon squarely presents the problem inherent in separation of powers:

> All legislative Powers herein granted shall be vested in a Congress of the United States.[40]
> The executive Power shall be vested in a President of the United States of America.[41] The President shall be Commander in Chief of the Army and Navy of the United States.[42]
>
> The judicial Power of the United States shall be

vested in one supreme Court, and in such inferior Courts as the Congress may from time to time ordain and establish.[43]

It has been accurately observed that "[p]erhaps no principle of American constitutionalism has attracted more attention than that of separation of powers. It has, in fact, come to define the very character of the American political system."[44] Indeed, James Madison deemed separation of powers to be "a first principle of free government."[45]

Madison's views were very much evident in an important 1983 case involving separation of powers, *Immigration and Naturalization Service* v. *Chadha*. In that case, Supreme Court Justice Lewis Powell made the separation of powers principle the fundamental premise of his concurring opinion:

> The Framers perceived that "[t]he accumulation of all powers legislative, executive, and judiciary in the same hands, whether of one, a few or many, and whether hereditary, self-appointed, or elective, may justly be pronounced the very definition of tyranny." *The Federalist No. 47*, p. 324 (J. Cooke ed. 1961) (J. Madison). Theirs was not a baseless fear. * * * During the Confederation, the States reacted by removing power from the executive and placing it in the hands of elected legislators. But many legislators proved to be little better than the Crown.
>
> One abuse that was prevalent during the Confederation was the exercise of judicial power by the state legislatures. * * * Jefferson observed that members of the General Assembly in his native Virginia had not been prevented from assuming judicial power, and "[t]hey have accordingly in many instances decided rights which should have been left

to judiciary controversy." *The Federalist No. 48*, p. 336 (J. Cooke ed. 1961) (emphasis in original) (quoting T. Jefferson, *Notes on the State of Virginia* 196 [London edition 1787]). * * * *It was to prevent the recurrence of such abuses that the Framers vested the executive, legislative, and judicial powers in separate branches.*[46] (My emphasis.)

Strictly speaking, the doctrine of separation of powers operates only "horizontally," by erecting functional barriers between the legislative, executive, and judicial branches of government. But there is a kind of separation of powers born of the federalism concept, one that operates "vertically." As Supreme Court Justice Anthony Kennedy explained, concurring in the 1998 case of *Clinton* v. *City of New York*:

> Separation of powers helps to ensure the ability of each branch to be vigorous in asserting its proper authority. In this respect the device operates on a horizontal axis to secure a proper balance of legislative, executive, and judicial authority. Separation of powers operates on a vertical axis as well, between each branch and the citizens in whose interest powers must be exercised. The citizen has a vital interest in the regularity of the exercise of governmental power. If this point was not clear before *Chadha*, it should have been so afterwards. * * * By [Congress] increasing the power of the President beyond what the Framers envisioned, the statute compromises the political liberty of our citizens' liberty which the separation of powers seeks to secure.[47]

In this sense, federalism, dividing the federal and state governments hierarchically, is a "separation of powers."

A Korean War–era Supreme Court case well illustrates the separation of powers principle in a conflict between the president (as commander in chief under Article II) and Congress (under Article I).

During that conflict, amidst serious labor disputes, President Harry Truman ordered his secretary of the interior to seize the major U.S. steel mills. Truman said he was concerned that strikes would affect the production of materiel essential for the war effort.

The case, *Youngstown Sheet and Tube* v. *Sawyer*, ended up in the Supreme Court.

The first point to note regarding separation of powers doctrine in *Youngstown* is that, once again, it would be the judicial branch refereeing a dispute between the other two branches of the federal government.

As to the president-versus-Congress aspect of the case, the Court ruled that the former, *acting alone*, lacked the power to seize private steel mills even under the rationale that labor strife was impeding a war effort the president was fighting as commander in chief. But this was not a pro-private property decision, because the Court ruled also that even though the mills were private property the president could seize them if Congress had authorized him to do so. But Congress had *expressly* denied that power to Truman, so he was powerless to act.

In the case of *Powell* v. *McCormack*, the Supreme Court was asked to interfere with the prerogatives not of the president, but of Congress. Adam Clayton Powell Jr.[48] held the Harlem district congressional seat in New York City. John McCormack, a Boston politician, was Speaker of the House of Representatives. Powell had a lock on his seat, and had served in Congress for years. He was also a playboy: women, a place in the Bahamas (with a speedboat to go with it), a no-show legislator in the House.

In 1967, serious allegations of corruption were leveled against Powell. Although he was re-elected, the House of Representatives refused to seat him. He sued, and eventually the case reached the Supreme Court.

There, Powell argued that under Article I, section 2, paragraph 2 of the Constitution—"No Person shall be a Representative who shall not have attained to the *Age* of twenty-five Years, and been seven Years a *Citizen* of the United States, and who shall not, when elected, be an *Inhabitant* of that State in which he shall be chosen"—the House was required to seat him. (My emphasis.) The separation of powers doctrine was involved because the Supreme *Court* was being asked to rule that one House of the federal *legislature* was required to seat an election-winner whom it wanted to exclude.

Lawyers for the House of Representatives argued that Article I, section 5, paragraph 1—"Each House [of Congress] shall be the Judge of the Elections, Returns and Qualifications of its own Members"—vested sole discretion in that body to seat or not seat Powell. He was, they said, presenting a "political question"—a constitutional law term having a very specific meaning. According to *Black's Law Dictionary*,[49] political questions are:

> Questions of which courts will refuse to take cognizance, or to decide, on account of their purely political character, or because their determination would involve an encroachment upon the executive or legislative powers.

Black's, citing the Supreme Court decision in the redistricting case of *Baker* v. *Carr*, adds that "[a] matter of dispute which can be handled more appropriately by another branch of the government is not a 'justiciable' matter for the courts." Because it's a "political question."

Did *Powell* v. *McCormack* present the Supreme Court with a political question? Did the case present "judicial business," as in the *Marbury* decision, or would a Court decision encroach upon legislative powers?

To answer that question, let's recall the bare-bones facts. The Constitution sets forth three requirements for election to the House: age, citizenship, and living in the state represented. There was no question that Powell satisfied them all. The House refused to honor that fact, effectively ignoring the Constitution's unambiguous command. Not surprisingly, the Supreme Court ruled that Powell's seating was not a political question because under the facts of the case, surely the dispute was judicial business (interpreting and enforcing the Constitution) and did not encroach upon any legitimate power possessed by the House.

Neither *Powell* nor *Youngstown Sheet and Tube*, both separation of powers decisions, simultaneously presented issues of federalism because no states were involved. Other cases do, among them one of the most notorious decisions (for more than one reason) in American constitutional history: *Griswold* v. *Connecticut*, handed down in 1965.

Griswold is a paradigmatic Living Constitution case. *Griswold* has it all: federalism, vertical separation of powers, judicial arrogance, distortion of the Bill of Rights, and judicial invention of textually non-existent "rights." The majority and concurring opinions in *Griswold* employ a method of constitutional legerdemain which, like sausage making, is not pretty to watch.

A Connecticut statute provided that "[a]ny person who uses any drug, medicinal article or instrument for the purpose of preventing conception shall be fined not less than fifty dollars or imprisoned not less than sixty days nor more than a year, or be both fined and imprisoned."[50]

Another section provided that "[a]ny person who assists, abets, counsels, causes, hires or commands another to commit any offense may be prosecuted and punished as if he were the principal offender."

It's important to recognize that the Connecticut law was the product of democratic processes. The voters elected the legislature. The legislature, with quorums present and on majority votes, enacted the law. The governor approved it. Democracy in action!

The Tenth Amendment has long been recognized to grant the states power to pass laws relating to the public health, welfare, public safety, and even morals. It was pursuant to that power that Connecticut enacted the anti-contraceptives law.[51]

Well, then, where in the federal Constitution is there a provision that says Connecticut could not pass such a law? And that a *federal court* could strike down the action of the Connecticut *state legislature and governor*?

Because the federal Constitution does not prohibit the states from enacting outrageous laws, the Court had to find some other way to hold the Connecticut statute unconstitutional. Chief Justice Earl Warren assigned the task to Associate Justice William O. Douglas, a darling of America's liberals.

In a barely three-page opinion, Douglas, a notorious Living Constitutionalist, prospected his way through the Bill of Rights. Although what he found was fool's gold, it glittered enough to satisfy six of his colleagues.

According to Douglas, prior cases of the Supreme Court "suggested that specific guarantees in the Bill of Rights"—dealing with speech, press, association, quartering soldiers, search and seizure, self-incrimination, and the education of one's children—"have *penumbras*, formed by *emanations* from those guarantees that help give them life and substance." (My emphasis.) On the basis of these "penumbras" and "emanations"—but not a shred of constitutional precedent or other legal authority—Douglas and a majority of the liberal Warren Court simply invented a constitutionally guaranteed "right of privacy." That's right, they *invented*, without even a nod to how the *federal* Supreme *Court* of the United States had the power to ride roughshod over a *state* statute enacted by its *legislature* and *governor*.

So much for federalism and, in a sense, "vertical" separation of powers.

For the seven-justice majority, Douglas wrote:

> We deal with a right of privacy older than the Bill of Rights—older than our political parties, older than our school system. Marriage [about which the Connecticut law said nothing] is a coming together for better or for worse, hopefully enduring, and intimate to the degree of being sacred. It is an association that promotes a way of life, not causes; a harmony in living, not political faiths; a bilateral loyalty, not commercial or social projects. Yet it is an association for as noble a purpose as any involved in our prior decisions.

Despite this pretentious mumbo jumbo, or perhaps because of it, neither Douglas nor any of his six colleagues had an answer to a simple question asked in Justice Potter Stewart's dissent (in which Justice Hugo Black joined):

What provision of the Constitution . . . make[s] this state law invalid? The Court says it is the right of privacy 'created by several fundamental constitutional guarantees.' With all deference, I can find no such general right of privacy in the Bill of Rights, in any other part of the Constitution, or in any case ever before decided by this Court. (My emphasis.)

Despite the clarity of Stewart's persuasive dissent—and because the seven-justice Warren Court majority wanted to rid Connecticut of what Stewart rightly characterized as an "uncommonly silly law"—the *Griswold* majority simply invented an ersatz "right to privacy." This anti-federalism, anti-democratic, anti-constitutional judicial invention would later be used by the Court in *Roe* v. *Wade* as precedent to support its invalidating the anti-abortion laws of every state in America.

As revealing as Douglas's stream-of-consciousness majority opinion was, still more revealing was the concurring opinion of Justices Arthur Goldberg, William Brennan, and Chief Justice Earl Warren. Agreeing with Douglas that the Connecticut law was unconstitutional, they disagreed with his reasons, unwilling to swallow his amorphous, undefined, ephemeral, penumbra/ emanation-driven "right of privacy." The trio's rationale for the Court's nullification of the Connecticut law was based instead on their own amorphous, undefined concept of something called a "fundamental right" (in this case the use of contraceptives), one apparently as important as the right to vote.

The fact that these three concurring justices voted to thwart the will of Connecticut voters, legislators, and governor was indefensible enough. Worse, by far, were the altruist-collectivist premises Goldberg, Warren, and Brennan revealed in the process—ironically, the very same premises that caused the law's enactment in the first place. Wrote Goldberg:

In determining which rights are fundamental, judges are not left at large to decide cases in light of *their* personal and private notions. Rather, they must look to the "*traditions* and [collective] *conscience* of our people" to determine whether a principle is "so rooted [there] * * * as to be ranked as fundamental." (My emphasis.)

A modest disclaimer. But while confessing that a *judge's* values are not the litmus paper by which "fundamental rights" are revealed, Goldberg openly deferred to "the traditions and [collective] conscience of our people"—a naked admission that rights are neither absolute nor recognized by and anchored in the Constitution. According to him, rights are what *society* (i.e., other people, maybe cannibals) decides they are. Goldberg and his two colleagues further incriminated themselves as Living Constitutionalists by their view of what Connecticut society had already decided in related aspects of sexual conduct:

> The State of Connecticut does have statutes, the constitutionality of which is beyond doubt, which prohibit adultery and fornication.
>
> * * *
>
> Finally, it should be said of the Court's holding today that it in no way interferes with a State's *proper* regulation of sexual promiscuity or misconduct. (My emphasis.)

Goldberg, Warren, and Brennan were, of course, motivated by altruist-collectivist principles about as controllable as a loose cannon on a rolling deck. How else to explain why they *denied* Connecticut the power to interfere with the use of contraceptives, while simultaneously *granting* the state the power to interfere with adultery, fornication, sexual promiscuity, and "misconduct"? What interests of whom were being sacrificed to whose?

But the Court's sacrifice of the interests of some to the collective others wasn't the end of the story *Griswold* told. Although it may be hard to believe, the Supreme Court majority actually endorsed, albeit implicitly, a forced-sterilization program—even for married couples. I am not making this up.

> . . . the Government, *absent a showing of a compelling subordinate state interest*, could not decree that all husbands and wives must be sterilized after two children have been born to them. (My emphasis.)

That's right. If such "a showing of a compelling subordinate state interest" *was* made, the government *could* "decree that all husbands and wives must be sterilized after two children have been born to them."

So much for "fundamental rights"! Or rights of any kind.

Justice John Marshall Harlan's concurring opinion was cast from the same mold, although his constitutional litmus paper was neither the majority's "right of privacy" nor the Goldberg concurrence's "fundamental rights"—two hollow Living Constitutionalist slogans more suitable for a political speech than a Supreme Court opinion. Harlan's concurring opinion put his constitutional chips on "basic values implicit in the concept of ordered liberty." That, in Harlan's view, is what justified the Court's invalidation of Connecticut's democratically enacted anti-contraception law. What he meant by "ordered liberty" is explained by what he said in the earlier case of *Poe* v. *Ullman*:

> . . . I would not suggest that adultery, homosexuality, fornication and incest are immune from criminal enquiry, however privately practiced. So much has been explicitly recognized in acknowledging the State's rightful concern for its people's moral welfare.

Thus, in Harlan's view of the matter, society (lots of people) can criminalize certain sexual practices, subordinating the preferences of others to the collective's judgment of what is "moral."52

Why, then, should Connecticut society not be able to criminalize the use of contraceptives? In what way does Connecticut's criminalization not invoke "the State's rightful concern for its people's moral welfare," about which Harlan is so solicitous? His answer:

> Adultery, homosexuality and the like are sexual intimacies which the State forbids altogether, but the intimacy of husband and wife is necessarily an essential and accepted feature of the institution of marriage, an institution which the State not only must allow, but which always and in every age it has fostered and protected. It is one thing when the State exerts its power either to forbid extra-marital sexuality altogether, or to say who may marry, but it is quite another when, having acknowledged a marriage and the intimacies inherent in it, it undertakes to regulate by means of the criminal law the details of that intimacy.
>
> * * *
>
> . . . requiring husband and wife to render account before a criminal tribunal of their uses of that intimacy, is surely a different thing indeed from punishing those who establish intimacies which the law has always forbidden and *which can have no claim to social protection.* (My emphasis.)

If we blend Douglas's *Griswold* majority opinion, the Goldberg-Warren-Brennan concurring opinion, and the Harlan concurring opinion, the result is this: "Society," on moral and other grounds, has a legitimate interest in marriage and sex.

Thus, society acting through government can criminalize the sexual conduct of some of its members, but because of tradition and a government interest in marriage, can't go so far as to prohibit the use of contraceptives by married heterosexuals.

According to Douglas and the others who joined his majority opinion, "emanations" and "penumbras" in virtually every provision of the Bill of Rights create a constitutional "right of privacy." According to the concurring opinion, this right is "fundamental," gleaned from the "*traditions* and [collective] *conscience* of our people." This sentiment was joined by Harlan, because in the name of morality, society traditionally approves of certain sexual acts and their practitioners while it disapproves of others.

We have not seen the last of *Griswold* v. *Connecticut*. We will revisit it in later chapters where it will become clear how its methodology and precedent status enabled the Court to further advance the march of the Living Constitution, the opposite of originalism. A Living Constitution is not only an anti-democratic and intellectually dishonest way to interpret our Constitution and federal statutes, it is also demonstrably capable of inventing dangerous ersatz "rights"—such as *Griswold*'s spurious "right of privacy"—which impose tremendous moral, legal, social, economic, political, and other costs on this nation and its citizens.

Griswold's interpretive methodology—imposed on the basic Constitution, on the Bill of Rights, on the Fourteenth Amendment, and on federal statutes—and the invention and institutionalization of "rights" have made possible the decades-long metastasis of the Living Constitution's malignant anti-federalism[53] and its anti–separation of powers doctrines into most areas of American constitutional and statutory law.

Nowhere is that malignancy more apparent than in the Supreme Court's decisions on the Commerce Clause.

3.
Congress
and Its Commerce and War Powers

If it can be said that any single event and the ensuing Supreme Court decision relating to it provided the genesis of today's bloated congressional power, at the expense of the Tenth Amendment, it is the Bank Controversy.

As Secretary of the Treasury in 1790, Alexander Hamilton proposed that Congress charter a national bank. Today—in light of the unaccountable Federal Reserve, the huge Treasury Department, the powerful Internal Revenue Service, and the vast array of other federal and quasi-federal financial entities— creation of a national bank wouldn't seem to be such a startling idea. In 1790, however, it was. Seen as an attempt to enlarge federal power over the country's financial affairs, Hamilton's proposal sparked a firestorm of opposition. Especially because many small farmers and Southern planters believed they would be at the mercy of (paraphrasing Lincoln) a government of the wealthy, by the wealthy, and for the wealthy. It looked to them as if Congress would be a tool of the commercial and mercantile interests, for which Hamilton was believed to be acting.

The Jeffersonians understood that the new nation might need a strong federal government to conduct foreign affairs, especially where the United States had to speak with one voice. But regulating domestic affairs in general and financial affairs in particular was different; essentially because of the Tenth Amendment and the Republicans' belief that state and local governments, closer to the people, were better suited to regulate financial affairs.

President Washington asked Secretary of State Jefferson and Treasury Secretary Hamilton for their opinions about the constitutionality of a national bank.

In support of the bank's constitutionality, Hamilton argued:

> every power vested in a government is in its nature *sovereign*, and includes, by *force* of the *term* a right to employ all the *means* requisite and fairly applicable to the attainment of the ends of such power, and which are not precluded by restrictions and exceptions specified in the Constitution, or not immoral, or not contrary to the *essential ends* of political society.
>
> . . . the powers contained in a constitution of government, especially those which concern the general administration of the affairs of a country, its finances, trade, defense &c., ought to be construed liberally in advancement of the public good.[54]

Although the syntax of Hamilton's argument, the product of 1791 writing style, could have been clearer, his meaning was apparent. Hamilton was arguing that subsumed within a delegated power are whatever means (i.e., other powers) may be necessary to implement that power—unless those means are expressly prohibited by the Constitution, are immoral, or are contrary to what society is all about. This argument would prove controlling in the later Supreme Court ruling on the bank's constitutionality, which for over two centuries has defined the scope of federal power.

Jefferson, speaking for the opposition, argued that congressional creation of the bank would be unconstitutional. Why? Because the power to incorporate a bank was not specifically delegated to Congress by Article I of the Constitution.

> I consider the foundation of the Constitution as laid on this ground—that all powers not delegated to the United States, by the Constitution, nor prohibited by it to the states, are reserved to the states or to the people.[55]

Jefferson was quoting the Tenth Amendment. Not only does the Constitution *prima facie* delegate to Congress specific, enumerated powers, but to make sure there's no misunderstanding, the Tenth Amendment is textually clear that if a power is not so delegated (or expressly prohibited to the states), it is reserved to the states and to their people.

He continued:

> To take a single step beyond the boundaries thus specially drawn around the powers of Congress, is to take possession of a boundless field of power, no longer susceptible of any definition.

After analyzing those powers of Congress that the Constitution did specifically enumerate—especially the Necessary and Proper Clause (about which more later)—Jefferson concluded that "[t]he present is the case of a right [really a power] remaining exclusively with the states . . . ."

Thus, the Bank Controversy squarely raised a question much more important than the narrow one of whether the Constitution had delegated to Congress the power to charter a bank. The more fundamental question was *how* the Constitution would be interpreted in order to ascertain *whether* Congress somehow possessed that textually absent power. The wrong answer to the "broad or narrow" construction question would have a weighty and lasting impact on individual rights and limited government.

Recall that the Constitution was conceived and created as a charter of enumerated, delegated powers. There is nothing in the Constitution—not even the Necessary and Proper Clause—to suggest that Congress (or, for that matter, any branch of the federal government) possesses unlimited power to legislate, let alone to sacrifice the interests of some individuals, for "advancement of the public good," as Hamilton argued.

Yet Hamilton's argument won. Washington signed the bank bill into law. The executive branch believed the Constitution could be broadly interpreted to advance the interests of some (then, the national bank and its proponents) at the expense of others (then, those who feared increased government power).

The worst thing about the Bank Controversy was that no one seemed to have given much thought to what effect a state (Jefferson) or federal (Hamilton) bank would have on individual rights and limited government. Hamilton and the federalists were trying to promote federalism, while Jefferson and the Republicans were trying to protect state power. Some choice!

The First Bank of the United States was chartered. Twenty years later, the charter lapsed and was not renewed.

In 1816, Congress chartered a Second Bank of the United States, and the bank established branches in several states. This action laid the groundwork for one of the worst Supreme Court decisions of all time, *M'Culloch* v. *Maryland*.

In 1818, the State of Maryland enacted a law that taxed the financial notes of all banks not chartered by the state; i.e., federal banks, including the Second Bank of the United States. The bank's Maryland branch refused to pay the tax; the State of Maryland sued to collect it; and eventually, the case ended up in the Supreme Court of the United States.

While ostensibly *M'Culloch* v. *Maryland* was about the legitimacy of the tax, the underlying issue for the Court was whether the congressional legislation creating the bank in the first place was constitutional. That question, in turn, depended on whether, under Article I, section 8 of the Constitution, Congress possessed the power to charter the bank.

Accordingly, the second paragraph of Chief Justice Marshall's opinion in *M'Culloch* began: "The first question made in the cause [case] is—has congress power to incorporate a bank?"

Marshall began his opinion by noting that there was a legislative precedent for the bank—the First Bank of the United States—although that fact said nothing about the *constitutionality* of either bank.

Next, after some irrelevant musings about the Constitution's origins, Marshall acknowledged that everyone agreed the federal government is "one of enumerated powers." Since Article I contained no express delegation of power to Congress to charter a bank, it would have seemed that the bank legislation was on its way to being held unconstitutional. But that was not to be. Far from it.

After considerable rambling, Marshall finally got to Article I, section 8's "Necessary and Proper Clause": Congress's power "[t]o make all Laws which shall be necessary and proper for carrying into Execution the foregoing Powers, and all other Powers vested in this Constitution in the Government of the United States, or in any Department or Officer thereof."

Focusing on the word "necessary," and channeling Alexander Hamilton, Marshall opined that:

> If reference be had to its use, in the common affairs of the world, or in approved authors, we find that it

frequently imports no more than that one thing is *convenient*, or *useful*, or *essential to another*.
* * *
The word "necessary" . . . has not a fixed character, peculiar to itself. It admits of all degrees of comparison; and is often connected with other words, which increase or diminish the impression the mind receives of the urgency it imports. A thing may be necessary, very necessary, absolutely or indispensably necessary. To no mind would the same idea be conveyed by these several phrases. (My emphasis.)

Marshall followed this linguistic exercise with a bit of mind reading, attributing to the Framers an intent to provide in the Necessary and Proper Clause a roaming commission in Congress to legislate on virtually any subject it chose. Although paying lip service to the principle that "the powers of the government are limited, and that its limits are not to be transcended," Marshall made one observation that more than any other synthesized his view of the Necessary and Proper Clause:

"Let the end be legitimate, let it be within the scope of the constitution, and all means which are appropriate, which are plainly adapted to that end, *which are not prohibited*, but consistent with the letter and spirit of the constitution, are constitutional." (My emphasis.)

There is much to criticize in John Marshall's opinion for the Supreme Court in *M'Culloch* v. *Maryland*: his unabashed allegiance to federalist principles, his rambling detours into constitutional history, his use of non sequiturs, his begging of questions, his tortured linguistic parsing of "necessary," his failure to satisfactorily come to grips with the Necessary and Proper Clause's other requirement, "proper."

But the worst aspect of *M'Culloch* is Marshall's too-slick reversal of the actual meaning of the Necessary and Proper Clause.

Article I, section 8 contains the bulk of Congress's delegated, enumerated, and thus limited powers. In the last paragraph of that section, the Necessary and Proper Clause allows Congress to "make all Laws which shall be necessary and proper *for carrying into Execution the foregoing Powers*, and all other Powers vested by this Constitution in the Government of the United States, or in any Department or Officer thereof." (My emphasis.)

Textually, the Necessary and Proper Clause is a mere *implementing* power, not itself an independent *source* of power. Yet, in construing what he might have more honestly called the "Convenient or Useful" Clause, Marshall turned the tables. No longer was the scope of Congress's power that which was *expressly* delegated to Congress in Article I, section 8's enumeration by the people through their states to the national government. Now, the virtually unlimited scope of that power was to be whatever was *"not prohibited"* to Congress by the Constitution.

And what does the Constitution expressly prohibit to Congress?

Not much:
- o Importation of slaves, and a tax on them of more than $10 each;
- o Enactment of bills of attainder and ex post facto laws;
- o Certain kinds of capitation, direct, and export taxes;
- o Port preferences;
- o Withdrawal of money from the treasury without appropriate legislative approval;
- o And, lest we forget, the granting of titles of nobility.

Thanks to Chief Justice John Marshall's "not prohibited" *M'Culloch* decision in 1819, virtually every conceivable subject has since been grist for Congress's Article I, section 8 mill—with severe consequences for republican institutions, individual rights, and limited government. Countless Supreme Court cases have relied heavily on *M'Culloch* v. *Maryland* to justify almost unlimited congressional power, especially when exercised under the Commerce Clause.

That Clause was rooted in what Alexander Hamilton had discussed in *Federalist* 22: that a serious defect in the Articles of Confederation was "the want of a power [in a central government] to regulate commerce." Such a lack would allow states to erect trade barriers against other states, causing a restriction in the free flow of commerce and the resulting restraint on economic growth. The Constitutional Convention's solution to that very real problem for the new nation was the Commerce Clause:

> The Congress shall have Power To . . . *regulate Commerce* with foreign Nations, and among the several States, and with the Indian tribes. (My emphasis.)

The two words I've emphasized—"regulate" and "Commerce"—would require interpretation by the Supreme Court.

The foundation for what would become a very broad interpretation of the Commerce Clause was laid in the 1824 case of *Gibbons* v. *Ogden.* The questions for the Supreme Court were whether the constitutional term "commerce" included *navigation* across the Hudson River, which separated New York and New Jersey, and what the limitations, if any, were on Congress's power to "regulate."

Marshall easily disposed of the navigation question. Navigation was commerce within the Commerce Clause:

> "The power of Congress, then, comprehends navigation, within the limits of every State in the Union; so far as that navigation may be, in any manner, connected with 'commerce with foreign nations, or among the several States, or with the Indian tribes.' It may, of consequence, pass the jurisdictional line of New-York . . . ."[56]

But what about the *regulatory* power over commerce delegated to Congress by Article I, section 8 of the Constitution? Marshall's answer:

> It is the power to . . . prescribe the rule by which commerce is to be governed. This power, like all others vested in Congress, is complete in itself, may be exercised to its utmost extent, and acknowledges no limitations, *other than are prescribed in the constitution*. These are expressed in plain terms, and do not affect the questions which arise in this case, or which have been discussed at the bar [by the lawyers during oral argument]. If, as has always been understood, the *sovereignty* of Congress, though limited to specified objects, is *plenary* as to those objects, the power over commerce with foreign nations, and among the several States, is vested in Congress as absolutely as it would be in a single *government*, having in its constitution the same restrictions on the exercise of the power as are found in the constitution of the United States. (My emphasis.)

There are two important points here. One is that Marshall, as he had said in *M'Culloch* v. *Maryland*, saw the power of

Congress restrained only by the limitations expressly "prescribed in the constitution"—a far cry from the Founders' textual grant of only specifically delegated powers.

Second, according to Marshall, Congress is "sovereign"—defined by *Black's Law Dictionary* as "[a] person, body or state in which independent and supreme authority is vested." That authority is "plenary"—meaning, according to *Black's*, "[f]ull, entire, complete, absolute, perfect, unqualified."

Thus, according to the Chief Justice and a majority of the Supreme Court of the United States, *the Commerce Clause grants the supremely independent Congress the power to exercise absolute power over anything of an interstate nature unless some provision of the Constitution expressly prohibits that regulation.*

As Marshall wrote:

> "[t]he genius and character of the whole government seem to be, that its action is to be applied to all the external concerns of the nation, and to those internal concerns which affect the States generally; but not to those which are completely within a particular state, which do not affect other states, and with which it is not necessary to interfere for the purpose of executing some of the general powers of the government. The completely internal commerce of the state then, may be considered as reserved for the state itself."

Modest sentiments from the arch-federalist Chief Justice: ones that, in reality, would be rarely observed.

Let's look at an interesting example.

As noted above, the Tenth Amendment reserves to the states the power to legislate for the public health, safety, welfare, and morals. This is the so-called police power (which has nothing to do with cops and squad cars). If those powers are reserved to the states by the Tenth Amendment, one would think that the federal government doesn't possess them.

But consider the case of *Champion* v. *Ames.*

If the Tenth Amendment and the reserved state police powers mean anything, gambling should hardly be a federal concern. Poker games, football pools, and horseracing are all inherently local activities. But wait. Marshall and other federalists could argue that the playing cards travel in interstate commerce, as do the gamblers and horses. Radio and television broadcasts of high-stakes poker, the Super Bowl and Kentucky Derby are certainly interstate commerce. So, why couldn't the federal government regulate those activities under the Commerce Clause? Or, for that matter, why not lotteries?

Well, once upon a time the federal government decided that it frowned on that particular form of gambling. The direct approach would have been for Congress simply to prohibit lotteries. But some congressional staff lawyer must have figured out—despite the ammunition provided a century earlier by John Marshall in *Marbury*, *Gibbons* and *M'Culloch*—that the lotteries' connection with interstate commerce was too tenuous to invoke the Commerce Clause as authority for the prohibition.

Congress's innovative solution was to enact the Federal Lottery Act of 1895, which prohibited not the lotteries themselves but rather the *interstate transportation of lottery tickets*. Obviously, if lottery tickets could not move in interstate commerce, the transportation ban would put a large dent in the lotteries themselves.

But how to justify the prohibition constitutionally?

Here's what the Court said:

> Lottery tickets are subjects of traffic and therefore are
> subjects of commerce[,] and the regulation of the
> carriage of such tickets from state to state at least by
> independent carriers or trains is a regulation of
> commerce among the several states.

Oh!

But what about that pesky textual problem, where the
Constitution delegates to Congress the power only to
regulate—not enact a total *prohibition*?

Well, had he still been around, Marshall would have responded
that there was nothing in the Constitution *prohibiting* Congress
from banning the interstate transportation of lottery tickets, and
that as a "sovereign," Congress "independently" possessed
"absolute" power over interstate commerce.

The *Champion* dissent argued, correctly but unsuccessfully,
that prohibiting the transportation of lottery tickets was in the
nature of a police power reserved to the states under the Tenth
Amendment, that under the Constitution's Article I, section 8,
Congress does not possess any general police powers, and that
traffic in lottery tickets was not "commerce."

Champion was only one of a plethora of tortuous decisions by
the Supreme Court that twisted the meaning of the Commerce
Clause's two most important words, "regulate" and
"interstate," in order to accomplish a "social good"—namely,
depriving degenerate lottery players of their gambling
pleasures because other people thought gambling was
"wrong."

To have their way, the anti-lottery forces enlisted the coercive
force of government.

Among the worst of those tortuous, flatly wrong decisions was the infamous case of *Wickard* v. *Filburn*. The Supreme Court's opinion in *Wickard* could just as easily have been written years earlier by Chief Justice Marshall himself, rather than in 1942 by Associate Justice Robert Jackson. In a sense, it was because Jackson's opinion in *Wickard* rests squarely on Marshall's opinion *M'Culloch* v. *Maryland* and *Gibbons* v. *Ogden*.

Wickard v. *Filburn* had its genesis in FDR's "New Deal" legislation. In 1938, the Agriculture Adjustment Act was passed. One reason for its enactment was to avoid surpluses of some foods (too much food?!) and shortages of others by establishing government control over farm production. The program was designed to support the price of farm commodities—an anti–free market, "command economy" scheme *par excellence*.

Every year, the federal bureaucrats used their crystal balls to determine how much wheat would be needed the next year. They then set production quotas.

Filburn was a small Ohio dairy and poultry farmer who also raised a small amount of winter wheat. Some he sold *locally*, some he fed to his *own* animals, some he milled into flour for his *own* consumption, and the rest he kept for the following year's seeding on his *own* land.

In 1940, based on the Act, its regulations, and what the clairvoyant government bureaucrats predicted, Filburn was informed that his 1941 wheat crop could occupy no more than eleven acres, with a harvest yield of no more than about twenty bushels per acre.

Recklessly throwing caution to the wind and willing to risk violating federal law, Filburn sowed and harvested an extra twelve acres. When the government assessed a penalty for his "farm marketing excess," he sued.

Eventually, the case reached the Supreme Court, where Filburn argued that the wheat marketing quota provisions of the Act were unconstitutional because they didn't constitute regulation of *interstate commerce*. Apparently, he hadn't read Marshall's opinions in *M'Culloch* and *Gibbons*.

Filburn conceded that Article I, section 8 of the federal Constitution vested Congress with the power to regulate interstate commerce, and that recently the Court had upheld a federal statute regulating the local production of goods simply because *later* they would enter the stream of interstate commerce. But, he argued, the Agricultural Adjustment Act was quite different. It went well beyond other federal laws by extending the reach of the Commerce Clause power to *local* farm production intended wholly for *local* consumption, which was not intended for later interstate commerce.

Filburn wanted to know how Congress could regulate wheat that would never move far off his farm. A fair question. One that might have given even the great John Marshall pause. But Justice Jackson was up to the task.

Although in Jackson's opinion for the Court he expressly acknowledged that the Agriculture Adjustment Act "extends federal regulation to *production not intended in any part for commerce* but wholly for consumption on the farm," (my emphasis) his concession didn't help farmer Filburn.

The core of Justice Jackson's opinion began by acknowledging that Filburn claimed the wheat quota

> " . . . is a regulation of *production* and *consumption* of wheat. Such activities are, he urges, beyond the reach of congressional power under the Commerce Clause, since they are *local* in character, and their effects upon interstate commerce are at most 'indirect.' In answer

92

[said Jackson] the Government argues that the statute regulates neither production nor consumption, but only marketing; and, in the alternative, that if the Act does go beyond the regulation of marketing it is sustainable as a 'necessary and proper' implementation of the power of Congress over interstate commerce."

Although Filburn's "production and consumption" argument was not to be taken lightly, instead of confronting it, Jackson simply dismissed the farmer's contention. "We believe," he wrote,

that a review of the course of decision under the Commerce Clause will make plain, however, that questions of the power of Congress are not to be decided by reference to any formula which would give controlling force to nomenclature such as 'production' and 'indirect' and foreclose consideration of the actual effects of the activity in question upon interstate commerce."

Beware!

Once the Supreme Court says explicitly that cases are "not to be decided by reference to any formula," and implies that the objective meaning of words must yield to "actual effects," it's obvious that the justices are going to *extend* the law. And that's exactly what Jackson was about to do.

As a predicate, Jackson observed that:

[t]he wheat industry has been a problem industry for some years. Largely as a result of increased foreign production and import restrictions, annual exports of wheat and flour from the United States during the ten-year period ending in 1940 averaged less than 10 per

cent of total production, while during the 1920s they averaged more than 25 percent. The decline in the export trade has left a large surplus in production which in connection with an abnormally large supply of wheat and other grains in recent years caused congestion in a number of markets; tied up railroad cars; and caused elevators in some instances to turn away grains, and railroads to institute embargoes to prevent further congestion.

Many countries, both importing and exporting, have sought to modify the impact of the world market conditions on their own economy. Importing countries have taken measures to stimulate production and self-sufficiency. The four large exporting countries of Argentina, Australia, Canada, and the United States have all undertaken various programs *for the relief of growers*. Such measures have been designed in part at least *to protect the domestic price received by producers*. Such plans have generally evolved towards control by the central government. (My emphasis.)

Even though the cat was now out of the bag as to the real purpose of the quotas, and even though Marshall in *Gibbons* v. *Ogden* had provided plenty of latitude for interpretation of the *commerce* element of the Commerce Clause, Jackson still had to find an *interstate* peg to hang the wheat quotas on. Necessity, once again, proved to be the mother of invention. Jackson wrote:

"One of the primary purposes of the Act in question was to *increase* the market price of wheat and to that end to *limit* the volume thereof that could affect the market. It can hardly be denied that a factor of such volume and variability as home-consumed wheat would have a substantial influence on price and market conditions." (My emphasis.)

In *Wickard*, an Associate Justice of the Supreme Court of the United States was claiming that homegrown, home-consumed wheat, never moving off Filburn's farm, let alone beyond the State of Ohio, would not merely have an "influence on price and market conditions," but a *substantial* one.

In what way?

Here was Jackson's explanation for, believe it or not, a *unanimous* Supreme Court:

> This may arise because being in marketable condition such wheat overhangs the market and if induced by rising prices tends to flow into the market and check price increases. But if we assume that it is never marketed, it supplies a need of the man who grew it which would otherwise be reflected by purchases in the open market. Home-grown wheat in this sense competes with wheat in commerce. The stimulation of commerce is a use of the regulatory function quite as definitely as prohibitions or restrictions thereon.

There is so much revealed in these four sentences that emphasizing individual words and phrases is inadequate to explain it all. To begin with, by Filburn's wheat "overhanging" the market, Jackson meant that the farmer's few paltry acres of the grain were somehow part of the worldwide universe of wheat from such places as neighboring states, Canada, Ukraine, even faraway Australia.

By itself, Jackson's musing was meaningless; however, Jackson built upon this flimsy foundation with a string of yet more speculative "maybes." With Filburn sitting on his drop-in-the bucket supply of homegrown wheat, *maybe* prices would rise. Ignoring his own uses for the wheat, *maybe* Filburn would be induced to sell it into the market. *Maybe*

Filburn's wheat would "check" price increases, but then again, *maybe* not.

Apparently, Jackson realized that these "maybes" were hardly the bedrock upon which the Court could ground a broad, far-reaching interpretation of the *interstate* Commerce Clause's regulation of purely *intrastate* activity. Accordingly, the justice conceded that Filburn's wheat might never leave his farm. In that case, according to Jackson, Filburn himself would consume it—and when he did, he wouldn't be buying wheat from Kansas (let alone Australia). Kansas is, of course, another state of the United States of America—which brings Jackson closer to what he needs: *interstate* commerce.

Indeed, Jackson wrote that "[h]ome-grown wheat in this sense competes with wheat in commerce." An interesting idea: not buying something interstate in some way is related to interstate commerce. [Below, I will deal with Mr. Obama's health care "reform," where not buying medical insurance somehow affects interstate commerce.]

Jackson's sophistry impaled Filburn on the horns of a dilemma he couldn't escape. If the farmer *sold* his wheat, it would affect interstate commerce. If he *consumed* his wheat, he wouldn't purchase other wheat that *was* in interstate commerce, and in thus "overhanging" the market, he was affecting interstate commerce. No matter what Filburn did, according to the Supreme Court, his wheat had a sufficient connection with interstate commerce to justify the congressional Agriculture Adjustment Act and the production quotas it imposed.

And what early precedents did Jackson rely on to magically justify converting purely *intrastate* activity into *interstate* commerce, and thus allow Congress to regulate the local production of agricultural products? Well, our two old friends from John Marshall's day, *M'Culloch* v. *Maryland* and *Gibbons* v. *Ogden*.

96

If those two cases could justify congressional legislation under the Commerce Clause to control Filburn's wheat, the clause could be, and has been, stretched to reach virtually any activity, economic and non-economic alike.

Unfortunately, *Wickard* is only one modern example of Congress' use of the Commerce Clause to sacrifice the private interests of some people (like the Filburns of the world) to others (needy bread-consumers in, say, Texas) anointed by the collective (here, Congress).

From the time of *Wickard* to the present, the Commerce Clause has been used by Congress and the Supreme Court to justify government *Wickard-like* control of transportation, communication, investments, banking, labor relations, power, energy, trade, food, drugs, and much more.

Understandably, it is this aspect of *Wickard* v. *Filburn*— concerning the scope and application of federal interstate commerce power—which has received the most notoriety in constitutional law circles. Yet, ethically more important is the unusually explicit collectivist-statist premise upon which the Agricultural Adjustment Act and the Supreme Court's decision in *Wickard* rests.

In essence, Filburn argued that by forcing him, and others similarly situated, into the market to purchase small amounts of needed wheat they were able to grow themselves, the government was hurting *them* in order to benefit *others*— consumers and commercial wheat farmers. Filburn wanted to know why small dairy/poultry farmers like him should be penalized to keep wheat prices high for commercial wheat farmers—why his interest in growing a little wheat for his own purposes should be sacrificed to the perceived need of other farmers to obtain a government-supported price higher than the free market would provide them.

The answer Filburn received from the Supreme Court was that "[i]t is the essence of regulation that it lays a restraining hand on the self-interest of the regulated and that advantages from the regulation commonly fall to others." Altruism-collectivism incarnate. And it was through an indefensible interpretation of the Commerce Clause that the Court justified Congress' socioeconomic allocation of those costs and benefits.

Wickard v. *Filburn*'s distortion of the Commerce Clause in economic cases was bad enough. In 1964, however, Congress and the Supreme Court teamed up to use the Commerce Clause as an engine of moral righteousness.

The Heart of Atlanta Motel—*a privately owned, local establishment*—had 216 rooms available to transient guests. Accessible to two interstate highways, the motel solicited business through national advertising and some fifty billboards and highway signs throughout Georgia. The motel served conventioneers from outside Georgia, and about 75 percent of its registered guests were from outside the state. The Heart of Atlanta Motel, however, was physically within the State of Georgia.

Ollie's Barbecue was a privately owned restaurant in Birmingham, Alabama, catering to a family and white-collar trade, specializing in barbecued meats and homemade pies. It had a seating capacity of 220 and was located on an Alabama *state* highway eleven blocks from an interstate. Bus stations and a railroad were not far away. Ollie's Barbecue purchased about half of its food from a local supplier who, in turn, procured it from outside Alabama. Ollie's Barbecue, however, was physically *within* the State of Alabama.

Both Heart of Atlanta Motel and Ollie's Barbecue had inflexible policies against accommodating Negroes as the establishments' owners believed that because the businesses belonged to them, they could indulge their racist attitudes and decline to serve whomever they pleased.

For many years preceding the civil rights movement of the sixties, a large number of people in the United States, Northerners and Southerners alike, rightly considered racial discrimination ignorant, vile, immoral, and un-American. This attitude included racism not only in the public sector, as reflected by such policies as the South's Jim Crow laws, but in the private sector as well, where it was not uncommon to find even Northern universities enforcing racial quotas against Negroes and even Jews.

Following World War II, gains started to be made against *official* racial discrimination at the federal, state, and local levels, and the Supreme Court's landmark 1954 school desegregation decision in *Brown* v. *Board of Education* was the spark that ignited the eventually successful organized civil rights movement.

But not everything that movement spawned was legitimate, as the *Heart of Atlanta* and *Katzenbach* (Ollie's Barbecue) cases prove.

Brown v. *Board of Education* had invoked the Equal Protection Clause of the Fourteenth Amendment—"No *State*[57] shall . . . deny to any person within its jurisdiction the equal protection of the laws" (my emphasis)—against *official, government* racial discrimination.

But that wasn't good enough for some people, who had no difficulty ignoring the crucial distinction between *public* and *private* discriminatory conduct. It wasn't enough for them— rightly—to attack *government* racial discrimination. They insisted on prohibiting and punishing also the *private* racially discriminatory choices made by all the Heart of Atlanta Motel– and Ollie's Barbecue–type establishments throughout the United States.

This public-private dichotomy is of utmost importance generally, and all the more so when racial discrimination is involved. It's axiomatic that *government*, at all levels, must not discriminate racially. However, as irrational and immoral as *private* racial discrimination is, the Constitution does not prohibit it. No more than it bars gigolos from marrying spinsters for their money, parental indifference to their children's spiritual needs, or religious bigotry. Indeed, *the very nature of a free country, embodied in its Constitution, distinguishes between public and private morality.*

As much as victims of racial discrimination had a *constitutional* right to nondiscriminatory treatment by their *government*, and a *moral* right to it from other *individuals*, those rights were not the same. To attempt a synthesis of the two—to hold that the Constitution required private individuals to eschew racial prejudice—was, in effect, to make government the arbiter of private morality.

It was also to erase the difference between public and private conduct, to compel some people to fulfill the aspirations of others (however legitimate) and, in so doing, to ignore the fact that it is a contradiction to try to vindicate supposed "rights" by violating the *actual* rights of others—let alone to sacrifice the private values and choices of some to the collective's moral philosophy—let alone by applying the compulsive force of statist government.

None of these distinctions or anything else, however, prevented some militant antidiscrimination forces from attempting to convert Negroes' *moral* rights into their *constitutional* rights concerning the use of *other people's* private property.

How could they accomplish that?

Since the antidiscrimination forces couldn't use the Fourteenth

Amendment against the motel and restaurant (no *state* was denying equal protection or due process), they tried another tactic. Instead of relying on the Constitution, they sought to enact a federal *statute*.

Thus, in the early sixties a broad-based federal Civil Rights Act was proposed. It was not to be based on the Fourteenth "state action" Amendment, but on an entirely different constitutional provision, the Commerce Clause.

One section of the proposed act was intended to prohibit *private* racial discrimination in a wide range of so-called public accommodations. Motels and restaurants, for example.

Although the bill had many congressional supporters, there were serious reservations about whether *Congress* could legitimately reach the *private* racially discriminatory practices of *local* business establishments. Senate hearings in 1963 spotlighted the problem:

> Attorney General [Robert] Kennedy: We base this [proposed legislation] on the commerce clause.

> Senator [Almer] Monroney: . . . many of us are worried about the use the interstate commerce clause will have on matters which have been for more than 170 years thought to be within the realm of local control under our dual system of State and Federal government [federalism].

> Senator Monroney: I strongly doubt we can stretch the interstate commerce clause that far . . . .

> Senator Monroney: If the court decisions . . . mean that a business, no matter how intrastate in its nature, comes under the interstate commerce clause, then we

can legislate for other businesses in other fields in addition to the discrimination legislation that is asked for here.

Attorney General Kennedy: If the establishment is covered by the commerce clause, then you can regulate; that is correct . . . .

Senator [Strom] Thurmond: Mr. Attorney General, isn't it true that all of the Acts of Congress based on the commerce clause . . . were primarily designed to regulate economic affairs of life and that the basic purpose of this bill is to regulate moral and social affairs?

Attorney General Kennedy: . . . I think that the discrimination that is taking place at the present time is having a very adverse effect on our economy.

Even though Kennedy was trying to invoke the Commerce Clause as the justification for the "public accommodations" section of the Act, he and the senators knew better:

Attorney General Kennedy: Senator, I think that there is an injustice that needs to be remedied. We have to find the tools with which to remedy that injustice . . . .

Senator [John Sherman] Cooper: I do not suppose that anyone would seriously contend that the administration is proposing legislation, or the Congress is considering legislation, because it has suddenly determined, after all these years, that segregation is a burden on interstate commerce. We are considering legislation because we believe, as the great majority of people in our country believe, that all citizens have an equal right to have access to goods, services, and facilities which are held out to be available for public use and patronage.

Senator [John] Pastore: I believe in this bill because I believe in the dignity of man, not because it impedes our commerce. I don't think any man has the right to say to another man, you can't eat in my restaurant because you have a dark skin; no matter how clean you are, you can't eat in my restaurant. That deprives a man of his full stature as an American citizen. That shocks me. That hurts me. And that is the reason why I want to vote for this law. Now it might well be that I can effect the same remedy through the commerce clause. But I like to feel that *what we are talking about is a moral issue*, an issue that involves the morality of this great country of ours.[58] (My emphasis.)

This scheme of curing the moral failings of private citizens, by an even more tortured interpretation of the Commerce Clause than already existed under the *M'Culloch-Gibbons-Wickard* axis of cases, found its way into a Senate Hearing Report:

The primary purpose of . . . [the "public accommodations" section of the Civil Rights Act], then, is to solve this problem, the *deprivation of personal dignity* that surely accompanies denials of equal access to public establishments. Discrimination is not simply dollars and cents, hamburgers and movies; it is the *humiliation, frustration and embarrassment* that a person must surely feel when he is told that he is unacceptable as a member of the public because of his race or color. (My emphasis.)

This was, of course, a confession that the Commerce Clause was being stretched beyond any legitimate meaning, which

103

was not a secret to most members of Congress. Indeed, they were not the only ones having serious reservations about extending federal Commerce Clause power so far as to control the private racial choices made by local business establishments.

One of America's most distinguished constitutional law authorities, Professor Gerald Gunther, informed the Department of Justice, unequivocally, that use of the Commerce Clause to bar *private* racial discrimination in *local* places of "public accommodation" would be unquestionably *unconstitutional.*

> The commerce clause "hook" has been put to some rather strained uses in the past, I know; but the substantive content of the commerce clause would have to be drained beyond any point yet reached to justify the simplistic argument that all *intra*state activity may be subjected to any kind of national regulation merely because some formal crossing of an interstate boundary once took place . . . . The aim of the proposed antidiscrimination legislation, I take it, is quite unrelated to any concern with national commerce in any substantive sense. It would, I think, pervert the meaning and purpose of the commerce clause to invoke it as the basis for this legislation.[59]

Despite the reservations of many knowledgeable people, the Civil Rights Act of 1964 was enacted, resting on the power granted to Congress in the Commerce Clause of Article I, section 8. Soon the constitutionality of the Act's "public accommodations" section was before the Supreme Court of the United States.

The question for the Court in *Heart of Atlanta* and *Katzenbach* was the same: Did Congress exceed its constitutionally delegated powers under the Commerce Clause when it compelled the private owners of local businesses to serve customers whom they declined to serve for racially motivated reasons?

With the ghosts of John Marshall and Robert Jackson looking over their shoulders, the nine Justices of the Warren Court *unanimously* upheld the "public accommodations" section of the Act as a constitutionally acceptable exercise of Congress's power under the Commerce Clause.

To reach that result, the Court relied on earlier cases in which it had allowed Congress to regulate such aspects of business as the sale of products, wages and hours, labor relations, crop control, and more—all because those aspects had some connection, no matter how tenuous, with interstate commerce.

Those precedents, together with the motel's and restaurant's albeit tenuous relationships with interstate commerce—through the former's customers and the latter's food purchases—were deemed sufficient by the Court to allow Congress to impose the Act's "public accommodations" prohibition on the two privately-owned local businesses. The Court's rationale in both *Heart of Atlanta* and *Katzenbach*, although lengthy, speaks for itself:

> While the Act as adopted carried no congressional findings the record of its passage through each house is replete with evidence of the burdens that discrimination by race or color places upon interstate commerce. * * * This testimony included the fact that our people have become increasingly mobile with millions of people of all races traveling from State to State; that Negroes in particular have been the subject of discrimination in transient accommodations, having to travel great distances to secure the same; that often

they have been unable to obtain accommodations and have had to call upon friends to put them up overnight . . . and that these conditions had become so acute as to require the listing of available lodging for Negroes in a special guidebook which was itself "dramatic testimony to the difficulties" Negroes encounter in travel. * * *

These exclusionary practices were found to be nationwide, the Under Secretary of Commerce testifying that there is "no question that this discrimination in the North still exists to a large degree" and in the West and Midwest as well. * * *

This testimony indicated a qualitative as well as quantitative effect on interstate travel by Negroes. The former was the obvious impairment of the Negro traveler's pleasure and convenience that resulted when he continually was uncertain of finding lodging. As for the latter, there was evidence that this uncertainty stemming from racial discrimination had the effect of discouraging travel on the part of a substantial portion of the Negro community. * * *

This was the conclusion not only of the Under Secretary of Commerce but also of the Administrator of the Federal Aviation Agency who wrote the Chairman of the Senate Commerce Committee that it was his "belief that air commerce is adversely affected by the denial to a substantial segment of the traveling public of adequate and desegregated public accommodations." We shall not burden this opinion with further details since the voluminous testimony presents overwhelming evidence that discrimination by hotels and motels impedes interstate travel. (*Heart of Atlanta Motel, Inc.* v. *United States*)

In *Katzenbach* v. *McClung*, the Court stated that

> Article I, s 8, cl. 3, confers upon Congress the power
> "to regulate Commerce * * * among the several
> States" and Clause 18 of the same Article grants it the
> power to make "all Laws which shall be necessary
> and proper for carrying into Execution the foregoing
> Powers." * * * This grant, as we have pointed out in
> Heart of Atlanta Motel "extends to those activities
> intrastate which so affect interstate commerce, or the
> exertion of the power of Congress over it, as to make
> regulation of them appropriate means to the
> attainment of a legitimate end, the effective execution
> of the granted power to regulate interstate commerce."
>
> * * *
>
> [Even if Ollie's Barbecue] activity be local and
> though it may not be regarded as commerce, it may
> still, whatever its nature, be reached by Congress if it
> exerts a substantial economic effect on interstate
> commerce." * * * [Here, the Court cited *Wickard* v.
> *Filburn*.] The activities that are beyond the reach of
> Congress are "those which are completely within a
> particular State, which do not affect other States, and
> with which it is not necessary to interfere, for the
> purpose of executing some of the general powers of
> the government." [Here, the Court cited *Gibbons* v.
> *Ogden*.] This rule is as good today as it was when
> Chief Justice Marshall laid it down almost a century
> and a half ago.
>
> * * *
>
> The power of Congress in this field is broad and
> sweeping; where it keeps within its sphere *and
> violates no express constitutional limitation* it has
> been the rule of this Court, going back almost to the
> founding days of the Republic, not to interfere. The
> Civil Rights Act of 1964, as here applied, we find to

be plainly appropriate in the resolution of what the Congress found to be a national commercial problem of the first magnitude. We find it in *no violation of any express limitations of the Constitution* and we therefore declare it valid. (My emphasis throughout.)

In sum, because Negroes were wrongly, indeed immorally, discriminated against by local, private, non-governmental businesses that had tenuous connections with interstate commerce, and because Congress wanted to rectify that situation as a moral imperative, the federal legislature justified "public accommodations" legislation on the basis of the Commerce Clause—even though United States senators, the attorney general of the United States, and eminent constitutional law scholars, let alone legal academics and practitioners, knew very well that the clause was never intended for that purpose and to use it to rectify a moral wrong was patently unconstitutional.

Even worse, if that's possible, is that the Supreme Court of the United States went along with the charade, building on Chief Justice Marshall's opinions in *M'Culloch* and *Gibbons*, Jackson's opinion in *Wickard*, and like opinions by other justices in the 150 years between *McCulloch* and *Heart of Atlanta/Katzenbach*.

And, ironically, all the players did so in the name of holier-than-thou" "morality."

Heart of Atlanta and *Katzenbach* raise a profoundly important question: If a core founding principle of this nation is the republican institution of federalism—as reflected in the delegation of enumerated powers to Congress and the Tenth Amendment's reservation of power to the states and its people—are there any limits to the statutory reach of the Commerce Clause power when Congress wants to employ it to intervene in matters of profoundly personal choice, using the clause as a tool to sacrifice some people to the needs of others?

Sadly, the answer is "no."[60]

On an almost equal footing for tortuous manipulation of the Commerce Clause is what the Supreme Court has done to the Constitution's war powers. Article I, section 8 provides that Congress shall have power "To declare War . . . To raise and support Armies . . . To provide and maintain a Navy; To make Rules for the Government and Regulation of the land and naval Forces."

For two and a half centuries, countless Americans have died in military service; beginning with the Civil War, many of them were draftees. Even the American colonists were familiar with conscription, the Revolutionary War having been waged in part by men who were drafted pursuant to the constitutions of nine states. However, because they had been drafted only into *state* militias, the national government was forced, when it needed soldiers, to requisition them from the states. Some people deemed this arrangement inconvenient, and sentiment arose for broader federal power over military affairs.

In the Constitution, the power of Congress to conscript is neither expressly denied nor granted. As noted above, Article I, section 8 expressly provides only general military powers for Congress: "To declare War . . . To raise and support Armies . . . To provide and maintain a Navy . . . ." Just how broad were these powers intended to be? The question was not tested for nearly 150 years, until World War I.

On May 18, 1917, President Woodrow Wilson signed into law the Selective Draft Act. It was intended to provide manpower to fight the stalemated trench warfare that had been draining the lifeblood of European countries for three years.
Ten men who were indicted under the Act for failing to register

for the draft launched a broad-based constitutional attack against it—the first and, until the Vietnam era, the last challenge of this kind ever made against the federal draft as such.[61]

Convicted in various federal district courts, the defendants finally reached the Supreme Court of the United States. There, they raised several constitutional objections to the draft, all unsuccessfully. Although it is significant that the defendants lost unanimously in the Supreme Court, much more significant is *how* the Court treated their constitutional arguments, and *why* they did so.

One of the defendants' major arguments was that Congress lacked the power to enact a law forcing men to fight. The Supreme Court countered that the Constitution granted that power when it authorized Congress to declare war and to raise and support armies. "As the mind cannot conceive an army without the men to compose it," said the Court, "on the face of the Constitution the objection that it does not give power to provide for such men would seem to be too frivolous for further notice." This equivocal non sequitur is so transparently dishonest as to make one embarrassed for the Court that uttered it. If the Colorado constitution provided that the state could "raise and support a police force," could it draft its citizens to serve if there weren't enough volunteers? Of course not; the state police would be recruited by being hired, just as Colorado hires its other employees.

At issue in the 1918 *Selective Draft Law Cases* was whether Congress possessed the all-encompassing power to strip men of their liberty and send them out to die. At issue was whether men could be fined or jailed for refusing to lay their lives on the line for a cause that was not theirs. But the Court evaded the defendants' "congressional power" argument, brushing it off as "too frivolous for further notice." This blatant refusal to address profound constitutional issues was a strategy the Court would employ consistently throughout the draft cases.

What the Court did, in attempting to dispose of the "congressional power" argument, was to set up a false alternative: the government must *either* draft men *or* do without an army.

There was of course a third, obvious choice, suggested to the Court by the defendants: Congress's delegated power to "raise" an army should properly be understood as calling for volunteer enlistments. Service for pay. But the Court responded that this choice "challenges the existence of all power, for a governmental power which has no sanction to it and which, therefore, can only be exercised provided the citizen consents to its exertion is in no substantial sense a power."

Exactly!

That's why America was founded on principles of individual rights, limited government, and delegated enumerated powers.

But the Supreme Court of the United States wasn't having any of it.

Give the government the power to do something, the Court was saying, and, *ipso facto*, it can use force to get what it wants. On that premise, the Constitution's delegation to Congress of the power to establish post offices would arguably allow the government to draft postal employees instead of hiring them in the free market like any other employer.

The defendants advanced still another argument. By reason of its religious exemption clauses (which exempted ministers and conscientious objectors from the draft), the Act violated the First Amendment's prohibition against government contributing to the establishment of religion. While there was merit to this argument —which the Court had a duty to consider—once again, the justices skirted the issue: ". . . we pass without anything but statement . . . [this] proposition . . . because we think its unsoundness is too apparent to require us to do more."

Cowards!

When the defendants addressed themselves to the Thirteenth Amendment—and cited as a barrier to the draft the Constitution's unequivocal prohibition of slavery and involuntary servitude—the Court evaded the argument by declaring that it was "refuted by its mere statement."

Dodging the issues allowed the Court to ignore its own precedent, a 1911 case where it had written:

> While the immediate concern was with African slavery, the [Thirteenth] Amendment was not limited to that. It was a charter of universal freedom for all persons, of whatever race, color or estate, under the flag. * * * The plain intention was to abolish slavery of whatever name and form and all its badges and incidents; to render impossible any state of bondage; to make labor free, by prohibiting that control by which the personal service of one man is disposed of or coerced for another's benefit which is the essence of involuntary servitude.

Apparently, the "charter of universal freedom," which was to "abolish slavery of whatever name and form and all its badges and incidents," was constitutionally and morally acceptable when the beneficiary was the government. In the 1918 draft law cases, the Court wrote:

> . . . as we are unable to conceive upon what theory the

112

exaction by government from the citizen of the performance *of his supreme and noble duty* of contributing to the defense of the rights and honor of the nation, as the result of a war declared by the *great representative body of the people*, can be said to be the imposition of involuntary servitude . . . we are constrained to the conclusion that the contention to that effect is refuted by its mere statement. (My emphasis.)

The defendants had anticipated this need-over-rights, altruist-collectivist-statist response. In a naive and overgeneralized attempt to show that freedom and conscription were mutually exclusive, the defendants argued, correctly, that compelled military service was "repugnant to a free government and in conflict with all the great guarantees of the Constitution as to individual liberty. . . ."

The Court's response amounted to a confession of its altruist-collectivist ethical values and its statist political philosophy:

But the premise of this proposition is so devoid of foundation that it leaves not even a shadow of ground upon which to base the conclusion. Let us see if this is not at once demonstrable. It may not be doubted that the very conception of a just government and its duty to the citizen includes the reciprocal obligation of the citizen to render military service in case of need and the right to compel it. . . . To do more than state the proposition is absolutely unnecessary. . . .

This explicit judicial endorsement of altruism-collectivism-statism was the work of nine justices who were unwilling to meet, and unable to discredit, one plausible legal argument after another.

113

There were, however, arguments of a different nature which the Supreme Court of the United States did find persuasive— arguments it relied upon as "proof" for the proposition that the draft was constitutional.

Look, said the Court, at the ". . . practical illustration afforded by the almost universal legislation to that effect now in force." Look at what other nations have done, the Court was saying. Thirty-three countries were cited in a footnote to its opinion— thirty-three governments which, prior to 1918, had subjected their citizens to the draft: Argentina, Austria-Hungary, Belgium, Brazil, Bulgaria, Bolivia, Colombia, Chile, China, Denmark, Ecuador, France, Greece, Germany, Guatemala, Honduras, Italy, Japan, Mexico, Montenegro, Netherlands, Nicaragua, Norway, Peru, Portugal, Rumania, Russia, Serbia, Siam, Spain, Switzerland, Salvador, Turkey.

The list includes every imaginable altruist-collectivist-statist social and political system: monarchies and dictatorships; banana republics and primitive backwashes; brutal Oriental despotisms and disjointed feudal kingdoms.

Missing from this list was a constitutional republic in which the government, created for the express purpose of protecting individual rights and institutionalizing limited government, derives its limited, delegated powers from the people.

Could our Supreme Court really have believed that American citizens were no more immune from the impact of altruist-collectivist and statist force than the helpless peasants under the heel of the Russian tsar, or the miserable serfs under the whip of Japanese feudal barons?

Could the Court have forgotten that so many immigrants "yearning to breathe free" had fled to America's shores precisely to avoid conscription in their native countries?

114

Could the Court have forgotten that America was founded on the moral principle of inalienable rights and a limited government of delegated powers, not on the antithetical altruist-collectivist-statist doctrines that have plagued the rest of the world from the beginning of time?

Would the Court ignore its own earlier precedents that in judging a law, *our* Constitution and *our* form of government must be its only guides?

It could, and it did. (Perversely, included in the Court's list of those countries that had draft laws—held up as an example for America to follow—was statist Germany, with which we were then at war!)

In addition to taking an international popularity poll on the draft issue, the Court attempted to justify conscription on the basis of three periods of United States history: pre-constitutional, the War of 1812, and the Civil War. It gave dubious interpretations to what had occurred during all three periods.

While in the pre-constitutional period it had been the practice of the states to draft men into the militia, and while it was true that the states had thus set an unfortunate precedent at a critical time in our history, it did not follow—as the Court implied—that the Constitution transferred this arbitrary power from the *states* to the *federal* government. The Constitution speaks for itself: the federal government was given no explicit power to raise and support an army by means of a national *draft*. The grant of power was, at best, equivocal.

The War of 1812 was cited by the Court because James Monroe, then Secretary of War, had written to Congress recommending compulsory federal draft legislation. (Ironically, we were then at war with the British because they

115

were impressing American seamen into their navy.) While the bill that was later introduced never passed, the Court speculated that, but for the intervention of peace, the United States would have had a draft law at that time. In fact, there is ample evidence that the bill had faced an uncertain future in both houses of Congress.

In citing the Civil War period, the Court placed considerable emphasis on an 1863 conscription law, suggesting that it was solid legal precedent.

Not true.

In the first place, the United States Supreme Court had never ruled on that law's constitutionality; the Civil War Draft Act was never challenged beyond the highest court of Pennsylvania. Second, that law provided for a financial alternative to the draft: draftees could find someone to take their place, or pay the Secretary of War up to three hundred dollars to find a substitute. (The essence of the Civil War Draft Act can thus be summed up as "your money or your life.") Third, that law expired before involuntary servitude had been outlawed by the Thirteenth Amendment, while the challenged World War I draft law was enacted *after* the Thirteenth Amendment.

Finally, the Supreme Court cited as authority *The Law of Nations*, a classic work written by an eighteenth-century scholar-diplomat named Emmerich de Vattel, without quoting from the book. The Court's reference was understandably oblique. It wouldn't have been a good tactic to quote from so revealing a political tract. Just how revealing can be gleaned from the following excerpt from *The Law of Nations*:

> Every citizen is *bound to serve* and defend the State as far as he is able. *Society cannot otherwise be preserved*; and this union for the common defense is

116

one of the first objects of all political association. Whoever is able to bear arms must take them up as soon as he is *ordered* to do so by the one who has the *power* to make war. . . . Since *every citizen or subject is obliged to serve the State*, the sovereign has the right, when the necessity arises, to conscript whom he pleases. (My emphasis.)

Since "society" is only a number of individuals in a given geographical area, what Vattel, the Supreme Court, and the colonists who sanctioned state militias really meant when they asserted that the draft was necessary to "preserve society" was that *some* people can be preserved only by forcing *other* people to preserve them.

And so, the draft became yet another vehicle by which our government claimed countless victims. In the twentieth century alone, hundreds of thousands of men, from the Argonne Forest to the jungles of Vietnam to the deserts of the Middle East, have fallen in mute testimony to the consequences of altruism-collectivism-statism. They have been victims not merely of powder and steel, but also of the idea that *man is a sacrificial animal whose life is held at the whim of the collective*, whose decisions are enforced by government's monopoly on physical force.

The *Selective Draft Law Cases* of 1918 are among the starkest examples of Ayn Rand's "inner contradiction," where statist government power (the conscription law) was used to sacrifice some men (the draftees) to the public (the collective) outcry for warm bodies to fill the trenches of France.

Another horrendous example of altruism-collectivism-statism at work was the event that gave rise to the case of *Korematsu* v. *United States*: the euphemistically named "relocation" of Americans of Japanese ancestry during World War II.

117

Americans! *Citizens!*

I won't dwell on the factual run-up to the case. Suffice it to say for our purposes that President Roosevelt and his complicit military decided to incarcerate virtually all Japanese-American citizens for the duration of World War II. By a 6–3 vote, the Supreme Court upheld the executive action (Congress had not passed an exclusion law), using the president's power as commander in chief as the constitutional source of power.

Racial animosity, of which there was plenty, was not the entire motivation. Envy and economics played a large role. Justice Murphy, in his dissenting opinion, included the following footnote.

> Special interest groups were extremely active in applying pressure for mass evacuation. See House Report No. 2124 (77th Cong., 2d Sess.) 154–6; McWilliams, Prejudice, 126–8 (1944). Mr. Austin E. Anson, managing secretary of the Salinas Vegetable Grower-Shipper Association, has frankly admitted that 'We're charged with wanting to get rid of the Japs for selfish reasons. We do. It's a question of whether the white man lives on the Pacific Coast or the brown men. They came into this valley to work, and they stayed to take over. . . . They undersell the white man in the markets. . . . They work their women and children while the white farmer has to pay wages for his help. If all the Japs were removed tomorrow, we'd never miss them in two weeks, because the white farmers can take over and produce everything the Jap grows. And we don't want them back when the war ends, either.' Quoted by Taylor in his article 'The People Nobody Wants,' 214 Sat. Eve. Post 24, 66 (May 9, 1942).

If we apply Ayn Rand's premise that America's inner contradiction has been the altruist-collectivist ethics, in the *Korematsu* case we quickly see it in full bloom: sacrificing the individual (here, the Japanese-American) to the common good (here, frightened and avaricious citizens)—accomplished by raw statism (here, the president and his military).

Taken together, the *Selective Draft Law Cases* and *Korematsu v. United States* make it impossible to doubt the validity of Rand's premise.[62]

The ghosts of John Marshall and Alexander Hamilton haunt the halls of the Supreme Court and, as we shall see again and again, their pernicious influence persists across the entire spectrum of its decisions.

4.
The President's Powers:
Domestic, Foreign, and War

Article II, paragraph 8 of the Constitution of the United States provides that "[b]efore he [the President of the United States] enter on the Execution of his Office, he shall take the following Oath or Affirmation:—'I do solemnly swear (or affirm) that I will faithfully execute the Office of President of the United States, and will to the best of my Ability, preserve, protect and defend the Constitution of the United States.'"[63]

What is the "Office of President of the United States" that George Washington and his successors swore to "execute"? What powers were delegated by the Founders to the President?

Principally, three:

> Article II, section 1, paragraph 1 provides that "[t]he executive Power shall be vested in a President of the United States of America."

> Article II, section 2, paragraph 1 provides that "[t]he President shall be Commander in Chief of the Army and Navy of the United States, and of the Militia of the several States, when called into the actual Service of the United States."

> Article II, section 2, paragraph 2 provides that "[h]e shall have Power, by and with the Advice and Consent of the Senate, to make Treaties . . . ."[64]

We saw something about the power of the presidency in the last chapter dealing with the power of Congress, because in

121

some instances the power of the national legislature and the President are connected. For example, Article I grants Congress the power to declare war, while Article II makes the President Commander in Chief.

As to the nature, scope and exercise of congressional and presidential power, from time to time the scales will tip to favor one side or the other. They will surely tip if a third party—i.e., the Supreme Court— puts its thumb on one side of the scale.

In examining the President's power, let's begin with section 1, paragraph 1 of Article II, the "executive power."

As I've noted earlier, a major deficiency of the Articles of Confederation was the lack of an executive branch. The Constitution sought to cure that deficiency by creating the position of President of the United States, to whom was delegated "executive" power. The term had a clear meaning to the Founders because in 1787, they were well aware of the existence and duties of colonial governors, whose principal task was implementing the Crown's policies through appointed subordinates.

Speaking of subordinates, Article II, section 2, paragraph 2, augmenting Article II, section 2, paragraph 1, provides that the President "shall nominate, and with the Advice and Consent of the Senate, shall appoint . . . Judges of the supreme Court, and all other officers of the United States, whose Appointments are not herein otherwise provided for, and which shall be established by Law; but the Congress may by Law vest the Appointment of such inferior Officers, as they think proper, in the President alone, in the Courts of Law, or in the Heads of Departments."

Which brings us to a very important contemporary question

arising under Article II: the appointment—without constitutional support or congressional approval—of what are politely called President Obama's "czars." The czars are personal advisors to the President, located in the White House and spread throughout the executive branch. By the end of 2011, there were about fifty of these *apparatchiks* already in existence, and approximately twenty more in the pipeline.

There are czars for Medicare/Healthcare, Weapons, Great Lakes, AIDS, Tobacco, Stimulus, Faith-Based Issues, Guantanamo Closure, War, Health Foods—and others, literally from A to Z, some of which defy the imagination: Autism, Disinformation, Income Redistribution, Radio-Internet Fairness, Asian Carp, and Zoning. (Doubtless, soon there will be a Queen-czar to oversee the work of the worker-czars.)

There are several important reasons why Obama's appointment of these czars is certainly anti-democratic and, in some instances, unconstitutional. Many of Obama's czars, who possess unprecedented authority over significant policy issues, are performing functions for which Senate confirmation is constitutionally required; that congressional oversight is being thwarted.

Obama has claimed that his czars are beyond the reach of the Freedom of Information Act and protected by the doctrine of "executive privilege" from being compelled to testify before Congress. There is example after example of czars bypassing, and even superseding, cabinet secretaries.

Obama's creation of these apparatchiks had become so flagrant that in February 2009, United States Senator Robert Byrd, the longest-serving senator—and a Democrat, no less—sent a letter to the President about his flouting of the Constitution. Byrd wrote, "The rapid and easy accumulation of power by White House staff can threaten the Constitutional system of checks and balances." He added, "At the worst, White House staff have taken direction and control of programmatic areas that are the statutory responsibility of Senate-confirmed officials."

Senator Byrd, who had the reputation of being a knowledgeable constitutional lawyer, could have added that even worse than a threat to separation of powers was Obama's statist disregard for much of the Constitution itself.

There is much more to say about Obama's czars, and the organization Judicial Watch rendered a great public service to constitutional government by publishing a forty-two-page report on the subject on September 15, 2011. The report, entitled *"A Judicial Watch Special Report: President Obama's Czars,"* can be accessed at http://www.judicialwatch.org/files/documents/2011/czar-report-09152011.pdf.

Here is Judicial Watch's devastating conclusion:

> The issue of presidential czars raises questions in four fundamental areas of governance: (1) the constitutionality of policy czars; (2) the degree to which the U.S. Senate is circumvented in the appointment of policy czars; (3) the political controversy that results from avoiding the Senate's vetting process; and (4) issues concerning the overall transparency of a government that operates through a system of czars.

> Objections to presidential czars can be leveled on a number of grounds, depending on the role of the particular czar. The most basic constitutional objection is that the activities of these "policy advisors" ran afoul of the Appointments Clause of the

U.S. Constitution. Some czars, such as former pay czar Kenneth Feinberg, effectively act with the authority of Officers of the United States, despite having never being confirmed.

In addition, presidential czar appointments to departmental positions have increased dramatically under the Obama administration. Many of the czars in departmental positions appear to report directly to the President and undermine the authority of Cabinet secretaries.

President Barack Obama has essentially doubled the number of czar positions created by executive order.

While Article II Section I of the U.S. Constitution authorizes the executive order as a means of ensuring effective operation of the government, the vague responsibilities bestowed upon many of these czars are confusing lines of authority in government. Furthermore, many of Obama's political operatives are usurping power from statutory officers. Such instances constitute a circumvention of constitutional oversight.

To date, congressional efforts to end funding for Obama's political operatives have been unsuccessful. A rider placed in the 2011 spending bill cutting non-defense appropriations and ending funding for certain highly controversial presidential advisor positions (climate change, the auto industry, health care, and urban affairs) was passed by both the House and Senate, and signed by President Obama in April 2011. But, according to press reports, "Obama pulled the rug out from under that provision" by issuing a signing statement essentially stating "he will continue to employ advisers as he sees fit."

This, according to Speaker Boehner's spokesman, Michael Steel, was "not surprising that the White House, having bypassed Congress to empower these "Czars' is objecting to eliminating them." [Footnote omitted.]

Judicial Watch has a major investigative program that seeks basic administrative information for each czar appointed by the Obama administration. After initially sending out 41 requests for the mission, budget, and staffing of individuals labeled "czars" by the media, Judicial Watch received responses for less than half of these czars. Only a few of these responses provided documents responsive to the initial request. Even executive agencies subject to the Freedom of Information Act, such as the Department of State and the Department of the Treasury, have ignored our requests.

As important as the czar issue is, however, the mess Obama has made of conducting America's foreign affairs is far worse: Iran, North Korea, Venezuela, Iraq, Afghanistan, and the Middle East. Regrettably, under Article II, he's had the constitutional power to make that mess.

The classic Supreme Court decision dealing with the President's foreign affairs power is the 1936 case of *United States* v. *Curtiss-Wright Export Corporation.* A joint congressional resolution—a resolution by both the Senate and the House of Representatives—gave President Roosevelt the authority to embargo the sale of arms by private American companies to Bolivia and Paraguay, which were fighting a massive territorial war in a remote border area of South America called the Chaco.

Based on what we already know about the Constitution

generally, about the power of Congress in particular, and what we'll soon see about the presidential treaty power, it was clear that when the Supreme Court decided the case it would rule that the United States "government" possessed the power to control private arms sales to the Chaco. But which branch, the President or Congress? And why?

The Constitution grants the *President* power over foreign affairs, as chief executive, commander in chief, treaty-maker, and appointer and receiver of ambassadors.

Congress is granted the power to provide for the common defense, establish a uniform rule of naturalization, define and punish piracy and felonies committed on the high seas and offenses against international law, declare war, raise and support armies, provide and maintain a navy, make rules to govern the land and naval forces, repel invasions, and "make all Laws which shall be necessary and proper for carrying into Execution the foregoing Powers, and all other Powers vested by this Constitution in the Government of the United States, or in any Department of Officer thereof."

And let's not forget Article I, section 7, paragraph 1: "All Bills for raising Revenue [to finance foreign affairs and wage wars] shall originate in the House of Representatives."

Against the backdrop of each branch's powers, in *Curtiss-Wright* the Supreme Court explained the nature and scope of presidential power over foreign affairs. To fully understand the Court's reasoning in this seminal case acknowledging the foundation of presidential power over foreign affairs, the following extensive quotation is necessary.

> Not only . . . is the federal power over external affairs in origin and essential character different from that over internal affairs, but participation in the exercise of the power is significantly limited. In this vast external realm, with its important, complicated,

delicate, and manifold problems, *the President alone has the power to speak or listen as a representative of the nation.* He makes treaties with the advice and consent of the Senate; *but he alone negotiates.*

Into the field of negotiation, the Senate cannot intrude; and Congress itself is powerless to invade it. As [Chief Justice John] Marshall said in his great argument of March 7, 1800, in the House of Representatives, "The President is the sole organ of the nation in its external relations, and its sole representative with foreign nations."

* * *

The Senate Committee on Foreign Relations at a very early day in our history (February 15, 1816), reported to the Senate, among other things, as follows:

> *The President is the constitutional representative of the United States with regard to foreign nations.* He manages our concerns with foreign nations and must necessarily be most competent to determine when, how, and upon what subjects negotiation may be urged with the greatest prospect of success. For his conduct he is responsible to the Constitution. The committee considers this responsibility the surest pledge for the faithful discharge of his duty. *They think the interference of the Senate in the direction of foreign negotiations is calculated to diminish that responsibility and thereby to impair the best security for the national safety.* The nature of transactions with foreign nations, moreover, requires caution and unity of design, and their success frequently depends on secrecy and dispatch.

It is important to bear in mind that we are dealing here not only with an authority vested in the President by an exertion of legislative [congressional] power, but with such an authority plus the very delicate, plenary, and exclusive power of the President as the sole organ of the federal government in the field of international relations—*a power which does not require as a basis for its exercise an act of Congress*, but which, of course, like every other governmental power, must be exercised in subordination to the applicable provisions of the Constitution.

It is quite apparent that if, in the maintenance of our international relations, embarrassment—perhaps serious embarrassment—is to be avoided and success for our aims achieved, *congressional legislation which is to be made effective through negotiation and inquiry within the international field must often accord to the President a degree of discretion and freedom from statutory restriction which would not be admissible were domestic affairs alone involved.* Moreover, he, not Congress, has the better opportunity of knowing the conditions which prevail in foreign countries, and this is especially true in time of war.

He has his confidential sources of information. He has his agents in the form of diplomatic, consular and other officials. Secrecy in respect of information gathered by them may be highly necessary, and the premature disclosure of it productive of harmful results. Indeed, so clearly is this true that the first President refused to accede to a request to lay before the House of Representatives the instructions, correspondence, and documents relating to the negotiation of the Jay Treaty—a refusal the wisdom of which was recognized by the House itself and has never since been doubted.

In his reply to the request, President Washington said:

> The nature of foreign negotiations requires caution,
> and their success must often depend on secrecy; and
> even when brought to a conclusion a full disclosure of
> all the measures, demands, or eventual concessions
> which may have been proposed or contemplated
> would be extremely impolitic; for this might have a
> pernicious influence on future negotiations, or
> produce immediate inconveniences, perhaps danger
> and mischief, in relation to other powers. The
> necessity of such caution and secrecy was one cogent
> reason for vesting the power of making treaties in the
> President, with the advice and consent of the Senate,
> the principle on which that body was formed
> confining it to a small number of members. To admit,
> then, a right in the House of Representatives to
> demand and to have as a matter of course all the
> papers respecting a negotiation with a foreign power
> would be to establish a dangerous precedent.
>
>   * * *
>
> In the light of the foregoing observations, it is evident
> that this court should not be in haste to apply a general
> rule which will have the effect of condemning
> legislation like that under review as constituting an
> unlawful delegation of legislative power. The
> principles which justify such legislation find
> overwhelming support in the unbroken legislative
> practice which has prevailed almost from the
> inception of the national government to the present
> day.[65] (My emphasis throughout entire quotation.)

In the 2003 case of *Garamendi* v. *United States*—the question
was whether a California law, requiring insurers doing
business there to disclose information about policies sold in

Europe between 1920 and 1945, interfered with the federal government's foreign affairs power—the Supreme Court of the United States looked back on *Curtiss-Wright Export Corporation* v. *United States*, reiterating the source and scope of presidential power over foreign affairs:

> Although the source of the President's power to act in foreign affairs does not enjoy any textual detail, the historical gloss on the "executive Power" vested in Article II of the Constitution has recognized the President's "vast share of responsibility for the conduct of our foreign relations." *Youngstown Sheet & Tube Co.* v. *Sawyer.*
>
> * * *
>
> While Congress holds express authority to regulate public and private dealings with other nations in its war and foreign commerce powers, in foreign affairs the President has a degree of independent authority to act.

Closely related to the President's "independent authority to act" regarding foreign affairs is his power to fight, but not necessarily initiate, a war.

First, it's clear from the constitutional text and subsequent decisions of the Supreme Court that the President and Congress have some kind of partnership regarding war powers. Which branch is the senior partner, however, is open to reasonable argument.

As noted above, Article I, section 8 expressly grants Congress substantial power over war and its attributes:

> Congress is granted the power to provide for the common defense, establish a uniform rule of naturalization, define and punish piracy and felonies committed on the high seas and offenses against

131

international law, declare war, raise and support armies, provide and maintain a navy, make rules to govern the land and naval forces, repel invasions and "make all Laws which shall be necessary and proper for carrying into Execution the foregoing Powers, and all other Powers vested by this Constitution in the Government of the United States, or in any Department of Officer thereof."

As Professors Nowak and Rotunda observe,

"The Commander-in-Chief Clause, read in concert with provisions vesting executive power in the President to see that the laws are faithfully executed and peace preserved, is read, as a matter of historical practice, to authorize the President to use military force where required to protect national interests, unless Congress prohibits such action. After all, the Constitution does not delegate to Congress the power to 'conduct' war or to 'make' war; it only delegates the power to 'declare' war."

The President-or-Congress war power question becomes murky in situations where the former acts unilaterally and the latter provides support but without a declaration of war.

Post–World War II, President Truman (wrapped in the United Nations flag) responded unilaterally to North Korean aggression with American troops, tens of thousands of whom died fighting a three-year "police action." Congress never declared war, but appropriated money and provided much of the manpower through the draft. Without both, money and men, Truman's "police action" could not have been fought for those three long years.

So, too, in Vietnam. During World War II, American intelligence agents trained indigenous Vietnamese forces to fight against the Japanese. After the war, when those forces escalated their insurrection against the French, Presidents Truman and Eisenhower provided some covert military assistance, which continued after 1954, when the country was partitioned and France pulled out. President Kennedy continued covert operations and added overt aid through the American Military Assistance Command.

When one of our patrol craft was supposedly fired on in 1964 by North Vietnamese in the Gulf of Tonkin, Congress, which for years had been supporting our military effort in Vietnam, enacted the Gulf of Tonkin Resolution authorizing President Lyndon Johnson to go full bore against the Communists of North Vietnam. Many argued that it was the equivalent of a declaration of war, but it wasn't.

Illustrating the point about a President-Congress war power partnership, and suggesting that Congress is the senior partner, is that when the American people eventually tired of the Vietnam War's costs in blood and treasure, President Nixon bailed out; Congress turned off the money; and the South Vietnamese were left to await the inevitable victory of the North Vietnamese Communists.

The War Powers Resolution of 1973 was supposed to prevent Korea- and Vietnam-like presidential military adventures by limiting the President's power to commit troops and requiring various reports to Congress, but it has never been invoked and many deem it an unconstitutional interference with the commander in chief's war powers.

President Carter launched the abortive Iran hostage rescue mission without asking Congress for permission.

President Reagan didn't seek Congress's approval before sending Marines to Lebanon, bombing Libya, or invading Grenada.

President George H. W. Bush didn't ask Congress for a declaration of war when he repelled Iraq's invasion of Kuwait, although both Senate and House supported him. And let's not forget his unilateral invasion of Panama to oust the threatening "President" Noriega.

President Clinton acted unilaterally in Somalia, Haiti, and the Balkans—and when he bombed that dangerous aspirin factory in Sudan.

There was no declaration of war when President George W. Bush ordered military action in Afghanistan and Iraq, although, again, both Senate and House supported him with appropriations and legislation.

Whether one characterizes the President's ability to commit the American military anywhere in the world as a "war power," it's plain that as commander in chief he can act unilaterally— until Congress stops him either by eliminating appropriations or by Joint Resolution condemning his actions.

The same congressional "check and balance" exists concerning the President's treaty power.

Article II, section 2, paragraph 2 provides that the President "shall have Power, by and with the Consent of the Senate, to make Treaties, provided two thirds of the Senators present concur . . ."

It's noteworthy that the Founders required not only Senate approval for treaties negotiated by the executive branch, but also that the approval vote be by a supermajority. This requirement reflects the importance the Founders attached to popular support for arrangements that would bind the United States to international responsibilities.

Although it appears that the President can unilaterally terminate a treaty—as President Carter terminated the 1954 United States–Taiwan Mutual Defense Treaty, and President George W. Bush ended the 1972 Anti-Ballistic Missile Treaty—that power pales by comparison to two important questions that arise under the treaty power.

The first is whether treaties are superior to the Constitution, the Bill of Rights, and domestic law.

For example, can a United Nations–engineered ban on "indecency" on radio and television, entered into by the President of the United States and two-thirds of the Senate, supersede the Constitution?

Another example: There is currently an attempt through the United Nations to limit if not eliminate domestic gun rights, to which the Obama Administration is very sympathetic. Could such a UN "law" trump the Second Amendment and the Supreme Court's *Heller* and *McDonald* decisions, which ruled that the Second Amendment and the Due Process Clause, respectively, constrained Congress and states from limiting citizens' right to bear arms?

Some people think so.

Article VI, paragraph 2 of the Constitution provides that "[t]his Constitution, and the Laws of the United States which shall be made in pursuance thereof; and all Treaties made, or which shall be made, under the Authority of the United States, shall be the supreme Law of the Land . . . ."

Note the significant phraseology, deliberately used by those accomplished lawyers at the Constitutional Convention of 1787: *Statutes* must be made *pursuant to the Constitution* and *treaties* must be made *under the authority of the United States.*

According to *The Heritage Guide to the Constitution,*

> The effectiveness of national treaties was a special
> concern of the Founding generation. This language
> ensured that treaties entered into by the United States
> prior to ratification of the Constitution . . . took
> precedence over conflicting state laws. The phrasing
> does not in any way imply that treaties are "supreme".
> The Supreme Court has declared that neither a treaty
> approved by the Senate nor *an executive agreement
> made under the President's authority* can create
> obligations that violate constitutional guarantees such
> as found in the Bill of Rights.[66] (My emphasis.)

"Executive agreement made under the President's authority"?
What's that?

Simply one of the most dangerous—indeed, mega-statist—
tools available to American presidents, enabling them to act in
circumvention of the Constitution.

Maxim Litvinov was foreign minister of the Soviet Union in
the years following the Bolshevik Revolution. A Comrade
Smirnoff, let's call him, was a resident of Moscow. But he kept
a checking account, in dollars, at Bank of America in New
York City because he did business internationally and spent
time in the United States, so it was convenient to have dollars
here. And probably he feared confiscation if the New York
funds were physically located in the Soviet Union. Whatever
the reason, Comrade Smirnoff had dollars in New York.

The Soviet government—"From each according to his ability,
to each according to his needs"—enacted a law to the effect
that Smirnoff's money, and all funds expatriated from the
Soviet Union, now belonged to the Communist state.

Theft.

Out-and-out confiscation.

The Soviets then tried to repatriate the money that was formerly Smirnoff's.

To their credit, the New York courts ruled that it was against the public policy of the state to sanction the Communists' theft of Smirnoff's funds, and thus refused to allow the Soviets to get their hands on the money.

While this tug-of-war was playing out, there was considerable agitation in the Soviet hierarchy and in the United States for the Democrat Roosevelt Administration to recognize the Bolshevik regime diplomatically, thus according it legitimate international status among the other nations of the world, and entitling the regime to other benefits.

"Well," FDR probably said to Litvinov, "if the Union of Soviet Socialist Republics wants diplomatic recognition from us, we have to get something in return. For example, let's have your government assign your interest in the money you stole from [our fictitious] Comrade Smirnoff [and countless other real Soviet citizens] to the government of the United States of America."

And that's what the Soviet government did. The United States, because of an "executive agreement," recognized the Communist regime and in turn owned the stolen funds.

There wasn't a treaty. Nothing went to the Senate, let alone was there a two-thirds vote. There was no vote, anywhere.

Nichevo.[67]

Now that the United States government had come into this windfall of other people's money, the federal government tried to obtain it.

137

To their credit, the state courts again ruled that the government stood in no better position, had no cleaner hands than the thieving Soviet Union. To let the federal government obtain the stolen money, the courts said, would violate New York public policy.

Inevitably, the case of *United States* v. *Belmont* reached the Supreme Court of the United States. The Court ruled the assignment of the stolen money from the Soviet Union to the United States government had been merely *incidental* to a clear foreign affairs arrangement by our federal government with a foreign country pursuant to the foreign affairs power of the President.

In effect, the Court ruled that when it came to foreign affairs, states (e.g., New York) don't exist; the Tenth Amendment is irrelevant. To put the point another way, the Communist government's assignment to the United States of Mr. Smirnoff's stolen New York money was simply a sideshow to diplomatic recognition of the Soviet Union, an important foreign affairs coup for both countries.

According to the Court, there are agreements the President can make on his sole authority and others he can make only with the consent of the Senate. This wasn't one of the latter. It wasn't a treaty and so didn't have to go through the check-and-balance Senate approval and constitutional formalities required for a treaty.

As the Supreme Court observed in the *Garamendi* case,

> At a more specific level, our cases have recognized that the President has authority to make "executive agreements" with other countries, requiring no ratification by the Senate or approval by Congress, this power having been exercised since the early years of the Republic. See Dames & Moore v. Regan . . . ;

138

United States v. Pink . . . ; United States v. Belmont . .
. ; see also L. Henkin, Foreign Affairs and the United
States Constitution 219, 496, n. 163 (2d ed. 1996)
("Presidents from Washington to Clinton have made
many thousands of agreements . . . on matters running
the gamut of U.S. foreign relations").

Making executive agreements to settle claims of
American nationals against foreign governments is a
particularly longstanding practice, the first example
being as early as 1799, when the Washington
administration settled demands against the Dutch
Government by American citizens who lost their
cargo when Dutch privateers overtook the schooner
Wilmington Packet. See Dames & Moore . . . . Given
the fact that the practice goes back over 200 years to
the first Presidential administration, and has received
congressional acquiescence throughout its history, the
conclusion "[t]hat the President's control of foreign
relations includes the settlement of claims is
indisputable." * * *

Over the years, President Roosevelt became adept at this semi-
secret (sometimes entirely secret) way of conducting foreign
affairs. Perhaps the worst exercise of the President's executive
agreement power was at the Yalta Conference as World War II
neared its end. Roosevelt met with Winston Churchill of Great
Britain and Joseph Stalin of the Soviet Union, and carved up
Eastern Europe and parts of the Far East. The Soviet Union's
hegemony over millions of innocent people was legitimized by
the stroke of an executive [agreement] pen.

There was no treaty. Nothing went to the Senate, let alone was
there a two-thirds vote. Not anywhere.

Nichevo. Again.

139

Nothing has changed since Roosevelt.

The late Egyptian President, Anwar el-Sadat, once claimed that as part of the 1978 Sinai Accord with Israel, he concluded secret agreements in which the *United States* pledged that *Israel* would not attack *Syria* and that every effort would be made to ensure *Palestinian* participation in the Middle East settlement. Mr. Sadat did not reveal whether the agreements were written or oral.

At the same time, *The New York Times* reported that the General Accounting Office had found that Congress hadn't been notified about thirty-four executive agreements between the United States and South Korea, despite Congress having enacted a reporting requirement.

According to Professor Henkin, cited by the Supreme Court in the *Garamendi* case above, Presidents have made literally thousands upon thousands of executive agreements, ranging from the prosaic to the crucial—with virtually no interference from the Supreme Court.

This isn't to say that the Court has been totally indulgent of presidential exercise of foreign affairs or war powers. Indeed, in the handful of terrorism cases of recent years the Supreme Court has severely limited presidential power.

These cases are significant for two reasons. First, for the limitations imposed on the President. Second, and even more significant, because of what they say about the Supreme Court's power to rearrange the principles of the constitutional separation of powers and in doing so shift war power from the commander in chief to the Court itself, effectively moving that power from Article II to Article III.

This brings us to the Supreme Court's post-9/11 terrorism

decisions that are complex and reveal a traditional liberal-conservative division—with Justice Anthony Kennedy dancing between the majorities and dissents.

Almost immediately after September 11, 2011, President George W. Bush, in his capacity as commander in chief, established by executive order, military commissions to try prisoners who were captured in what was then called the War on Terror. There would be no constitutional rights for those who were captured abroad. In the view of the Bush Administration, the Guantanamo Bay naval base in Cuba was not considered part of the territorial United States. It was "offshore."

Military commissions had existed since George Washington. Even Franklin Roosevelt had convened them during World War II. During that war, Nazi saboteurs, including at least one American citizen, were quickly tried and hanged.

The first "War on Terror" case to reach the Supreme Court involved the would-be "dirty bomber," an American citizen named Jose Padilla, who was arrested in the United States. Because Padilla's attempt to be released pursuant to a writ of habeas corpus had been brought in the wrong federal court, the Supreme Court was able to decide the case on a jurisdictional issue and avoid ruling on the more important questions raised by the facts of the case, among them presidential war powers.

Next came the case of *Hamdi* v. *Rumsfeld*, also involving an American citizen. The Supreme Court ruled that the President did have the power to designate captured fighters as "enemy combatants" and hold them until the end of hostilities, whenever that might be. It also ruled that as an American citizen, Hamdi was entitled to due process. Among all the justices' opinions, only Clarence Thomas had the correct understanding of the President's war powers: *"The power to designate captured Americans as enemy combatants lay with*

141

*the president, and the courts had no role except to ascertain
whether he had made a good-faith determination."*

According to Thomas:

> The Executive Branch, acting pursuant to the powers
> vested in the President by the Constitution and with
> explicit congressional approval, has determined that
> Yaser Hamdi is an enemy combatant and should be
> detained. This detention falls squarely within the
> Federal Government's war powers, and we lack the
> expertise and capacity to second-guess that decision.
> As such, petitioners' habeas challenge should fail . . . .
> The plurality [opinion] reaches a contrary conclusion
> by failing adequately to consider basic principles of
> the constitutional structure as it relates to national
> security and foreign affairs and by using the balancing
> scheme of *Mathews* v. *Eldridge. . . . I do not think that
> the Federal Government's war powers can be
> balanced away by this Court.* Arguably, Congress
> could provide for additional procedural protections,
> but until it does, we have no right to insist upon them.
> But even if I were to agree with the general approach
> the plurality takes, I could not accept the particulars.
> The plurality utterly fails to account for the
> Government's compelling interests and for our own
> institutional inability to weigh competing concerns
> correctly. (Emphasis in original.)

Justice Thomas then invoked Supreme Court precedent (and
Alexander Hamilton in *The Federalist)* for the proposition that
there is no more compelling government interest than the
nation's security. Indeed, Thomas reminded his colleagues that
the Preamble of the Constitution expressly provides that the
purpose of union is "to provide for the common defence."
(Spelling as in the Preamble.)

He cited Chief Justice John Marshall for the proposition that the president has primacy as "the sole organ of the nation in its external relations, and its sole representative with foreign nations," which is why Article II, section 1 provides that he "shall be Commander in Chief" of the armed forces and "places in him the power to recognize foreign governments."

Citations of Supreme Court cases followed in Thomas's opinion, all reiterating that the combination of the national interest and the President's constitutional power vests in him substantial power apart from, and beyond, that of Congress in matters of national security.

> Several points, made forcefully by [former Supreme Court] Justice Jackson, are worth emphasizing. First, with respect to certain decisions relating to national security and foreign affairs, the courts simply lack the relevant information and expertise to second-guess determinations made by the President based on information properly withheld. Second, even if the courts could compel the Executive to produce the necessary information, such decisions are simply not amenable to judicial determination because "[t]hey are delicate, complex, and involve large elements of prophecy." * * * Third, the Court in *Chicago & Southern Air Lines* and elsewhere has correctly recognized the primacy of the political branches in the foreign-affairs and national-security contexts.

> For these institutional reasons and because "Congress cannot anticipate and legislate with regard to every possible action the President may find it necessary to take or every possible situation in which he might act," it should come as no surprise that "[s]uch failure of Congress . . . does not, 'especially . . . in the areas of foreign policy and national security,' imply

'congressional disapproval' of action taken by the Executive." * * *

Rather, in these domains, the fact that Congress has provided the President with broad authorities does not imply—and the Judicial Branch should not infer—that Congress intended to deprive him of particular powers not specifically enumerated.* * *

As far as the courts are concerned, "the enactment of legislation closely related to the question of the President's authority in a particular case which evinces legislative intent to accord the President broad discretion may be considered to invite measures on independent presidential responsibility."

After considerable discussion about the relative powers of the President and the Court, the transcending importance of national security, and detailed consideration of historical and judicial precedents, Thomas's unwavering conclusion was that "the Government's detention of Hamdi as an enemy combatant does not violate the Constitution. By detaining Hamdi, the President, in the prosecution of a war and authorized by Congress, has acted well within his authority [Article II]."

Unlike Yaser Hamdi, Shafik Rasul, (and others) were captured fighting, or otherwise acting against the United States, *outside* our borders. They were incarcerated at the United States Guantanamo naval base, and eventually sought habeas corpus relief to challenge their detention.

Writing for a five-justice majority in the *Rasul* case, Justice John Paul Stevens—joined by Justices O'Connor, Souter, Ginsburg and Breyer (Justice Kennedy concurred in the result, and Justice Scalia dissented, joined by Chief Justice Rehnquist and Justice Thomas)—noted that "The [trial] court held, in reliance on our [1950] opinion in *Johnson* v. *Eisentrager* . . .

that 'aliens detained outside the sovereign territory of the United States [may not] invoke a petition for a writ of habeas corpus.'" In other words, the federal district court from which enemy combatant Shafik Rasul sought habeas corpus followed Supreme Court precedent, as it was bound to do.

Rasul then appealed to the United States Court of Appeals for the District of Columbia Circuit. According to Justice Stevens, "[t]he Court of Appeals affirmed, reading Eisentrager to hold that 'the privilege of litigation' does not extend to aliens in military custody who have no presence in 'any territory over which the United States is sovereign' . . . . It held that the District Court lacked jurisdiction over petitioners' [Rasul's and others'] habeas [corpus] actions . . . ." In other words, the Court of Appeals was also bound by the Supreme Court's *Eisentrager* precedent.

But while the federal district courts and the federal courts of appeals are bound by Supreme Court precedent, the High Court itself is not—despite the venerable and important principle of *stare decisis* ("to abide by, or adhere to, decided cases).

Justice Stevens's ruling for the Court's majority was that "the habeas corpus statute, 28 U.S.C. Section 2241, extends to aliens detained by the United States military overseas, outside the sovereign borders of the United States and beyond the territorial jurisdictions of all its courts." In dissent, Justice Scalia, for himself, Chief Justice Rehnquist and Justice Thomas, wrote:

> This is not only a novel holding; it contravenes a half-century-old precedent on which the military undoubtedly relied . . . . The Court's contention that Eisentrager was somehow negated by [the Braden case of 1973]—a decision that dealt with a different issue and did not so much as mention Eisentrager—is

implausible in the extreme. This is an irresponsible overturning of settled law in a matter of extreme importance to our forces currently in the field.

Thus did the Supreme Court's liberals, aided and abetted by the turncoat Sandra Day O'Connor and the waffling Anthony Kennedy, open the doors of every federal district court in the United States to the Guantanamo enemy combatant detainees, many of them alleged killers captured on the battlefield and elsewhere around the world, their murderous hands at least figuratively, and sometimes literally, soaked with the blood of Americans, our allies, and innocent civilians. All because the Court's liberals had no qualms about degrading presidential war power.

The speciousness and indefensibleness of the *Rasul* decision, its nature and scope, and the danger it poses to America in general and the then-called War on Terror in particular, was eloquently exposed by Justice Antonin Scalia's lengthy and comprehensive dissent.

Scalia proved that the *Eisentrager* decision had been *de facto* and dishonestly overruled by the Stevens majority opinion based on illogic and bad history—and with no explanation of why that case had been wrongly decided a half-century earlier. "Today," Justice Scalia wrote, the Court "springs a trap on the Executive . . . ."

Scalia's dissent also observed: that ". . . the Court boldly extends the habeas statute to the four corners of the earth" and that "[t]he consequence of this holding . . . is breathtaking. It permits an alien captured in a foreign theater of active combat to bring a Section 2241 [habeas corpus] action against the Secretary of Defense" and that "[f]rom this point forward, federal courts will entertain petitions from these [Guantanamo] prisoners, and others like them around the world, challenging

146

actions and events far away, and forcing the courts to oversee one aspect of the Executive's conduct of a foreign war."

Well said, but to no avail.

Then Scalia confronted the Stevens majority with language from the now *de facto* overruled, decades-old *Eisentrager* case itself, where the Supreme Court had observed that:

> To grant the writ to these prisoners [held in Germany] might mean that our army must transport them across the seas for hearing. This would require allocation for shipping space, guarding personnel, billeting and rations. It might also require transportation for whatever witnesses the prisoners desired to call as well as transportation for those necessary to defend legality of the sentence. The writ, since it is held to be a matter of right, would be equally available to enemies during active hostilities as in the present twilight between war and peace. Such trials would hamper the war effort and bring aid and comfort to the enemy. They would diminish the prestige of our commanders, not only with enemies but with wavering neutrals. It would be difficult to devise more effective fettering of a field commander than to allow the very enemies he is ordered to reduce to submission to call him to account in his own civil courts and divert his efforts and attention from the military offensive abroad to the legal defensive at home. Nor is it unlikely that the result of such enemy litigiousness would be conflict between judicial and military opinion highly comforting to enemies of the United States.

As if these potential consequences of the Stevens majority ruling were not dangerous enough, consider this irony: Justice

Scalia correctly observed that "today's clumsy countertextual reinterpretation [of the federal habeas corpus statute] . . . confers upon wartime prisoners greater habeas rights than domestic detainees." Why?

> "The latter must challenge their present physical confinement in the district of their confinement; see Rumsfeld v. Padilla [above] . . . whereas under today's strange holding Guantanamo Bay detainees can petition in any of the 94 federal judicial districts. * * * For this Court to create such a monstrous scheme in time of war, and in frustration of our military commanders' reliance upon clearly stated prior law, is judicial adventurism of the worst sort."

In typical liberal fashion, once the Stevens majority wreaked havoc on the President's war power, on the military, and the country, those justices—with typical detachment—simply walked away from the potential consequences. "Whether and what further proceedings may become necessary after [the Government] make[s] their response to the merits of [the Guantanamo] detainees' claims are matters we need not address now," Stevens dismissively noted.

But unlike the cloistered liberals of the Supreme Court— irony— four of the six justices in the Stevens majority were appointed by *Republican* presidents—the rest of America must face the music.

Armed with the Supreme Court's *Hamdi* (due process) and *Rasul* (habeas corpus) decisions, and aided and comforted by radical lawyers and their America-hating colleagues, the flotsam and jetsam of Guantanamo Bay and perhaps other enemy combatants, held from Afghanistan to who-knows-where-else, can now shop around among our ninety-four federal judicial districts in search of judges sympathetic to tales of mistaken identity and religious persecution—anything to justify release of the habeas corpus petitioners. Federal judges like that haven't been hard to find.

To paraphrase Godfather Don Corleone: Radical lawyers with word processors can do more harm than 100 terrorists with machine guns.

This observation proved to be correct in the next terrorist case, *Hamdan* v. *Rumsfeld,* decided by a 5–3 vote of the Supreme Court.[68]

The case had its genesis in November 2001, when our military and the Northern Alliance were fighting the Taliban in Afghanistan. At that time, President George W. Bush issued an Order relating to the "Detention, Treatment, and Trial of Certain Non-Citizens in the War Against Terrorism."

The Order applied to non-citizens whom the President had "reason to believe" (1) were members of al Qaeda or (2) had engaged or participated in terrorist activities aimed at or harmful to the United States.

The Order provided that such persons would be tried by military commissions.

Under the military commission rules, among other provisions was that an "enemy combatant" and his lawyer could be excluded from any part of the proceedings that were closed by the tribunal's presiding officer to protect classified information and intelligence operations, for the physical safety of participants, and in the name of other national security interests.

As to evidence, everything was admissible if, in the presiding officer's opinion, it would have probative value to a reasonable

149

person. The enemy combatant need never be told of the evidence against him.

Finally, the enemy combatant and his lawyer could be denied access to classified and other protected information if the presiding officer determined that it was probative.

Remember this: military commission trials are not any part of the American civilian justice system. They try enemy combatants, and are military proceedings. They do not try civilian criminals.

In 2001, Salim Ahmed Hamdan was captured on the battlefield in Afghanistan, and in 2002 was sent to Guantanamo Bay.

In 2003, the President determined that Hamdan was subject to the Military Commission Order, though specific charges had not yet been made against him. A military lawyer was appointed to represent Hamdan.

After various procedures and sparring in other venues, Hamdan's case reached the Supreme Court of the United States, where there were two questions: "[1] Whether the military commission convened to try Hamdan has authority to do so, and [2] whether Hamdan may rely on the Geneva Conventions in these proceedings." In other words, [1] jurisdiction and [2] whether the military commission squared with the requirements of the Geneva Conventions.

The jurisdictional question need not concern us here; the Court ruled that the military commission had the power to entertain and decide the case. [69]

As to the Geneva Conventions question, the Court ruled that they applied to Hamdan. Under them, the Court ruled further that the structure of President Bush's military commissions, and the rules they operated under, were inadequate to safeguard Hamdan's rights under the Universal Code of Military Justice and, for good measure, international law.

Why?

Writing for the liberal majority again, Justice Stevens ruled that Congress had not authorized that *particular type* of military commission, and that it suffered fatally from certain specific structural and procedural deficiencies—deficiencies considered illegal by Common Article 3 of the Geneva Conventions.

Justice Thomas's dissent agreed with Justice Scalia on the originalist-driven jurisdictional issue, leaving Thomas to address the Geneva Conventions–military commission issue. In so doing, Thomas stood firmly on grounds of separation of powers in general and the war power of the President specifically.

Thomas led off with a broad stroke. The Court's opinion, he wrote, "openly flouts our well-established duty to respect the Executive's judgment in matters of military operations and foreign affairs. The Court's evident belief that *it* is qualified to pass on the '[m]ilitary necessity' . . . of the Commander in Chief's decision to employ a particular form of force against our enemies is so antithetical to our constitutional structure that it simply cannot go unanswered."

He followed with an explanation of the role of each branch of government in the "conduct of war," and then "emphasize[d] the complete congressional sanction of the President's exercise of his commander-in-chief authority to conduct the present war." Because of that, Thomas argued, the Court's duty to "defer to the Executive's military and foreign policy judgment is at its zenith; it does not countenance the kind of second-guessing the Court repeatedly engages in today." Thomas reminded Stevens and the others what, in an earlier terrorist case, Thomas had said in dissent about military and foreign policy judgments.

> They are and should be undertaken only by those directly responsible to the people whose welfare they advance or imperil. They are decisions of a kind for which the Judiciary has neither aptitude, facilities nor responsibility and which has long been held to belong in the domain of political power not subject to judicial intrusion or inquiry.

The balance of Thomas's dissent was devoted to a rebuttal of each of the Stevens points, culminating near the end with this lengthy, comprehensive statement:

> Today a plurality of this Court would hold that conspiracy to massacre innocent civilians does not violate the laws of war. This determination is unsustainable. The judgment of the political branches [Congress and the President] that Hamdan, and others like him, must be held accountable before military commissions for their involvement with and membership in an unlawful organization dedicated to inflicting massive civilian casualties is supported by virtually every relevant authority, including all of the authorities invoked by the plurality today. It is also supported by the nature of the present conflict.

> We are not engaged in a traditional battle with a nation-state, but with a worldwide, hydra-headed enemy, who lurks in the shadows conspiring to reproduce the atrocities of September 11, 2001, and who has boasted of sending suicide bombers into civilian gatherings, has proudly distributed videotapes of beheadings of civilian workers, and has tortured

152

and dismembered captured American soldiers. But according to the plurality, when our Armed Forces capture those who are plotting terrorist atrocities like the bombing of the Khobar Towers, the bombing of the U.S.S. Cole, and the attacks of September 11— even if their plots are advanced to the very brink of fulfillment—our military cannot charge those criminals with any offense against the laws of war. Instead, our troops must catch the terrorists "red handed" . . . in the midst of the attack itself, in order to bring them to justice. Not only is this conclusion fundamentally inconsistent with the cardinal principal of the law of war, namely protecting non-combatants, but it would sorely hamper the President's ability to confront and defeat a new and deadly enemy.

After seeing the plurality overturn longstanding precedents in order to seize jurisdiction over this case [see Justice Scalia's dissent in footnote 68] . . . it is no surprise to see them go on to overrule one after another of the President's judgments pertaining to the conduct of an ongoing war. Those Justices who today disregard the commander-in-chief's wartime decisions, only 10 days ago [in another end-of-the-term case] deferred to the judgment of the Corps of Engineers with regard to a matter much more within the competence of lawyers, upholding that agency's wildly implausible conclusion that a storm drain is a tributary of the waters of the United States. * * * It goes without saying that there is much more at stake here than storm drains. The plurality's willingness to second-guess the determination of the political branches that these conspirators must be brought to justice is both unprecedented and dangerous.

The bright side of the *Hamdan* decision, if there be one, is that the Court's decision *does recognize the legitimacy of military commissions*, albeit ones different from the one convened to try Hamdan.

That, however, doesn't change the fact that in an extreme exercise of judicial usurpation and arrogance, the *Hamdan* majority justices made a mockery of the Constitution's separation of powers and significantly intruded into the President's power as chief executive and commander in chief. The implications of this judicial intrusion—exalting the power of federal courts to micromanage a war while further limiting the President's freedom of action by forcing him to negotiate with Congress about his conduct—do not auger well for America's war against Islamic jihad.

The last terrorism case decided by the Supreme Court before this book was published was *Boumediene* v. *Bush*, a 5–4 decision where, in dissent, Justice Scalia wrote that "for the first time in our Nation's history, the Court confers a constitutional right to habeas corpus on alien enemies detained abroad by our military forces in the course of an ongoing war."

- o   Note that they receive United States *constitutional habeas corpus*, not protection under the Geneva Conventions or other international law.
- o   Note that they are *alien enemies*, not American citizens.
- o   Note that they are detained *abroad*, not in the United States (or Guantanamo).
- o   Note that it is during *wartime*, not while they are engaged in some kind of domestic criminality.

Justice Kennedy, for a five-justice majority, ruled that the right to seek a writ of habeas corpus under constitutional and federal statutory law *was available to enemy combatants and prisoners held at Guantanamo* (none of whom need be American citizens). Although Congress might be able to

154

suspend that remedy, it could not do so without providing some mechanism for what the writ itself would provide. Since the Detainee Treatment Act did not provide that mechanism, it was unconstitutional.

In dissent, Chief Justice Roberts wrote:

> Today the Court strikes down as inadequate the most generous set of procedural protections ever afforded aliens detained by this country as enemy combatants. The political branches [Congress and the President] crafted these procedures [the Detainee Treatment Act] amidst an ongoing military conflict, after much careful investigation and thorough debate. The Court rejects them today out of hand, without bothering to say what due process rights the detainees possess, without explaining how the statute fails to vindicate those rights, and before a single petitioner [prisoner] has even attempted to avail himself of the law's operation. And to what effect? The majority merely replaces a review system designed by the people's representatives with a set of shapeless procedures to be defined by federal courts at some future date. One cannot help but think, after surveying the modest practical results of the majority's ambitious opinion, that this decision is not really about the detainees at all, but about control of federal policy regarding enemy combatants.
>
> * * *
>
> So who has won? Not the detainees. The Court's analysis leaves them with only the prospect of further litigation to determine the content of their new habeas right, followed by further litigation to resolve their particular cases, followed by further litigation before the D.C. [District of Columbia] Circuit—where they could have started had they invoked the DTA

155

[Detainee Treatment Act] procedure. Not Congress, whose attempt to "determine—through democratic means—how best" to balance the security of the American people with the detainees' liberty interests . . . has been unceremoniously brushed aside. Not the Great Writ [of habeas corpus], whose majesty is hardly enhanced by its extension to a jurisdictionally quirky outpost, with no tangible benefit to anyone. Not the rule of law, unless by that is meant the rule of lawyers, who will now arguably have a greater role than military and intelligence officials in shaping policy for alien enemy combatants. And certainly not the American people, who today lose a bit more control over the conduct of this Nation's foreign policy to unelected, politically unaccountable judges.

If the detainees have not won, if Congress has not won, if the principle of habeas corpus has not won, if the rule of law has not won, if the American people have not won—and, one can add, if the President as commander in chief has not won—who has?

Chief Justice Roberts told us. The *Boumediene* decision is "not really about the detainees at all, *but about control of federal policy regarding enemy combatants*," and that "today's opinion has . . . shift[ed] responsibility for those sensitive foreign policy and national security decisions *from the elected branches* [Congress and the President] *to the Federal Judiciary*." To "unelected, politically unaccountable judges." (My emphasis.)

In that shift of responsibility, the more narrow loss is of the President's war powers. Much worse is the violation of separation of powers—an imbalance now allowing the Supreme Court of the United States to put its thumb on the scale and weigh more heavily the so-called rights of terrorists at the expense of innocent Americans whose safety and other interests are to be sacrificed on the altar of state—in this case, *judicial*—power.

We will examine the nature and extent of that power in the next chapter.

5.
The Judiciary and Its Powers

Even though by now I've had a lot to say about the judiciary—Chief Justice John Marshall establishing the Supreme Court's power of judicial review; the judicial relationship to federalism and separation of powers; the frequent explicit appearance and institutionalization of Ayn Rand's "inner contradiction," originalism, and more—there's still much to say about other aspects of judicial power: the "nuts and bolts" of the *exercise* of such power, which has serious substantive consequences for individual rights and limited government.

Article III, section 1 delegates judicial power: "The *judicial Power* of the United States, shall be vested in one supreme Court, and in such inferior courts as the Congress may from time to time ordain and establish."

Section 2 provides that "[t]he judicial Power shall extend to all *Cases*, in Law and Equity, arising under this Constitution, the Laws of the United States, and Treaties made, or which shall be made, under their Authority . . . ."

I've emphasized the words "judicial Power" and "Cases" because while they appear to be innocuous and easily defined terms, they aren't.

Loosely speaking, "judicial power" is the power to decide, something that courts have done as long as anyone can remember. Our modern judicial system—actually two systems: state and federal—is hierarchical. At the bottom of the ladder are trial courts, essentially fact-finding forums (with or without juries) where the judge acts as the referee of legal issues (Was certain evidence admissible?) rather than the decider of factual questions (Was the traffic light red or green?).[70]

159

A rung above the trial courts are appeal courts, whose job is to make sure the lower courts correctly applied the law. (Were the jury instructions correct?)

At the top of the judicial ladder are the highest courts of each state and, above them, the Supreme Court of the United States. They determine for themselves what cases they hear, and are usually interested only when important legal questions are presented. The Supreme Court of the United States wears two hats (or robes). As the highest court in the federal system, it interprets federal statutes. It also interprets the Constitution of the United States of America in cases coming from both state and federal courts.

Note that Article III vests judicial power only over *cases*; if a dispute isn't a *case*, there's nothing to apply judicial power to. The constitutional requirement that there be a case applies a textual *limitation* on the exercise of judicial power. For the judicial power to be exercised, there must be "judicial business" afoot.

But even if there is judicial business, courts can't be expected to be bottomless vessels into which endless disputes are poured. There are limitations on what judicial business courts, especially the Supreme Court, will entertain—some limitations are constitutionally required, some are self-imposed.

Essentially, there are seven such limitations, one of which is minor compared to the others (see Note 73).

Advisory opinions. Simply stated, when a court is asked to render an advisory opinion, there is in no sense a "case." There are no legally adverse parties, the facts are not settled and subject to change. Mere curiosity about the answer to a legal question is not "judicial business." Courts don't give advice; they decide adversely concrete cases and create finality in the disputes before them.

Recall that when President Washington asked for the opinions of Hamilton and Jefferson in the Bank Controversy, the two secretaries were members of the executive branch, not judges.

Imagine a President seeking an opinion from the Supreme Court about whether he could be impeached without first being indicted, or whether a bill being considered by Congress is constitutional. If courts issued advisory opinions, they would be violating separation of powers.

Political questions. According to Professors Nowak and Rotunda, "[t]he political question doctrine states that certain matters are really political in nature and best resolved by the body politic rather than suitable for judicial review." In other words, the controversy, as otherwise legitimate as it may be, is not really "judicial business."

 The cases brought to challenge the legality of the Vietnam War are examples of non-justiciable "political questions." So, too, would be a legal challenge to congressional committee assignments and the seniority system in Congress. Also, whether the President should withdraw troops from Afghanistan. In all these situations and others like them, there are other means within the democratic process that should resolve these kinds of questions.

Ripeness. This is one of the most important limitations on the exercise of judicial power, because premature judicial adjudication would embroil courts in hypothetical disagreements, which are not yet judicial business. Here's how Justice Thomas explained the ripeness doctrine in *National Parks Hospitality Association* v. *Department of Interior*:

> Ripeness is a justiciability doctrine designed "to prevent the courts, through avoidance of premature adjudication, from entangling themselves in abstract

disagreements over administrative policies, and also to protect the agencies from judicial interference until an administrative decision has been formalized and its effects felt in a concrete way by the challenging parties." * * * The ripeness doctrine is "drawn both from Article III limitations on judicial power and from prudential reasons for refusing to exercise jurisdiction . . . ."

Determining whether administrative action is ripe for judicial review requires us to evaluate (1) the fitness of the issues for judicial decision and (2) the hardship to the parties of withholding court consideration. * * * "Absent [a statutory provision providing for immediate judicial review], a regulation is not ordinarily considered the type of agency action 'ripe" for judicial review under the [Administrative Procedure Act (APA)] until the scope of the controversy has been reduced to more manageable proportions, and its factual components fleshed out, by some concrete action applying the regulation to the claimant's situation in a fashion that harms or threatens to harm him.

* * *

Recall Article III, which vests "*judicial* Power." (My emphasis.)

Obviously, there is no bright line separating ripe from unripe cases. So how to tell, especially if in a given case the judges themselves disagree, as often happens?

Ultimately, the issue of ripeness requires a subjective decision that's very fact intensive. Courts need to know factually what has happened so far in the controversy in order to know

162

whether there is "judicial business."
As an example, let's take one of my cases.

A Southwestern state enacted comprehensive election "reform" legislation. One section of the statute provided that no contributions received in a *federal* election campaign could be used by the candidate in a *state* election campaign. Doing so was a crime, even though in the case of *Buckley* v. *Valeo* the Supreme Court had ruled that spending money in connection with an election is a protected constitutional right under the First Amendment.

On the one hand, we were confronted by the prohibitory criminal statute, and on the other, the Supreme Court's *Buckley* ruling that spending money in an electoral contest was protected free speech.

I represented a congressman who had in his war chest some federally raised money, and was considering running for governor. So we sued.

I alleged that the statute violated the First Amendment.

The state attorney general argued that our claim was not yet "ripe." That

> "until such time as the congressman can represent to
> the court that he intends to run for a state elective
> office, this matter is not ripe for adjudication. Neither
> he nor his campaign committee demonstrate any
> concrete hardship until his plans concerning state
> elective office are more definite."

A classic ripeness argument.

The federal district judge agreed with the state:

"because the plaintiff has expressed no firm interest in spending money in connection with a state election campaign and has shown no definite interest in running for state elective office, he is not currently forced to choose between violating the law and pursuing his First Amendment rights. There is no impact on him which is sufficiently direct and immediate. In its current posture, this case fails to portray him suffering substantial hardship as a result of my withholding judicial review.

Of course, if he sometime in the future presents a more detailed and solid factual record regarding his intention to spend funds in connection with a state election campaign, he would not be precluded from again seeking relief in this court."

How generous.

I appealed to the United States Court of Appeals for the Tenth Circuit, and won. Said the court:

The facts presented to the district court undoubtedly show the existence of the . . . statute has created a direct and immediate dilemma with respect to [the] Congressman['s] exercise of his First Amendment liberties. * * * [He] has, however, as a result of the statute, grown reluctant to solicit funds in the usual manner, i.e., for unrestricted purposes. This has had the further effect of reducing the likelihood that [he] will be able to obtain funds from contributors due to the limited use for which those funds could be put under the statute. The dilemma thereby created is this: If [he] is to either inform potential contributors of the statutorily imposed restrictions on the use to which their donations can be put, or if [he] expresses a

generalized intent of following all applicable laws
regarding campaign contributions and expenditures,
he will at the same time be impairing his ability to
effectively exercise his First Amendment liberties.

The Tenth Circuit reversed the trial court 2–1.[71]

The **ripeness** issue was thus crucial to the determination of the
underlying free speech issue. If we hadn't prevailed on
ripeness, the statute would have remained in place and the
congressman would have been unable to use his federally
raised money for a state election campaign.[72] Ripeness can
control the substantive outcome of a case.

Mootness. There may have been a real case, but now is it too
late? Is there no longer a dispute? Do the parties have what
they wanted?

In the context of Article III, mootness means that there's
nothing left to decide. There *was* once something to decide, but
there's nothing left anymore. Something has happened after a
lawsuit has begun; a settlement, for example. Or an essential
party has died. The essence of mootness is that if the posture of
the case at the beginning were the way it is today, would it had
been brought? Having said this, however, the *application* of
the mootness doctrine is more difficult than merely stating it.

Roe v. *Wade* is one of the most notorious cases in American
jurisprudence. Roe was pregnant when the case began in 1970.
The Supreme Court decided the case in 1973, when *Roe*
obviously was no longer pregnant. So the question is, how was
the Court able to decide the case? Why wasn't the mootness
doctrine applied?

Justice Blackmun's answer was that

> when, as here, pregnancy is a significant fact in the
> litigation, the normal 266-day human gestation period
> is so short that the pregnancy will come to term before
> the usual appellate process is complete. If that
> termination makes a case moot, pregnancy litigation
> seldom will survive much beyond the trial stage and
> appellate review will be effectively denied. Our laws
> should not be that rigid. Pregnancy often comes more
> than once to the same woman and in the general
> population. If man is to survive it will always be with
> us." * * * "Pregnancy provides a classic justification
> or a conclusion of non-mootness. It truly could be
> capable of repetition yet evading review.

Contrast the mootness result in *Roe* with that of *DeFunis* v.
Odegaard. DeFunis had challenged a law school minority
admission program on the ground that it was racially
discriminatory. While the case was in the courts, however, he
attended classes.

In the Supreme Court, with DeFunis about to graduate,
somehow his case was not "capable of repetition yet evading
review." His case was moot.

How to reconcile *Roe* and *DeFunis*? Cynics might believe that
the Court, for policy reasons, wanted to decide *Roe* and
legalize abortion, but didn't want to decide *DeFunis* and face
the affirmative action question.

Standing to sue. In situations where all the other requirements
for justiciability are satisfied, is there a party who is
sufficiently affected so as to invoke the judicial process?
Obviously, the Constitution does not contemplate a situation
where *no one* can sue, under any circumstances. Nor a

166

situation where *anyone* can sue, under any circumstances. Someone must be able to sue about something.

The courts sit with their hands on a valve. If it's turned too far to the left, on, everyone can sue. Too far to the right, off, no one can sue. Where's the middle ground?

The case of *Baker* v. *Carr* established that in non-taxpayer lawsuits involving personal legal questions, to have standing to sue, a party must have a personal stake in the outcome "to assure concrete adverseness which sharpens the presentation of issues."

Easy to say. But within this formulation is the difficult but essential question of whether the party has sustained an adequate personal *injury*. At that point the inquiry breaks down into sub-questions that are complex even for constitutional lawyers. So suffice it to say for our purposes that as a constitutional requirement under Article III, and a prudential hand-on-the-valve consideration, federal courts, especially the Supreme Court, have long wrestled with both the concept of standing to sue and its application in real cases.[73]

Abstention. A court can abstain only from cases that satisfy all the criteria of justiciability. The case cannot request an advisory opinion, present a political question, be unripe, have a plaintiff who lacks standing to sue, or be moot. Once a case is deemed justiciable, only then will a court examine whether the self-imposed doctrine of abstention—whose genesis is in the federalism principle—should be applied.

Let's focus on federalism again for a moment. Recall that there are two spheres of government, state and federal. There are two sets of laws, state and federal. There are two judicial systems, state and federal. The federal government is empowered by the delegations made to it in the Constitution;

the states, by nature of their sovereignty and the explicit recognition of their reserved power under the Tenth Amendment.

Abstention becomes an issue at the federal trial level. *All the constitutional and self-created limitations have been satisfied: the court possesses jurisdiction.* Jurisdictionally, either the case arises under the Constitution or a federal statute, or involves parties from different states.

 Even when a federal district court does have jurisdiction and there are no other impediments to its exercise, courts today abstain infrequently. Abstention usually happens in two kinds of cases.

First, where a federal constitutional question could be substantially affected by a state court ruling on its own state law.

Second, less legally but more politically, where, according to Nowak and Rotunda, there exist "difficult questions of state law bearing on policy problems of substantial public import whose importance transcends the result in the case" then before the court.

To illustrate, let's look at the case of *Boehning* v. *Indiana Employees Association.*

A state employee, a woman named Musgrave, had allegedly done something that constituted grounds for being fired. She sought a pre-termination hearing, was denied one, and was then fired for cause.

Musgrave brought a *federal* civil rights lawsuit in an Indiana *federal* district court, alleging that she had a *federal civil right* —specifically, Fourteenth Amendment procedural due process—to a pre-termination hearing.

168

This certainly sounds like a valid case. All the Article III and self-imposed requirements had been met and the court had jurisdiction.

But it abstained!

Why?

Because there was an Indiana statute which might have provided Musgrave with a pre-termination hearing. The problem, however, was that no one knew what the Indiana statute meant because it had not yet been interpreted by the state court.

When the case reached the Supreme Court of the United States, it upheld the trial court's abstention because, from its own independent research, the Court found another state statute (the Indiana Administrative Adjudication Act) that might also have granted Musgrave a pre-termination hearing. If either statute did that, the state pre-termination hearing would eliminate entirely the need for federal relief, let alone a constitutional ruling on Fourteenth Amendment procedural due process.

This result is unadulterated federalism. The Tenth Amendment at work. The Supreme Court deferred to the State of Indiana and to statutes enacted by the State Legislature and approved by the governor. If it turned out that after Musgrave jumped through all the Indiana hoops she had no pre-termination hearing entitlement under *state* law, she could return to the *federal* trial court with a Fourteenth Amendment due process claim.[74]

6.
Intergovernmental Relations

Recall that during the Articles of Confederation period a potentially fatal problem was that some states enacted trade barriers against other states, a problem sought to be cured by the Constitution.

How does the Constitution provide that the states have to get along? Through interstate collaboration and interstate obligations.

Federalism is, in effect, a "vertical" relationship between the federal government and the states. Intergovernmental relations deal principally with the "horizontal" relationship of the states to each other.

There's one interstate collaboration requirement I want to mention in passing, and two I want to discuss.

Article I, section 10, paragraph 3 provides that "[n]o state shall, without the Consent of Congress . . . enter into any Agreement or Compact with another State." The Framers were concerned about some states ganging up on others. (Despite the clear language of this section, the Supreme Court has ruled that only compacts that encroach on federal supremacy have to be approved by Congress. A safeguard for federalism.)

Article IV, section 1 provides that "[f]ull Faith and Credit shall be given in each State to the public Acts, Records, and judicial Proceedings of every other State . . . ." This section serves as strong glue to hold the states together "horizontally" in our federal union

Because the "public Acts" and "Records" part of the section can get very complicated, let's focus on the more important "judicial Proceedings."

Let's say that someone gets divorced in New Mexico and then moves to California. Is the New Mexico divorce decree good in California or, if he wants to remarry there, does he risk being charged with bigamy? If a New York creditor obtains a judgment in that state and the debtor then moves to Missouri, can the creditor enforce the judgment there?

If the New Mexico divorce decree and the New York money judgment were unenforceable in other states, the problems for the federal union would be unimaginable.

The Full Faith and Credit Clause solves that problem. Here's how.

Let's use "F1" to designate the state where a judgment was obtained (e.g., the divorce decree or the money judgment) and "F2" for the state where the judgment is sought to be enforced.

It's obvious that if the F1 judgment was obtained underhandedly—e.g., the plaintiff engaged in some kind of fraud on the court, or the defendant was never served with papers—it should not be enforced in F2.

So the question is what criteria does the F1 judgment have to satisfy in order to be enforceable in F2?

The Supreme Court answered that question in the case of *Durfee* v. *Duke*.[75] The Court acknowledged that Article IV plainly provides that the Full Faith and Credit Clause generally requires every state (F2) to give a judgment at least the effect it would be accorded in the state which rendered it (F1). If it's good in F1, it has to be good in F2.

But what makes the judgment good?

First, that F1 had jurisdiction.[76] If no jurisdiction, no full faith and credit.

Next, the F1 judgment is enforceable in F2 if in F1 the issues before the court were "fully and fairly litigated" and decided there with "finality."

The Supreme Court's decision was not only sound, but it provided a workable, commonsensical test for enforcement of an F1 judgment. The need for courts to determine rights of litigants is an integral part of our system, and with fifty states in the union, chaos would ensue if a judgment in F1 was unenforceable in F2, let alone in F3 through F48. Indeed, unenforceability of the F1 judgment elsewhere would require relitigation of all the F1 issues—a situation hardly conducive to a federal union of coequal states. There would never be finality for the determination of rights and responsibilities.

I'll demonstrate this point with an actual case.

When I first began practicing law in 1959, I was retained to collect a very large judgment that had been rendered in a New York (F1) divorce case. Soon after the defendant lost in the Big Apple, he moved to Reno, Nevada, and then to San Francisco, California. I sued on the New York judgment in San Francisco. The debtor argued that the New York (F1) judgment was no good in California (F2) because it was no good in New York.

Why?

Because, he argued, under *Durfee* v. *Duke,* the New York case had not been "fully and fairly litigated" there.

I went back to the New York trial records looking for proof of "fully and fairly litigated." I found that in the New York courts

173

the defendant had not only had a lawyer, appeared in the case, participated in the proceedings beginning on the day he was served with the summons and the complaint, made motions, and interposed affirmative defenses to his wife's complaint, but also had counterclaimed, thereby starting a new lawsuit of his own.

The defendant had done everything he possibly could have done in the New York litigation. He had even waived his right to appeal the judgment. No case had ever been more "fully and fairly litigated" in F1.

In that case and most other full faith and credit cases, we see vindication of the Framers' wisdom as they sought to meld this nation into a true union of *United* States.

As difficult as it is to imagine the Constitution not having a Full Faith and Credit Clause, it's equally hard to contemplate no Article IV, section 2, paragraph 2: "A Person charged in any State with Treason, Felony, or other Crime, who shall flee from Justice, and be found in another State, shall on Demand of the executive Authority [the governor] of the State from which he fled, to be delivered up, to be removed to the State having Jurisdiction of the Crime." The Extradition Clause.

The constitutional principle served by the Extradition Clause again demonstrates the "horizontal" relationship of the states. It requires one state to respect another state, and contributes more glue to cement the union.

Sometimes overlooked in discussions of the federalism, separation of powers, judicial review, delegated power, and state collaboration/obligation aspects of the Constitution are its provisions furthering those core elements. I refer to the Constitution's express *prohibitions* on the conduct of the federal government and the states (other than those of the Bill of Rights, which I'll discuss in later chapters).

174

Let's begin with Article 1, section 9, which contains a host of prohibitions. First, habeas corpus. "The Privilege of the Writ of Habeas Corpus shall not be suspended, unless when in Cases of Rebellion or Invasion, the public Safety may require it." This text seems pretty clear, but let's see how the section actually plays out in the real world. (By the way, this is the only place in the Constitution where habeas corpus is mentioned.)

When reading the section, the first question coming to mind is "shall not be suspended" by whom? The Constitution doesn't say. Is it the President, Congress, courts, the states? Note where the Framers put the suspension power, in Article I: "All legislative Powers herein granted shall be vested in a Congress of the United States . . . ." So only Congress can suspend the writ. This provision was derived from the English system of law, where only Parliament could suspend the writ.

President Lincoln learned this lesson in the case of *Ex parte Merryman*, when Chief Justice Roger Taney reminded the chief executive/commander in chief that only Congress had the power to suspend the writ.[77]

Article 1, section 9, clause 3 provides that "[n]o bill of Attainder or ex post facto Law shall be passed." The two are not the same, although the provisions are often mistakenly referred to interchangeably. A bill of attainder is punishment without a judicial trial. For example, in the mid-1940s, Congress passed an Act prohibiting the payment of compensation to certain specifically named government employees who had been charged with subversive activities. That was a bill of attainder. Legislative punishment without a trial.

An ex post facto [literally, "after the fact"] law is one that makes an act criminal that was innocent when done, or which imposes a greater punishment than the law provided when it was committed.[78]

175

Even with all the recent discussion about the Tenth Amendment being the counterweight to the powers delegated to Congress—"The powers not delegated to the United States by the Constitution, *nor prohibited by it to the States* (my emphasis), are reserved to the States respectively, or to the people"— there has been little attention paid to those prohibitions.[79] Even though, as we'll see presently, Minnesota's violation of one of them produced one of the worst altruist-collectivist-statist decisions in Supreme Court history.

Article I, section 10, paragraph 1, prohibits states from enacting any law "impairing the Obligation of Contracts." This is among the most important provisions of the Constitution attempting to safeguard the sacredness of private property.

Every day of our lives we come into contact with scores if not hundreds of other people. We interact with loved ones, fellow workers, casual acquaintances, total strangers, landlords, employers, clerks, physicians. Most of these interactions are voluntary.

To the extent that voluntarily chosen relationships create important benefits and obligations, the details have to be objectified and easily recalled. Hence, many are expressed in formal contracts.

Contracts embody the voluntary arrangements of free people. Without contracts, little or nothing would ever be accomplished. Because enforceable private choices are a cornerstone of individual rights, contracts are indispensable to objectify and protect those choices. For this reason, the Founders specifically provided in Article I, section 10 that state governments were prohibited from enacting any law "impairing the Obligation of Contracts." This provision was designed to insert itself between contracting parties and the states, preventing the latter from rewriting (or nullifying) private agreements either for the government's own purposes or for anybody else's benefit.

The genesis of the Contract Clause is found in debtor relief laws. Early on, first colonies and then states enacted laws simply wiping out debt, at the great expense of creditors. These debtor relief laws were altruism, collectivism, and statism at their naked essence. One man's debt is another man's asset. Wipe out the debt, and government has stolen the asset.

Traditionally, however, there were certain exceptions prohibiting government interference with contract rights.

First, states (and the federal government, in the Fifth Amendment) possess the power to condemn private property for public use if "just compensation" is paid.

The second exception is the state police power. As noted earlier, under the Tenth Amendment it was long understood that the states had the power to legislate regarding the public health, safety, welfare, and morals. For example, if two people make a contract that Party A has a license to dump raw sewage on Party B's lawn, obviously the government has the power to step in and nullify that contract to abate the public health and safety dangers.

If someone decides when they buy a nursing home that to save money they're going to make a contract to remove the sprinkler system, the fire marshals will promptly nullify that agreement as a threat to the residents' safety. As far as morals are concerned, a lease on a bordello where prostitution is illegal will be void on public policy grounds despite the Contract Clause.

Let's look at two cases involving state impairment of contracts and see what the Supreme Court did with them. Let's see whether in America a contract is worth the paper it's written on.

The first case is *Blaisdell* v. *Home Building & Loan Association*, the poster case for impairment of contracts.

Mr. and Mrs. John H. Blaisdell sat down with the Home Building & Loan Association and mortgaged a two-story residential building in Minneapolis, Minnesota.

A mortgage is simply another name for a certain kind of contract. The owner (or would-be owner) of real property (the "mortgagor") pledges that property to a lender (the "mortgagee") as security for a loan. Usually, the proceeds of the loan are used to purchase the property. A common example is the financing arrangement for the purchase of a home. (There also can be "chattel" mortgages for personal property, such as financed purchases of automobiles.)

The Blaisdells' mortgage (contract) with their lender contained customary, rather simple terms.

In return for putting up their property as collateral, the Blaisdells received money from the lender. The Blaisdells agreed to repay the loan in regular monthly installments of principal and interest.

If the Blaisdells didn't make the payments—if they defaulted on their contractual agreement—the lender could protect its creditor position by foreclosing on the property and selling it at auction.

This is exactly what's happening today across the country: loan contracts are being breached because of non-payment, and lenders are availing themselves of the legal remedy of foreclosure in order to protect, at least to some extent, the money they loaned.

Back to the Blasidells and the bank.

If the foreclosure sale netted more than the amount Home Building & Loan Association was owed, the excess proceeds would go to the Blaisdells. If it netted less, the Blaisdells would owe the lender the difference (a "deficiency").

Another provision of the mortgage contract—automatically inserted as a requirement of Minnesota law—was a one-year redemption period following a foreclosure sale, during which the Blaisdells could reacquire the property for the price at which it had been sold.

The buyer at the foreclosure sale could get good title only when the one-year redemption period had expired without the Blaisdells having exercised their statutory right of redemption. (Let's put aside for now by what right the Minnesota legislature could enact a law requiring private contracts to include a right of redemption—a state power whose source is far from clear or defensible.)

For a few years, the Blaisdells made their regular mortgage payments. Then they stopped.

A foreclosure sale followed, and the lender "bought" the property for exactly the amount then owed on the mortgage. The sale yielded no excess proceeds for the Blaisdells, and no deficiency was owed by them to Home Building & Loan Association, which now owned the property subject to the Blaisdells' one-year statutory right of redemption.

Because the foreclosure sale occurred on May 2, 1932, the Blaisdells had until May 2, 1933 to redeem the property.

But a few weeks before that date, providence, in the guise of the State of Minnesota Legislature, intervened. On April 18,

1933, a mere fourteen days before the one-year redemption period was set to expire, the state enacted the "Minnesota Mortgage Moratorium Law," which rewrote the contractual agreement between the Blaisdells and Home Building & Loan Association.

Why?

As the Minnesota Legislature explained,

> Whereas, the severe financial and economic depression existing for several years past has resulted in *extremely low prices* for the products of the farms and the factories, a great amount of *unemployment*, an almost complete *lack of credit* for farmers, business men and property owners and a general and *extreme stagnation of business, agriculture and industry*, and

> Whereas, many owners of real property, by reason of said conditions, are unable, and it is believed, will for some time be *unable to meet all payments* as they come due of taxes, interest and principal of mortgages on their properties and are, therefore, *threatened with loss of such properties* through mortgage foreclosure and judicial sales thereof, and

> Whereas, many such properties have been and are being bid in at mortgage foreclosure . . . sales for prices much below what is believed to be their real values and often for *much less than the mortgage* or . . . indebtedness, thus entailing deficienc[ies] . . . against the mortgage[es] . . . . and

> Whereas, it is believed, and the Legislature of Minnesota hereby declares its belief, that the conditions existing as hereinbefore set forth has

created an *emergency* of such nature that justifies and validates legislation for the extension of the time of redemption from mortgage foreclosure and execution sales and other relief of a like character; and

Whereas, The State of Minnesota possesses the right under its police power to declare a *state of emergency* to exist, and

Whereas, the inherent and fundamental purposes of our government is to *safeguard the public and promote the general welfare of the people*; and

Whereas, under existing conditions the *foreclosure of many real estate mortgages* by advertisement would prevent fair, open and competitive bidding . . . and

Whereas, it is believed, and the Legislature of Minnesota hereby declares its belief, that the conditions existing as hereinbefore set forth have created an *emergency* of such a nature that justifies and validates changes in legislation providing for the temporary manner, method, terms and conditions upon which mortgage foreclosure sales may be had or postponed and jurisdiction to administer equitable relief in connection therewith may be conferred upon the District Court,

* * *

Section 1. *Emergency Declared to Exist*. In view of the situation . . . the Legislature of the State of Minnesota hereby declares that *a public economic emergency does exist* in the State of Minnesota. (My emphasis throughout entire quotation.)

Sound familiar?

181

Just substitute for the "Minnesota Legislature" the "Congress (and President) of the United States," and these words, and the rationale behind them, could have been written today.

In order to implement the state's newly declared mortgagor/debtor-relief policy, the Minnesota Mortgage Moratorium Act mandated that foreclosure sales could be postponed, and the redemption period extended until May 1, 1935—two years after the Blaisdells could have redeemed their mortgaged property under the law that existed when they made their contract with the bank.

Taking advantage of the Moratorium Act, the Blaisdells asked a Minnesota court to enter an order extending their redemption period.

The court—apparently recognizing that Article I, section 10 of the federal Constitution expressly prohibits a state from enacting any law "impairing the obligation of contracts," and realizing that the Moratorium Act did just that—refused to grant the extension.

So the Blaisdells appealed.

The Minnesota Supreme Court reversed the lower court and granted the two-year extension (conditioned on the Blaisdells paying "rent" of forty dollars each month).

Consider what had happened.

The Blaisdells had put up their real estate as security for a loan from Home Building & Loan Association. The loan had been defaulted. The lender had to repurchase the property and then wait almost a year until the statutory redemption period expired before it could have clear title.

Near the end of that period, the Minnesota Legislature rewrote the Blaisdell–Home Building & Loan mortgage contract, the net result being that the lender would have to wait a minimum of another two years before obtaining the property—all the while receiving "rent" instead of the contractually agreed-upon mortgage payments.

We know why the Minnesota Legislature enacted the Moratorium Act. But what was the rationale of the Supreme Court of Minnesota for upholding it?

According to the later opinion of the Supreme Court of the United States, which I'll get to in a moment, the Minnesota court upheld the moratorium law because it was

> . . . an *emergency* measure. Although conceding that the obligations of the mortgage contract were impaired [despite the prohibition of Article I, section 10], the [Minnesota Supreme Court] decided that what it thus described as an impairment was, notwithstanding the contract clause of the federal Constitution, within the police power of the state as that power was called into execution by the *public economic emergency* which the Legislature had found to exist. (My emphasis.)

Actually, the Minnesota Supreme Court had been even more explicit, and arrogant, about what motivated its decision:

> In addition to the weight to be given the determination of the Legislature that *an economic emergency exists which demands relief*, the court must take notice of other considerations. The members of the Legislature come from every community of the state and from all the walks of life. They are familiar with conditions generally in every calling, occupation, profession, and business in the state. Not only they, but the courts

183

must be guided by what is common knowledge. It is common knowledge that in the last few years *land values have shrunk enormously.* Loans made a few years ago upon the basis of the then going values cannot possibly be replaced on the basis of present values. (My emphasis.)

Justice Olsen of the Minnesota Supreme Court, in a concurring opinion, added the following:

The present *nationwide and world wide business and financial crisis* has the same results as if it were caused by flood, earthquake, or disturbance in nature. It has deprived millions of persons in this nation of their employment and means of earning a living for themselves and their families; it has *destroyed the value of and the income from all property on which thousands of people depended for a living*; it actually has resulted in the *loss of their homes* by a number of our people, and threatens to result in the loss of their homes by many other people in this state; it has resulted in such *widespread want and suffering* among our people that private, state and municipal agencies are unable to adequately relieve the want and suffering, and *Congress has found it necessary to step in and attempt to remedy the situation by federal aid.* Millions of the people's money were and are yet *tied up in closed banks and in business enterprises.*" (My emphasis.)

In other words, by "common knowledge" things were rough for depression-era borrowers—just as they are today for some, especially those who tried to game the system by purchasing homes without adequate means to pay for them, in the expectation that the real estate bubble would everlastingly get bigger and bigger and never burst—let alone for the wheelers

184

and dealers on Wall Street whose voracious appetite for "investment" vehicles could be satisfied only by more and more rotten paper debt.

But times were tough for Home Building & Loan Association (and other lenders) too, so it appealed the case to the Supreme Court of the United States, to protect itself, its stockholders, and its depositors.

There, Chief Justice Charles Evans Hughes authored the Court's majority opinion upholding the constitutionality of the Minnesota Mortgage Moratorium Law.

A significant portion of his opinion consists of a survey of some of the Court's previous cases, on the basis of which Hughes enunciated a startlingly candid conclusion:

> It is manifest from this review of our decisions that there has been a growing appreciation of *public needs* and of the necessity of finding ground for *a rational compromise between individual rights and public welfare.* The settlement and consequent contraction of the public domain, the pressure of a constantly increasing density of population, the interrelation of the activities of our people and *the complexity of our economic interests,* have inevitably led to an increased use of the organization of society in order to protect the very bases of individual opportunity. Where, in earlier days, it was thought that only the concerns of individuals or of classes were involved, and that those of the state itself were touched only remotely, it has later been found that *the fundamental interests of the state are directly affected*; and that the question is no longer merely that of one party to a contract as against another, but of the use of reasonable means to *safeguard the economic structure upon which the good of all depends.* (My emphasis.)

185

What Chief Justice Hughes was saying couldn't be clearer. Postulating an increasingly complicated social environment in which "the good of all" was the standard of value, Hughes held that "public needs," "public welfare" and "fundamental interests of the state" trumped, and had to be protected from, something perniciously antithetical: "individual rights." Necessary, according to Hughes and the Court's majority, was a "rational compromise between individual rights and public welfare."

Since the nature of a compromise is "a settlement in which each side gives up some demands or makes concessions," the concept can have no application to individual rights, which are either absolute or nonexistent.

Indeed, the majority's idea of a compromise—between the sanctity of contracts supposedly guaranteed against government impairment by a specific provision of the Constitution (Article I, section 10) and the "public welfare" that allegedly required a two-year mortgage moratorium—was to allow Minnesota to rewrite the core provision of the Blaisdells' contract with their lender, namely repayment of the loan.

So much for compromise—and contracts, and, for that matter, individual rights and limited government.

Unfortunately, the dissenting opinion by Justice Sutherland went unheeded.

With my bracketed explanatory and other comments and more modern paragraphing (the latter to enhance clarity for today's readers), here's much of Justice Sutherland's very lengthy dissent. Despite its length, for those who love the Constitution and its attempt to safeguard the sanctity of contracts and the individual rights and limited government that make them possible, it is important, indeed essential, reading. (I have

186

made no substantive changes in the thrust of Justice Sutherland's opinion.)

> Few questions of greater moment than that just decided [by this Court] have been submitted for judicial inquiry during this generation.

> He simply closes his eyes to the necessary implications of the decision who fails to see in it the potentiality of future gradual but ever-advancing encroachments upon the sanctity of private and public contracts.

> The effect of the Minnesota legislation, though serious enough in itself, is of trivial significance compared with the far more serious and dangerous inroads upon the limitations of the Constitution which are almost certain to ensue as a consequence naturally following any step beyond the boundaries fixed by that instrument. And those of us who are thus apprehensive of the effect of this decision would, in a matter so important, be neglectful of our duty should we fail to spread upon the permanent records of the court the reasons which move us to the opposite view.

> [The "Contract Clause"] . . . is in grave danger, because the majority decision legitimizes violation of a private contract (the mortgage) and, more broadly, limitations expressly embodied in the Constitution are even more threatened.

> A provision of the Constitution, it is hardly necessary to say, does not admit of two distinctly opposite interpretations. It does not mean one thing at one time and an entirely different thing at another time. [Justice Brennan and his band of "Living Constitutionalists" notwithstanding.]

If the contract impairment clause, when framed and adopted [by the Founders], meant that the terms of a contract for the payment of money could not be altered in invitum ["against an unwilling party; against one not assenting"] by a state statute enacted for the relief of hardly pressed debtors to the end and with the effect of postponing payment or enforcement during and because of an economic or financial emergency, it is but to state the obvious to say that it means the same now. [A wonderful "originalist" statement.]

This view, at once so rational in its application to the written word, and so necessary to the stability of constitutional principles, though from time to time challenged, has never, unless recently, been put within the realm of doubt by the decisions of this court.

The true rule was forcefully declared in Ex parte Milligan, in the face of circumstances of national peril and public unrest and disturbance far greater than any that exist today. In that great case, this court said that the provisions of the Constitution there under consideration had been expressed by our ancestors in such plain English words that it would seem the ingenuity of man could not evade them, but that after the lapse of more than seventy years they were sought to be avoided. 'Those great and good men,' the Court said, 'foresaw that troublous times would arise, when rules and people would become restive under restraint, and seek by sharp and decisive measures to accomplish ends deemed just and proper; and that the principles of constitutional liberty would be in peril, unless established by irrepealable law.

The history of the world had taught them that what

was done in the past might be attempted in the future.' And then, in words the power and truth of which have become increasingly evident with the lapse of time, there was laid down the rule without which the Constitution would cease to be the 'supreme law of the land,' binding equally upon governments and governed at all times and under all circumstances, and become a mere collection of political maxims to be adhered to or disregarded according to the prevailing sentiment or the legislative and judicial opinion in respect of the supposed necessities of the hour:

> The Constitution of the United States is a law for rulers and people, equally in war and in peace, and covers with the shield of its protection all classes of men, at all times, and under all circumstances. No doctrine, involving more pernicious consequences, was ever invented by the wit of man than that any of its provisions can be suspended during any of the great exigencies of government. Such a doctrine leads directly to anarchy or despotism . . . .

Chief Justice Taney, in Dred Scott v. Sandford [among the most reprehensible decisions of all time in its principal holding] said that, while the Constitution remains unaltered, it must be construed now as it was understood at the time of its adoption; that it is not only the same in words but the same in meaning, 'and as long as it continues to exist in its present form, it speaks not only in the same words, but with the same meaning and intent with which it spoke when it came from the hands of its framers, and was voted on and adopted by the people of the United States. Any other rule of construction would abrogate the judicial

character of this court, and make it the mere reflex of the popular opinion or passion of the day.' * * *
* * *

An application of these principles to the question under review . . . , removes any doubt . . . that the contract impairment clause denies to the several states the power to mitigate hard consequences resulting to debtors from financial or economic exigencies by an impairment of the obligation of contracts.

A candid consideration of the history and circumstances which led up to and accompanied the framing and adoption of this clause will demonstrate conclusively that it was framed and adopted with the specific and studied purpose of preventing legislation designed to relieve debtors especially in time of financial distress. Indeed, it is not probable that any other purpose was definitely in the minds of those who composed the framers' convention or the ratifying state conventions which followed . . . .
* * *

The present exigency is nothing new.
From the beginning of our existence as a nation, periods of depression, of industrial failure, of financial distress, of unpaid and unpayable indebtedness, have alternated with years of plenty. *The vital lesson that expenditure beyond income begets poverty, that public or private extravagance, financed by promises to pay, either must end in complete or partial repudiation or the promises be fulfilled by self-denial and painful effort, though constantly taught by bitter experience, seems never to be learned*; and the attempt by legislative devices to shift the misfortune of the debtor to the shoulders of the creditor without coming into conflict with the contract impairment clause has been persistent and oft-repeated.

The defense of the Minnesota law is made upon grounds which were discountenanced by the makers of the Constitution and have many times been rejected by this Court. That defense should not now succeed because it constitutes an effort to overthrow the constitutional provision by an appeal to facts and circumstances identical with those which brought it into existence.

With due regard for the processes of logical thinking, it legitimately cannot be urged that conditions which produced the rule may now be invoked to destroy it.

The lower court, and counsel for the [debtor Blaisdells] in their argument here, frankly admitted that the statute does constitute a material impairment of the contract, but contended that such legislation is brought within the state power by the present emergency. If I understand the opinion just delivered, this court is not wholly in accord with that view. The opinion concedes that emergency does not create power, or increase granted power, or remove or diminish restrictions upon power granted or reserved. It then proceeds to say, however, that, while emergency does not create power, it may furnish the occasion for the exercise of power.

I can only interpret what is said on that subject as meaning that, while an emergency does not diminish a restriction upon power, it furnishes an occasion for diminishing it; and this, as it seems to me, is merely to say the same thing by the use of another set of words, with the effect of affirming that which has just been denied.

It is quite true that an emergency may supply the occasion for the exercise of power, dependent upon the nature of the power and the intent of the Constitution with respect thereto. The emergency of war furnishes an occasion for the exercise of certain of the war powers. This the Constitution contemplates, since they cannot be exercised upon any other occasion.

The existence of another kind of emergency authorizes the United States to protect each of the states of the Union against domestic violence.

But we are here dealing, not with a power granted by the Federal Constitution, but with the state police power, which exists in its own right. Hence the question is, not whether an emergency furnishes the occasion for the exercise of that state power, but whether an emergency furnishes an occasion for the relaxation of the restrictions upon the power imposed by the contract impairment clause; and the difficulty is that the contract impairment clause forbids state action under any circumstances, if it have the effect of impairing the obligation of contracts. That clause restricts every state power in the particular specified, no matter what may be the occasion. It does not contemplate that an emergency shall furnish an occasion for softening the restriction or making it any the less a restriction upon state action in that contingency than it is under strictly normal conditions.

The Minnesota statute either impairs the obligation of contracts or it does not.

If it does not, the occasion to which it relates becomes immaterial, since then the passage of the statute is the exercise of a normal, unrestricted, state power and requires no special occasion to render it effective.

If it does, the emergency no more furnishes a proper occasion for its exercise than if the emergency were nonexistent. And so, while, in form, the suggested distinction seems to put us forward in a straight line, in reality it simply carries us back in a circle, like bewildered travelers lost in a wood, to the point where we parted company with the view of the state court.

If what has now been said is sound, as I think it is, we come to what really is the vital question in the case: Does the Minnesota statute constitute an impairment of the obligation of the contract now under review? (My emphasis throughout.)* * *

According to Justice Sutherland, it did!

Justice Sutherland's dissent in *Blaisdell* is virtually unknown today even, or especially, among the professoriate and legal profession. It is a devastating rebuttal to Hughes's majority opinion, a resounding paean to originalism, and the prescient canary in the coalmine for what can happen to the sanctity of contracts at the hands of state legislatures and the Supreme Court. Sadly, the 5–4 majority decision in *Blaisdell* has in subsequent Contract Clause cases, killed the canary.

Although since the Blaisdell decision in 1934 there has been some amelioration of states' power to nullify the Contract Clause, the *Blaisdell* precedent still stands. Thus, if today's real estate situation worsens and the government's jawboning and arm-twisting of lenders proves inadequate to forestall foreclosures, no one should be surprised if Congress enacts a federal Mortgage Moratorium Act, or President Obama decrees one by Executive Order.

But today, mortgages are only a relatively small part of the financial meltdown problem. Now, the financial undertow caused by oceans of toxic debt paper is sucking under banks, credit card providers, the auto industry, and God knows who else. Now, it appears that the world financial and economic structure is drowning.

And what life preserver may Congress and the President, in their infinite stupidity and disdain for individual rights, limited government, and the free market, throw into the churning debt waters? Using the Minnesota Mortgage Moratorium Act as a template and the Supreme Court's decision in *Blaisdell* v. *Home Building & Loan Association* as precedent, it will be a Federal Debt Relief Act. In effect, bankruptcy without bankruptcy.

Or, better put, more of the poison that caused the disease.

Let's look at another case, *Shelley* v. *Kraemer*. It begins with what is called a "covenant." A covenant is simply a contractual agreement between two or more people or entities either to do, or to refrain from doing, something. For example, the purchaser of a house agrees with the seller that the former won't cut down any of the trees. The covenant is recorded, and future buyers are on notice and bound by it. A racially restrictive covenant prohibits subsequent owners from selling to specified classes of persons.

In the late 1800s and the early twentieth century, racially restrictive covenants were not uncommon in this country, and usually were aimed at excluding Negroes, Chinese, Indians, Jews, Mexicans and others who were considered unacceptable. That some Americans discriminated in this manner was morally reprehensible (as were the policies of the Heart of Atlanta Motel and Ollie's Barbecue). But if the principles of private property and liberty of contract mean anything, the racists should have had a constitutional right to withhold their property from anyone they wanted, for whatever reason.

The *Shelley* case involved some thirty landowners in St. Louis. In 1911 they had voluntarily entered into restrictive covenants with each other concerning their own property. They mutually agreed that for fifty years, their property could be owned only by Caucasians. The covenant was recorded in the recorder's office just like a deed. It was intended to encumber the land like a mortgage, and provide actual notice to prospective purchasers that certain resale of the properties were prohibited.

For our purposes, let's put aside the racist motive for the covenants, which were simply part of a conventional real estate transaction, like a recorded easement running with the land that one property owner might give another for access to a beach.

Thirty-five years pass, with fifteen more to run on the fifty-year covenant.

In violation of one of the covenants, a sale is made to a Negro family.

The non-selling covenantors go to court seeking an injunction to prevent the Negro buyers from taking possession of the property, and to divest them of title.

How are the buyers supposed to defend? They could invoke the Equal Protection Clause of the Fourteenth Amendment to the Constitution of the United States because attempted enforcement of the restrictive covenant is obviously racial discrimination.

But wait!

The Fourteenth Amendment is clear: "No *state* shall make or enforce any law which shall . . . deny to any person within its

195

jurisdiction the equal protection of the laws." (My emphasis.) But the covenantors weren't the "state." They were just a group of private property owners, with no connection to the State of Missouri. As a matter of fact, every court that had previously looked at racially restrictive covenants over the previous eighty years had upheld them because no action by the states was involved. The Fourteenth Amendment didn't protect people against non-state action. The Supreme Court itself had said so in the earlier Civil Rights Act cases.

When the *Shelley* case reached the Supreme Court of the United States, Chief Justice Fred Vinson acknowledged that although the *state* was prohibited under the Fourteenth Amendment from discriminating against buyers in these circumstances, the discriminatory racial covenants' restriction stemmed "in the first instance" from a contract between private persons only. So the Court concluded that "standing alone," the contract could not be regarded as a violation of any rights guaranteed by the Constitution.

Uh-oh. "Standing alone"? What was Vinson getting at?

He said that so long as the purposes of those covenants were satisfied by *voluntary* adherence to their terms, there was no problem; the Fourteenth Amendment hadn't been violated.

Of course not.

This was a foursquare ruling that the private racially restrictive covenants were valid and thus not unconstitutional (but remember the "standing alone"). So far, the decision was a victory for private contracts. Given the proper function of courts in our supposed democratic, individual-rights, limited-government system, that should have been the end of the case.

No such luck. The Court was heading somewhere else; you

have a hint from my comments. But how was Vinson going to get there?

The tip-off is Vinson's pointed qualification that the restrictive covenant was constitutional, "standing alone." In other words, since the Fourteenth Amendment prohibited only *states* from racially discriminating, and since the State of Missouri had no part in creating the restrictive covenants, no constitutional rights of the Negro purchasers had been violated *up to that point*. But, said Vinson, the Court is "called upon to consider whether *enforcement* by state courts of the restrictive agreements may be deemed to be the acts of the states."

Wait a second. Isn't that what courts do? Don't courts enforce contracts everyone admits are valid? Isn't that why courts exist? Vinson himself, for the Court's majority, had said the covenants were valid.

Well, be that as it may, in the end, the Supreme Court ruled

> "that the action of state courts and judicial officers in their official capacities is to be regarded as *action of the state* within the meaning of the Fourteenth Amendment is a proposition which has long been established by decisions of this court." (My emphasis.)

Notwithstanding the fact that this statement, and all of Vinson's other arguments, were so easily discredited, the Supreme Court's decision was that any court's judicial enforcement of a private non-state restrictive covenant was now deemed an act of the state that denied the purchasers equal protection of the law under the Fourteenth Amendment.

So much for individual rights, limited government, and the Contract Clause of the Constitution. The landowners' contract

197

rights, supposedly protected by the Contract Clause—rights that are a subset of liberty and property rights—were cynically sacrificed to the desire of the Negro purchasers to live where they weren't wanted.

As we shall see, even the Bill of Rights would not have protected the covenantors.

7.
Prohibitions on Congress and the States: The Bill of Rights and the Fourteenth Amendment

Recall that at the Constitutional Convention of 1787 there was great concern about the creation of a powerful federal government. Despite that concern, when two of the delegates, Elbridge Gerry and George Mason, tried to introduce the subject of a bill of rights they were unsuccessful—even though some state constitutions already contained them in one form or another.

Recall also the ratification debates, opposition to the proposed Constitution because it lacked a bill of rights, Alexander Hamilton's argument in *Federalist* 84 against a bill of rights, and the many proposals for one that came from the state ratifying conventions and elsewhere.

As we know, Hamilton's argument prevailed, and the Constitution was ratified without a bill of rights. Then, in the First Congress, James Madison solved the "don't enumerate rights" problem with the Ninth Amendment, which said that the enumeration in the Constitution of certain rights (First through Eighth Amendments) shall not be construed to deny or disparage others retained by the people.

Finally, recall that at the First Congress, Madison introduced an amendment designed to protect the rights of conscience, press, and criminal jury trial against violation by the *states*. Madison's was an explicit attempt to reach *state* action via prohibitions in the bill of rights.

199

His proposed amendment was rejected, with the consequence that the Bill of Rights contains no prohibitions against the states. Indeed, the First Amendment begins with the unequivocal statement that "*Congress* shall make no law. . . ." (My emphasis.) Considering the explicit rejection of Madison's "state" amendment, the first word of the Bill of Rights, and universal understanding in 1791—about the scope of amendments First through Nine—there is no doubt that the Bill of Rights was intended to apply only to the federal government.

In the 1833 case of *Barron* v. *Baltimore*—our old friend John Marshall was still Chief Justice—the Supreme Court expressly ruled that the Bill of Rights applied only to the federal government. This was some *forty-two years* after the promulgation of the Bill of Rights in 1791.

In 1833, there were still judges and others who were alive when the First Congress adopted the Bill of Rights. They knew very well what its purpose was. I cannot emphasize this strongly enough, in light of where I'm going with my discussion of the Bill of Rights.

As Hamilton had noted in *Federalist* 84,

> It has been several times truly remarked that bills of rights are, in their origin, stipulations between kings and their subjects, abridgements of prerogative in favor of privilege, reservations of rights not surrendered to the prince. Such was Magna Carta obtained by the barons, sword in hand, from King John. Such were the subsequent confirmations of that charter by succeeding princes. Such was the *Petition of Right* assented to by Charles I, in the beginning of his reign. Such, also, was the Declaration of Right presented by the Lords and Commons to the Prince of

Orange in 1688, and afterwards thrown into the form of an act of parliament called the Bill of Rights. It is evident, therefore, that, according to their primitive signification, they have no application to constitutions professedly founded upon the power of the people, and executed by their immediate representatives and servants. Here, in strictness, the people surrender nothing; and as they retain every thing they have no need of particular reservations. "WE, THE PEOPLE of the United States, to secure the blessings of liberty to ourselves and our posterity, do *ordain* and *establish* this Constitution for the United States of America." Here is a better recognition of popular rights, than volumes of those aphorisms which make the principal figure in several of our State bills of rights, and which would sound much better in a treatise of ethics than in a constitution of government.

In Magna Carta's stipulation 39 (of 63) King John agreed that "[n]o freemen shall be taken or imprisoned or disseised [dispossessed] or exiled or in any way destroyed, nor will we go upon him nor send upon him, except by the lawful judgment of his peers or *by the law of the land*." (My emphasis.)

According to *Black's Law Dictionary*, "[b]y the law of the land is most clearly intended the general law which hears before it condemns, which proceeds upon inquiry, and renders judgment only after trial. * * * The meaning is that every citizen shall hold his life, liberty, property, and immunities under the protection of general rules which govern society."

From the concept of "by the law of the land" evolved the early concept of "due process of law": "No man of what state or condition he be, shall be put out of his lands or tenements nor taken, nor disinherited, nor put to death, without he be brought

201

to answer by due process of law," which originated in a 1355 English restatement of the 1215 Magna Carta.

Just as Magna Carta, the 1355 English statute, and early state constitutions with similar provisions make abundantly clear, "due process of law" related exclusively to fair *procedure*.

And so, in 1791, the Fifth Amendment to the Constitution of the United States of America provided that no person shall "be deprived of life, liberty, or property without due process of law."

I am emphasizing the *procedural* nature of due process because *procedure* is wholly different from *substance*. Whether an accused has the right to an indictment first rather than summary trial (procedure) is quite different from whether soliciting a prostitute should be a crime (substance). This important distinction between procedure and substance becomes very important in American constitutional law.

If there is any doubt about the *procedural* nature of due process, we need only examine its position in the overall architecture of the Bill of Rights.

The Fourth Amendment deals exclusively with the criminal *procedure* of searches and seizures.

The Fifth Amendment—of which the Due Process Clause is part—deals exclusively with four other *procedural* protections, three of which are indictment, double jeopardy, and self-incrimination.

The Sixth Amendment deals, *procedurally*, with speedy and public trials, impartial jury, notice of the charges, confrontation by witnesses, compulsory process, and assistance of counsel.

This architecture simply leaves no doubt that the Fifth Amendment's due process protection was intend to be solely of a *procedural* nature—and to operate only against the federal government.

There is no better and finer explication of procedural due process than in the case of *Jones* v. *Flowers,* where Justice Clarence Thomas dissented.[80] First the facts of the *Jones* case:

> When . . . [Jones] failed to pay his property taxes for several consecutive years, [the] Commissioner of State Lands in Arkansas, using the record address that Jones provided to the State, sent Jones a letter by certified mail, noting his tax delinquency and explaining that his property would be subject to public sale if the delinquent taxes and penalties were not paid. After [Jones] failed to respond, the State also published notice of the delinquency and public sale in an Arkansas newspaper. Soon after . . . Linda K. Flowers submitted a purchase offer to the State, it sent [Jones] a second letter by certified mail explaining that the sale would proceed if the delinquent taxes and penalties were not paid.
>
> [Jones] argues that the State violated his rights under the Due Process Clause of the Fourteenth Amendment because, in [Jones's] view, the State failed to take sufficient steps to contact him before selling his property to Flowers. [Jones] contends that once the State became aware that he had not claimed the certified mail, it was constitutionally obligated to employ additional methods to locate him.

The question for the Court was whether procedural due process of law requires that "when mailed notice of a tax sale is returned unclaimed, the State must take additional reasonable

203

steps to attempt to provide notice to the property owner before selling his property, if it is practicable to do so." The 5–3 majority's answer was "yes."

Unfortunately for the Court's reputation, especially because the majority opinion was written by Chief Justice John Roberts, one hunts in vain for a reason why the Due Process Clause of the Fourteenth Amendment required Arkansas to do more than it did. Roberts and his four predictable liberal colleagues seemed to be saying that because the stakes were high—loss of a person's home—the state *should* have done more simply because it *could* have done more.

Justice Thomas, however, was having none of it. His dissent shredded Roberts's majority opinion.

Thomas began by referring to various Court precedents: "Balancing a State's interest in efficiently managing its administrative system and an individual's interest in adequate notice, this Court has held that a State must provide notice reasonably calculated, under all the circumstances, to apprise interested parties of the pendency of the action."

He continued: "The methods of notice employed by Arkansas were reasonably calculated to inform [Jones] of proceedings affecting his property interest and thus satisfy the requirements of the Due Process Clause. The State mailed a notice by *certified* letter to the address provided by petitioner. The certified letter was returned to the State marked 'unclaimed' after *three* attempts to deliver it. The State then *published a notice* of public sale containing redemption information in the Arkansas Democrat Gazette newspaper. After Flowers submitted a purchase offer, the State sent yet *another certified letter* to petitioner at his record address. That letter, too, was returned to the State marked 'unclaimed' after *three* delivery attempts." (Emphasis in original.)

204

Thomas dug deeply into the United States Postal Operations manual to show that its regulations require notices to be left at the delivery address of every delivery attempt.

He reminded the majority that Jones had a "statutory duty to pay his taxes and to report any change of address to the state taxing authority."

There was more, but suffice to say that Thomas also decimated the majority's attempt to rely on Supreme Court precedent.

In the end, Thomas's dissent comes down to this: creating new "constitutional" *rights*, and thus "constitutional" *duties*, for the states is a problematic enterprise, especially through the too-flexible means provided by the [procedural] Due Process Clause of the Fourteenth Amendment.

"If 'title to property,' he wrote, 'should not depend on [factual] vagaries' . . . then certainly it cannot turn on 'wrinkle[s]' caused by a property owner's own failure to be a prudent ward of his [own] interests. The meaning of the Constitution should not turn on the antics of tax evaders and scofflaws. Nor is the self-created conundrum in which [Jones] finds himself a legitimate ground for *imposing additional constitutional obligations on the State*. The State's attempts to notify [Jones] by certified mail at the address that he provided and, additionally, by publishing notice in a local newspaper satisfy due process. (My emphasis.)

Jones v. *Flowers* was a Due Process Clause case under the Fourteenth Amendment, but, as Thomas's dissent makes clear, it was a *procedural* due process case.

Which brings me to one of the most grotesque distortions of a constitutional provision ever engineered by the Supreme Court: the notion of "substantive" due process. Here's where this abomination originated.

205

The first state legislatures had considerable power, especially over property rights. Anti-creditor confiscation laws are an example. There was also a flood of paper-money laws, which reduced the purchasing power of state citizens.

The new federal judiciary wanted to stop the predatory state legislation. How to do it? The courts invoked extra-constitutional principles, such as those found in the writings of English philosopher John Locke and others on the subject of natural law.

For example, in 1795, four years after the Bill of Rights was enacted, Justice William Paterson of the new Supreme Court of the United States had this to say in the case of *Vanhorne's Lessee* v. *Dorrance*:

> . . . the right of acquiring and possessing property, and having it protected, is one of the natural, inherent, and unalienable rights of man. Men have a sense of property: Property is necessary to their subsistence, and correspondent to their natural wants and desires; its security was one of the objects that induced them to unite in society. No man would become a member of a community in which he could not enjoy the fruits of his honest labour and industry. The preservation of property then is a primary object of the social compact, and, by the late Constitution of *Pennsylvania*, was made a fundamental law. Every person ought to contribute his proportion for public purposes and public exigencies; but no one can be called upon to surrender or sacrifice his whole property, real and personal, for the good of the community, without receiving a recompence in value. This would be laying a burden upon an individual, which ought to be sustained by the society at large. The *English* history does not furnish an instance of the

kind; the Parliament, with all their boasted omnipotence, never committed such an outrage on private property; and if they had, it would have served only to display the dangerous nature of unlimited authority; it would have been an exercise of power and not of right. Such an act would be a monster in legislation, and shock all mankind. The legislature, therefore, had no authority to make an act divesting one citizen of his freehold, and vesting it in another, without a just compensation. *It is inconsistent with the principles of reason, justice, and moral rectitude*; it is incompatible with the comfort, peace, and happiness of mankind; it is contrary to the principles of social alliance in every free government; and lastly, it is contrary both to the letter and spirit of the Constitution. (Spelling as in the original. The word "Pennsylvania" was emphasized in the original. All other emphases are mine.)

As rousing as Justice Paterson's words were, many believed that while the Court's reliance on "the letter . . . of the Constitution" (if an appropriate provision could be found) would suffice as the basis of a pro-property decision, the Supreme Court of the United States should do better in support of its conclusion than to rest on "principles of reason, justice, and moral rectitude," "the comfort, peace, and happiness of mankind," and "the principles of social alliance in every free government," let alone on the "spirit of the Constitution." These empty slogans, whatever they meant, were non-constitutional.

As the right to vote became more widespread and the power of legislatures grew, property rights became more threatened. They were being sacrificed to the collective's need for such things as debtor relief laws and other transfers of private property.

207

In response, a firmer basis was sought upon which to ground judicial protection of property rights; ideally, some *specific* provisions of constitutions themselves, both state and federal. The idea was to move the protection of private rights—liberty, property, contract—away from the popularly elected legislatures and put them in the courts, where it was hoped that lawyers and judges could safeguard them.

But how? How to defend, on purely constitutional grounds, property and other rights by reference to constitutions themselves? Remember that at the beginning on the federal level, the only provision of the Bill of Rights that mentioned the word "property" was the procedural Due Process Clause of the Fifth Amendment.

This is where the constitutional slippery slope began. Because some textual justification was sought, and because the Due Process Clause of the Fifth Amendment ("No person shall . . . be deprived of life, liberty, or property without due process of law") was the only place in the Bill of Rights where property was mentioned, that amendment was chosen to carry the burden of determining whether government action was "substantively" constitutional. Whether it was "OK." This, despite the fact that due process clauses had always applied only to form, process, procedure—not to substance.

But how would this shift of due process gears become accepted constitutional doctrine, especially since everyone knew that due process was synonymous only with procedure?

How was *procedural* due process to be transmogrified into a *substantive* tool by which the *content* of legislation could be judged? A tool that would enable courts to decide the undefined "rightness" or "wrongness" of legislation based on the values of judges? How were the *policy* choices of politically accountable legislatures—social, economic, fiscal, cultural, political, sexual, etc.—to be evaluated for their constitutionality by the politically unaccountable courts?

For example, by what criteria was a court to decide, not whether somebody could be tried for gambling in a court where the judge was prosecutor and jury (which would obviously be a *procedural* deprivation of the defendant's rights), but rather whether the legislature possessed the police power to make gambling illegal in the first place (a substantive question).

Understanding this distinction between procedural and substantive due process is essential to understanding what the Supreme Court has done to our individual rights and the promise of limited government.

Let's go a bit further down the slippery slope. In the mid-1800s, New York enacted a statewide prohibition law and applied it retroactively to liquor in existence when the law was passed. Property rights in existing inventories of liquor were destroyed.

In the New York Court of Appeals (the state's highest court), the majority opinion in the case of *Wynehamer* v. *The People of the State of New York* was written by Judge George Comstock. He expressly repudiated all the arguments against the prohibition law on the basis of natural law, fundamental liberty, common sense, and natural rights—none of which found textual support in either the constitution or statutes of the State of New York.

To the contrary, Comstock wrote that there was nothing *outside* the state constitution to render the prohibition law unconstitutional that couldn't be found *inside* the state constitution: "[T]here is no process of reasoning by which it can be demonstrated that [the prohibition law] is void upon principles and theories outside the [state] constitution, which will not also and by an easier deduction, bring it in direct conflict with the constitution itself."

In other words, people whose property (or liberty or contracts) has been taken from them don't have to seek protection in "natural law." Nor "fundamental liberty." Nor "common sense." Nor "natural rights." Because there is textual protection right here in the constitution of the State of New York.

What part of the New York constitution was Judge Comstock alluding to in his "outside-inside" point?

New York's constitution contained a due process clause, which like all the others everywhere was exclusively *procedural*. So Comstock would protect against the retroactive confiscation of Mr. Wynehamer's liquor by invoking "due process."

But wait! Due process of law had never before been interpreted to operate against the *substance* of a statute, to somehow determine whether it was "right," "moral," "commonsensical" or otherwise acceptable to courts.

No matter.

The next year, invoking the Fifth Amendment to the federal Constitution, the amoeba-like division of procedural due process into one part itself and another part substantive due process became a reality in the morally corrupt, patently indefensible *Dred Scott* decision.

Chief Justice Roger Taney ruled that Section 8 of the Missouri Compromise, excluding slavery from the American territories, was void under the Fifth Amendment. But not because the *procedure* for enacting or enforcing that law was not "due process," but because the Supreme Court regarded as unjust the inability of slave owners to take their "property" (i.e., slaves) from one place to another.

> . . . an act of Congress which deprives a citizen of his
> liberty or property, merely because he came himself
> or brought his property into a particular territory of
> the United States and who had committed no offense
> against the laws could hardly be dignified with the
> name of due process of law.

Thus, in its 7–2 *Dred Scott* decision, the Supreme Court of the
United States declared that slavery was constitutional in the
territories based solely on the reason that Section 8 of the
Missouri Compromise was "unfair," "unjust," "unreasonable,"
"inequitable"—choose any synonym you like. Just not "right,"
by whatever subjective standard Taney and his six colleagues
had in mind (if they had any at all).

The *Dred Scott* decision legitimized the Fifth Amendment's
Due Process Clause as having a substantive power to invalidate
laws enacted by Congress. The writing was on the wall: the
Law of the Land/Due Process Clause that since Magna Carta
had been utilized to consecrate specific modes of *procedure*
was judicially transformed into a general, subjective check on
any legislation capable of having a detrimental effect on life,
liberty, property or contracts.

Putting aside the immorality of human slavery, let alone that
seven members of the Supreme Court and countless Americans
could countenance a slave as someone else's "property," the
Dred Scott decision opened the courthouse doors to a principle
which, when fully developed, was and continues to be
destructive of individual rights and limited government. Two
wrongs not only don't make a right, two wrongs are doubly
wrong.

Now for a bit of historical context.

In the time of the *Wynehamer* and *Dred Scott* cases, there was an important political development afoot in the United States. Those decisions, and a growing number of others like them, were jurisprudential fodder for the spread of Jacksonian democracy. This newly articulated doctrine of popular sovereignty trumpeted the supremacy of legislatures. *Vox Populi.* The Voice of the People.

With good reason, many Americans considered this trend very dangerous. Governments were dabbling in railroads, canals, manufacturing, banks, steamships, and many other commercial activities. Creditors and other owners of property were so justifiably concerned about the nearly unlimited power of state legislatures, they turned for help to the courts.

But there was a serious problem beyond that of substantive due process. The only Due Process Clause was found in the Fifth Amendment, which restrained only the *federal* government, not the *states*. Unlike New York, not every state constitution had a due process clause.

Then, in 1868, American constitutional law, the protection of individual rights, and the Founders' attempted institutionalization of limited government changed forever.

The Fourteenth Amendment was ratified on July 9, 1868: ". . . nor shall any *State* deprive any person of life, liberty, or property, without due process of law . . . ." (My emphasis.)

Now courts could apply substantive due process not only to laws enacted by Congress, but also to *state* legislation.

One hundred ten years later, I reviewed a book by Harvard Law School Professor Raoul Berger, entitled *Government by Judiciary: The Transformation of the Fourteenth Amendment.*

Here are a few of my comments, which are a good introduction to the substantive due process phenomenon on the state level.

> Raoul Berger has written one of the most important books in the literature of American constitutional law, and one of the most disturbing. The book's first sentence expresses his thesis, drawn from his exhaustive examination of the Fourteenth Amendment's background and legislative history: "The Fourteenth Amendment is the case study par excellence of what Justice Harlan described as the Supreme Court's 'exercise of the amending power,' its *continuing revision of the Constitution under the guise of interpretation*. (My emphasis.)

In *Government by Judiciary*, Professor Berger proves conclusively that the Fourteenth Amendment's Due Process Clause was intended to deal with the same *procedural* deprivation of rights as was the Fifth Amendment's Due Process Clause, whose development and application began with Magna Carta.

In my review, I wrote also that "[i]n Chapter 11 Berger piles proof upon proof to demonstrate that neither in 1789 nor in 1866 did due process 'comprehend judicial power to override legislation on substantive or policy grounds' . . . ." He then quotes Alexander Hamilton: "The words 'due process' have a precise technical import, and are only applicable to the process and proceedings of the courts of justice; they can never be referred to an act of the legislature."

As we've seen, Hamilton was correct, but it didn't matter. Following ratification of the Fourteenth Amendment, every state law, especially those adversely affecting liberty, individual rights, contract and property, were now fair game for anybody wanting to attack the law on the basis of the

213

Fourteenth Amendment's Due Process Clause.

However, despite *Dred Scott*, *Wynehamer*, and some similar cases, the Supreme Court majority refused for many years to apply the Due Process Clause of the Fourteenth Amendment to anything except alleged *procedural* deprivations of rights.

But there were murmurs. The pot was bubbling. Litigants were aware of how "due process" arguments might help them. Lawyers discussed them. Articles appeared in the professional literature.

In 1878, ten years after the enactment of the Fourteenth Amendment, a case entitled *Davidson* v. *New Orleans* reached the Supreme Court. Justice Samuel Miller wrote for the majority:

> While the Fourteenth Amendment has been part of the Constitution, as a restraint upon the power of the State, only a very few years, the docket of this court is crowded with cases in which we are asked to hold that state courts and state legislatures have deprived their own citizens of life, liberty, or property without due process of law. There is here abundant evidence that there exists some strange misconception of the scope of this provision as found in the Fourteenth Amendment. In fact, it would seem, from the character of many of the cases before us, and the arguments made in them, that the clause under consideration, due process, is looked upon as a means of bringing to the test of the decision of this court the abstract opinions of every unsuccessful litigant in a State court the *justice* of the decision against him, and of the *merits* of the legislation on which such a decision may be founded. (My emphasis.)

214

Despite Justice Miller's analysis, there continued to be pro–substantive due process dissents in a variety of cases. Finally, in the late 1800s, the earlier substantive due process dissents finally became law. In the case of *Mugler* v. *Kansas*, the Supreme Court majority ruled that due process had substantive clout and could subjectively test the fairness, reasonableness, justness of state legislation—based, of course, on the personal values of judges.

The first Justice John Harlan wrote:

> It does not at all follow that every statute enacted ostensibly for the promotion of these ends, that is police power and health, safety, welfare, and morals, is to be accepted as a legitimate exercise of the powers of the state.

True.

> There are, of necessity, limits beyond which legislation cannot rightfully go.

True, again.

> While every possible presumption is to be indulged in favor of the validity of the statute, the courts must obey the Constitution rather than the law-making department of the government, and must, upon their own responsibility, determine whether, in any particular case, these limits have been passed.

And again, true. *But by what criteria are the limits ascertained and applied?*

Here's one answer. In the 1890 case of *Chicago, Milwaukee & St. Paul Railway Company* v. *Minnesota*, the Supreme Court ruled that the validity of railroad rates fixed by state administrative commissions were not final. Their "reasonableness" was a matter for judicial review. Why? The Court said that if rates were "unreasonable," the railroad was deprived of the lawful use of its property and thus of the property itself, without—guess what?—*substantive due process of law*.

The constitutional standard by which to assess government interference with personal and property rights had become "reasonableness" in the eyes of the beholders: judges. Life, liberty, property and contract interests were now to be protected, or not protected, throughout the United States of America by this subjective notion.

Two years later, in 1892, the American Bar Association had a meeting. The general counsel of the railroad (whom we can safely assume was an economic conservative) delivered a paper he'd written entitled "Limitations on the legislative power in respect to personal rights and private property." What did he argue for? Why, for the "right" of railroads to make "reasonable profits"—a determination, he said, for *judicial* rather than *legislative* determination. Well, with friends like these, free Americans didn't need enemies.

Note what has happened. Seeking protection from state legislative excesses regarding liberty, property and contract, lawyers attempted to shift their battles into the courts, where the traditional *procedural* due process clauses would acquire *substantive* meaning and test the "reasonableness" of those excesses. Altruist-collectivist-statist legislation would be judged by subjective standards, usually reflecting the personal values of the judges.

The sad truth is that proponents of substantive due process were trading short-term gains for long-term jurisprudential instability and destruction of the very values of individual rights and limited government they naively thought they were protecting. It wasn't only that they didn't know what they were doing. Worse, as we shall see, the values of most of them were the same altruist-collectivist-statist values they thought they were fighting.

In the 1898 case of *Smith* v. *Ames*, the Court would hold that public utilities had the "right" to "reasonable profits." Nobody asked embarrassing questions such as "Reasonable to whom?" "Why?" "For how long?" "How much?" "By what standard?"

Few of the economic-conservative businessman, lawyers, and judges who heralded what they called the "new constitutional mandate" for laissez-faire apparently realized, or cared about, the destructive idea they were advancing. The profit deemed reasonable by one court in 1898 might well be deemed unreasonable by another court on another day, or in another decade. And they didn't realize the implications of reasonable profits defined not by the free market but by a legislature or a court.

Liberty, property and contract rights were to be protected not because they were absolute, not because they were inalienable, and not because government had no right to violate them. Instead, they were going to be protected, or not, depending on whether interference with them would be deemed "unreasonable" by a court. They would be protected by a legal fiction, a judicial invention called "substantive due process of law," by a standard of "reasonableness" (or "justness" or "unjustness"). There was no *objective* standard of what was, and what was not, reasonable—much less what "rights" were.

Let's look at a case that exemplifies the combination of substantive due process and altruism-collectivism-statism. With a nod to Charles Dickens, here's my take on the case of *Muller* v. *Oregon*.

217

It's December 1902, cold and snowing. Bob Gotcher's wife needs money for Christmas because the family anticipates that all they're going to get from Bob's employer, Mr. Ebenezer Scrooge, is a lump of coal. Mrs. Gotcher wants to buy her little boy, Tiny Tim, a sled. She goes looking for work and comes upon a "help wanted" sign outside the Grand Laundry. She tells the manager, Mr. Muller, that she needs work because poor crippled Tiny Tim will be devastated if he doesn't get a sled for Christmas.

"Well," says Mr. Muller, "I'll tell you what; we've got work for a starcher.[81] But it's fifteen-hour-a-day work, it's hard, and you're going to have to stand most of the time." "Oh no," says Mrs. Gotcher, "I don't care. We have to get that sled." And Muller says, "Well, that's great, because I'm down one starcher." Each was glad to have the other. A win-win situation.

So, Mrs. Gotcher went to work; she and the Grand Laundry had made a contract. A few months later, the Oregon Legislature in its wisdom enacted a law whose first section said: "No female shall be employed in any mechanical establishment or factory or laundry in this state more than 10 hours in any one day." If a female was so employed, the employer would be guilty of a misdemeanor. Uh-oh.[82]

In September 1905, Mr. Muller was charged with violating the statute. He was convicted and fined.

Eventually, the case of *Muller* v. *Oregon* reached the Supreme Court. There, the question for the justices was whether an adult American woman in the early twentieth century could freely choose to work more than ten hours a day, whatever her reasons, or whether government (here, the State of Oregon) knew better what was good for American women such as Mrs. Gotcher and could impose its collectivist, majoritarian values

218

on her and on the laundry's owner.

The Supreme Court upheld the Oregon statute, to the loud cheers of the liberals/progressives of that day, who applauded the justices' enlightened concern for working women who apparently either did not know, or could not protect, their own interests.

But if the decision's partisans (especially women) had paid attention to the Court's *reasons* for its decision in *Muller* v. *Oregon*, they probably would not have cheered so loudly, if at all. Indeed, if they really understood the decision, they should have been appalled. Even scared.

Muller v. *Oregon* was a *unanimous* decision—one that today's feminists should take no comfort from. To quote the Court:

> That woman's physical structure and the performance of material functions places her at a disadvantage in the struggle for subsistence is obvious. This is especially true when the burdens of motherhood are upon her. Even when they are not . . . continuance for a long time on her feet at work . . . tends to injurious effects upon the body, and, as healthy mothers are essential to vigorous offspring, *the physical well-being of women becomes an object of public interest and care in order to preserve the strength of the race.* (My emphasis.)

This patronizing, collectivist view of American working women was not all the Court had to say about the weakness of women and their relationship to a paternalistic state.

> Still again, history discloses the fact that *woman has always been dependent upon man.* He established his control at the outset by superior physical strength, and this control in various forms . . . has continued to the

present. * * * It is still true that in the struggle for subsistence she is not an equal competitor with her brother [meaning, any man]. Though limitations upon personal and contractual rights may be removed by legislation *there is that in her disposition and habits of life which will operate against a full assertion of those rights*. (My emphasis.)

It was bad enough that in upholding the statute the Court, which allegedly worried about "subsistence," was limiting the working hours of those trying to subsist. Much worse was the Court's view of working women as weak, timid, and dependent—even cowardly, in being unable or unwilling to assert their "rights." Lest there be any doubt that that's what the *unanimous* Court was saying:

[Woman] is so constituted that she will rest upon and look to [man] for protection; that her physical structure and a proper discharge of her maternal functions—having in view not merely her own health, but *the well-being of the race*—justify legislation to protect her from the greed as well as the passion of man. The limitations which this statute places upon her contractual powers, upon her right to agree with her employer as to the time she shall labor, are not imposed solely for her benefit, *but for the benefit of all*. (My emphasis.)

This is nothing short of altruism-collectivism-statism squared.[83]

No doubt some will say that the connection between the Supreme Court's rationale in *Muller* v. *Oregon* and the Nazi "Master Race" program is, at best, tenuous.

They are mistaken.

To hold women's "physical well-being" and their production of "vigorous offspring" to be matters of "public interest" so as to "preserve the strength and vigor of the race" is to consider women, as did the Nazis, a mere state resource—important to the government for their procreational capacity, to be nurtured much like livestock, and for the same reason.

The rationale underlying the Supreme Court's decision in *Muller* v. *Oregon* transcends mere altruism, collectivism, and even statism, "isms" that deny and negate any possibility of individual rights or a limited government. In *Muller*, the Supreme Court gave voice to a doctrine evil in its intent and murderous in its application: the belief that human beings, in that case women, were mere resources to be used, abused, and ultimately disposed of for the public good by those holding political power.

Muller v. *Oregon* was decided by the Supreme Court of the United States in 1908. Less than three decades later, the case's rationale was on display in Hitler's Nazi Germany.

In those three decades here in the United States, the final bricks would be put in place to complete the jurisprudential edifice that would become known as the Living Constitution.

It may have been a major achievement for lawyers and judges to imbue the two Due Process Clauses with the substantive power to rule on the constitutionality of legislation, but a major question remained. How could the protections of the Bill of Rights—speech, double jeopardy, right of assembly, right to bear arms, and the rest—*which protected against only the federal government* be made applicable to the states and, coupled with substantive due process, anoint the courts, especially the Supreme Court, as the final arbiters on individual rights and limited government?

Although in *Muller*, invoking due process didn't help the

defendant, in *Gitlow* v. *New York*, it did. It's *Gitlow* that put in place the final brick: the "Incorporation Doctrine."

In *M'Culloch* v. *Maryland* we saw how Chief Justice John Marshall laid the foundation for an expansive view of the power of the federal government, with the concomitant reduction of the powers reserved to the states by the Tenth Amendment.

In *Morrison* v. *Olson* we saw how the Founders' dominating principle of separation of powers has come to be devalued almost to the point of irrelevance.

In *Griswold* v. *Connecticut* we saw how an arrogant Supreme Court, worshiping at the altar of the Living Constitution, deconstructed federalism (a *federal* court holding unconstitutional a *state* law) and disregarded vertical separation of powers (a federal *court* holding unconstitutional a law enacted by the political representatives (*legislature* and *executive*) of a state).

Worse, still, than *Griswold*'s utter disregard for federalism and separation of powers is that the tools the Court used—various distorted and mal-applied provisions of the Bill of Rights— exist as prohibitions on *only* the federal government ("*Congress* shall make no law . . ."), having no force against the states.

But tell that to "Living Constitutionalists" such as the late Justice William J. Brennan, Jr.

What has made it possible for them and their distorted view of the Constitution to prevail and thrive is the so-called Incorporation Doctrine—a judicial construct at which the Founders, federalist and anti-federalist alike, would doubtless have scoffed.

An examination of the Incorporation Doctrine begins with an undeniably valid premise: The Bill of Rights was intended by Madison, who introduced it, by the Congress that approved it, and by the states that ratified it to apply only to actions by the federal government. Indeed, as I have said repeatedly, the First Amendment begins by reciting, "Congress shall make no law . . . ."

Never was a political intent, or a legal statement, clearer. So much so that even those who would have it otherwise concede, as they must, that in the early days of the Supreme Court of the United States, the Court ruled squarely that the Bill of Rights was *not* applicable to the states

How, then, has the Supreme Court been able to hold unconstitutional *under the federal Constitution* acts of the *states* allegedly violating such rights as free speech, protection against double jeopardy, and many other guarantees found in the *federal* Bill of Rights?

The answer lies in the Incorporation Doctrine and the Due Process Clause of the Fourteenth Amendment: "[N]or shall any *State* deprive any person of life, liberty, or property, without due process of law." (My emphasis.)

Even though the federal Bill of Rights contains at least thirty specific "rights" types of guarantees—one of which is the Fifth Amendment's *own* Due Process Clause—in a series of cases beginning with *Gitlow* v. *New York* in 1925, the Supreme Court ruled that the Fourteenth Amendment's Due Process Clause, as the centerpiece of the "Living Constitution," "incorporates" many of those same guarantees, thus making them applicable to state action.

Ironically, indeed fittingly, it all began with a New York Communist.

Benjamin Gitlow was an interesting character. At 18, he was a

223

Socialist. At 22, he was the first president of the Retail Clerks Union of New York, and at 26, Gitlow was elected to the New York State Assembly.

In 1919, Socialists of a more revolutionary flavor, like Gitlow and the legendary John Reed, had founded the Communist Labor Party, which later became the Communist Party of the United States. Gitlow ran as the Communist candidate for Vice President of the United States in 1924 and 1928.

Before his quixotic quest for high political office, Gitlow spent three years in New York's Sing Sing prison on a conviction for violating that state's 1902 criminal anarchy law. That statute, wrongly, made it a crime to encourage the violent overthrow of the United States government.

Gitlow's indictment was in two counts. The first charged that the defendant had

> "advocated, advised and taught the duty, necessity and propriety of overthrowing and overturning organized government by force, violence and unlawful means, *by certain writings* therein set forth entitled 'The Left Wing Manifesto'; the second that he had *printed, published and knowingly circulated and distributed a certain paper* called 'The Revolutionary Age,' containing the writings set forth in the first count advocating, advising and teaching the doctrine that organized government should be overthrown by force, violence and unlawful means." (My emphasis.)

Initially at his trial, and later in two New York appellate courts, and eventually in the Supreme Court of the United States, Gitlow argued that the criminal anarchy statute as written and applied to him violated the Due Process Clause of the Fourteenth Amendment.

But not because there were any *procedural* irregularities in either the law or in the way it was applied against him. No, indeed. Gitlow argued that the statute was "substantively" unconstitutional because it punished what Gitlow rightly characterized as "pure speech."

In effect, though not explicitly, Gitlow was invoking the *First Amendment* (which applies only to action by the *federal* government) against a *New York state* law, which could be attacked only by the Due Process Clause of the *Fourteenth Amendment. As we have seen, the First Amendment is very different from the Due Process Clause of the Fourteenth Amendment.*

Both New York appellate courts held the criminal anarchy statute *constitutional.*

So did the Supreme Court, which wrongly upheld Gitlow's conviction for pure speech.

Even worse, in doing so the Court made a statement that set the stage for later "incorporation" of virtually every provision of the Bill of Rights into the Fourteenth Amendment's due process guarantee—thereby endowing that previously purely *procedural* amendment ("due *process*") with the power to test the *substantive* ("rightness" or "wrongness") content of all state laws:

> For present purposes we may and do assume that freedom of speech and of the press—which are protected by the First Amendment from abridgment by Congress—are among the fundamental personal rights and "liberties" protected by the due process clause of the Fourteenth Amendment from impairment by the States.

225

In other words, lurking somewhere within the Due Process Clause of the Fourteenth Amendment was First Amendment "content," and the former's guarantee that no state shall "deprive any person of life, liberty, or property, without due process of law" really meant that "no state shall abridge the freedom of speech." And if a state law affecting speech was challenged on the ground that it did abridge free speech, the Supreme Court had the power to assess the substantive content of that law (e.g., punishing anarchists' pure speech) to ascertain if it passed constitutional muster, by some standard or other.

That left open the question of what criteria—what litmus paper—the Court would use to decide whether, *substantively*, a state law was constitutional or not.

> The *Gitlow* Court began by observing that there was no absolute right of free speech (or press) under the First Amendment:

> It is a fundamental principle, long established, that the freedom of speech and of the press which is secured by the Constitution, does not confer an absolute right to speak or publish, without responsibility, whatever one may choose, or an unrestricted and unbridled license that gives immunity for every possible use of language and prevents the punishment of those who abuse this freedom. * * * Reasonably limited . . . this freedom is an inestimable privilege in a free government; without such limitation, it might become the scourge of the republic.

So, according to the Supreme Court in 1925, free speech was a mere "privilege," subject to "limitation."

"Limitation," OK. But by what *standard? To what is pure speech subordinated?*

226

The Supreme Court of the United States wasn't bashful about its answer:

> That a State in the exercise of its police power may punish those who abuse this freedom by utterances inimical to the *public* welfare, tending to corrupt *public* morals, incite to crime, or disturb the *public* peace, is not open to question. (My emphasis.)

Having concluded that Gitlow's over-the-top Communist ranting was indeed "inimical to the public welfare," the Supreme Court upheld his conviction and sentence, uttering some hyperbole of its own:

> The State cannot reasonably be required to measure the danger from every such utterance in the nice balance of a jeweler's scale. A single revolutionary spark may kindle a fire that, smoldering for a time, may burst into a sweeping and destructive conflagration.

Even though the Supreme Court upheld the New York criminal anarchy statute, and with it Gitlow's conviction, more important for the future of constitutional law was that the Court tested that law not by the Constitution's *procedural Fourteenth* Amendment ("[N]o *state* shall deprive any person of life, liberty, or property, without *due process of law*"), but instead, by the *First* Amendment ("*Congress* shall make no law . . . abridging the *freedom of speech* . . .") *via* the Fourteenth—and that the essence of the Court's test was whether "substantively" the statute was "inimical to the public welfare" and thus constitutionally within New York's power to protect that public. (My emphasis.)

Gitlow's right to free speech was to be silenced (i.e., sacrificed) to the welfare (i.e., need for security) of others (i.e.,

227

the collective) under state law backed by government force (i.e., statism).

Justice Oliver Wendell Holmes authored a dissent for himself and Justice Louis Brandeis.

Most interesting about that dissent is that Holmes and Brandeis shared their colleagues' view that the Fourteenth Amendment's *Due Process* Clause contained First Amendment "content" which, through "incorporation," would be read into the Fourteenth.

Why, then, did they dissent?

Not because they believed New York was powerless to punish subversive speech, for they found no fault with the statute itself.

And not because they believed the Court lacked the judicial power to evaluate the *substantive* content of the statute, for they assumed that the Fourteenth Amendment's Due *Process* Clause could *substantively* test the constitutional appropriateness of the criminal anarchy statute.

Holmes and Brandeis dissented because they disagreed with their colleagues only about whether, under the facts of the case, Gitlow's speech was truly "inimical to the public welfare." If it was, he could be sent to Sing Sing. If not, he should have been set free.

For Holmes and Brandeis, those facts were to be assessed under the test the Court had developed in the earlier World War I free speech case of *Schenck* v. *United States*, where Schenck and others went to prison for protesting conscription. In *Schenck*, Holmes had written for the majority that "[t]he question in every case is whether the words used are used in such circumstances and are of such a nature as to create a clear and present danger that they will bring about the substantive evils that [the State] has a right to prevent."

In *Gitlow*, Holmes and Brandeis thought not; there was, in their opinion, no "clear and present danger."

> It is said that this manifesto was more than a theory, that it was an incitement. Every idea is an incitement. It offers itself for belief and if believed it is acted on unless some other belief outweighs it or some failure of energy stifles the movement at its birth. The only difference between the expression of an opinion and an incitement in the narrower sense is the speaker's enthusiasm for the result. Eloquence may set fire to reason. But whatever may be thought of the redundant discourse before us it had no chance of starting a present conflagration. *If in the long run the beliefs expressed in proletarian dictatorship are destined to be accepted by the dominant forces of the community*, the only meaning of free speech is that they should be given their chance and have their way. (My emphasis.)

Thus, Holmes and Brandeis, too, subscribed to their colleagues' belief that the Fourteenth Amendment "incorporated" the free speech guarantee of the First Amendment, and that state action allegedly violating "due process" could be examined substantively by the judicial power of the Supreme Court in order to ascertain whether the law under attack was constitutionally acceptable. By whatever standard nine justices saw fit to apply.

During the ensuing years, "incorporation" of virtually all other provisions of the Bill of Rights has occurred—violating individual rights, limited government, federalism, separation of powers, the appropriate role of the judiciary, and erasing the difference between the explicit provisions of the Bill of Rights and the more amorphous, and formerly procedural, Due Process Clause of the Fourteenth Amendment.

To get a better handle on just what the substantive due process litmus paper developed into, let's take a look at the 1920s case of *Palko* v. *Connecticut*.

Connecticut had a statute allowing the government to appeal in a criminal case. Palko had been indicted for second-degree murder; he appealed; the Connecticut Supreme Court reversed and ordered a new trial; and this time he was convicted of first-degree murder.

He appealed again, and eventually his case reached the Supreme Court of the United States. There, he argued that his second trial and conviction violated the Double Jeopardy Clause of the Fifth Amendment. *Fifth Amendment?* But that applies only to action by the *federal* government. No matter. Let's remember the Incorporation Doctrine.

Justice Benjamin Cardozo, for the eight justice majority:

> . . . the due process clause of the Fourteenth Amendment may make it unlawful for a state to abridge by its statutes the freedom of speech which the First Amendment safeguards against encroachment by the Congress . . . or the like freedom of the press . . . or the free exercise of religion . . . or the right of peaceable assembly, without which speech would be unduly trammeled . . . or the right of one accused of crime to the benefit of counsel . . . . In these and other situations immunities that are valid as against the federal government by force of the specific pledges of particular amendments have been found to be implicit in *the concept of ordered liberty*, and thus,

through the Fourteenth Amendment, become valid as against the states. (My emphasis.)

"Ordered liberty," no less.
Cardozo elaborated: "A scheme of ordered liberty. A principle of justice so rooted in the traditions and conscience of our people as to be ranked as fundamental."

Let's ask a few questions. The protection of individual rights and the existence of a limited government depend upon the answers to these questions. What is meant by "justice"? How does a Supreme Court justice ascertain the "traditions and conscience of our people"? And whatever those are, and however determined, which of them are "fundamental" and how do we know that they are? These Cardozo-inspired questions sound like Winston Churchill's observation about Soviet Russia. That it's a "riddle wrapped in a mystery inside an enigma."

Sad to say—because he was, after all, a Justice of the Supreme Court of the United States—Cardozo's opinion is utter mumbo jumbo. "Ordered liberty" is worse than no test at all because it provides all courts, and especially the Supreme Court of the United States, with a roving commission to translate the policy values of nine unelected and unaccountable philosopher kings/queens into what is supposed to pass for constitutional law. *Overriding the voters of the states. Overriding the governors. Overriding the legislatures. That our republican system, and the rights of any American, should rest on such indefensible clichés is scandalous (and depressing) in the extreme.*[My emphasis]

Back to Professor Raoul Berger: "As in the case of the Chinese mandate from heaven, we learn a right is fundamental only after the Court attaches that label. Ordered liberty is too vague to describe a national objective. It says that order and liberty are both to be sought, but provides no standard for reconciling the eternal conflict between them. * * * It is a vehicle for whatever meaning the Court gives it, and thus enables the Court to apply its own conceptions of public policy."

Don't take my, or Professor Berger's, word for it. Supreme Court Associate Justice Byron White himself once observed that "ordered liberty" is "[n]o more than a means whereby a majority of the Court can impose its own philosophical predilections upon State legislatures or Congress."

All of this leaves us with one more question: What has been incorporated? The answer: virtually every provision of the Bill of Rights.

Not only have they been incorporated, "emanations" and "penumbras" (to quote Justice William O. Douglas again) from specific Bill of Rights provisions have, in turn, created other non-textual "rights" that the Founders in their wildest dreams could not have imagined.

Which brings us back to *Griswold* v. *Connecticut* and that case's progeny, the infamous stain on over two hundred years of Supreme Court decisions, *Roe* v. *Wade.*

My earlier discussion of *Griswold* leaves no doubt that far from being a victory for "choice," individual rights, and limited government, the decision—rooted as it was in altruism-collectivism-statism and its utter disregard of federalism, separation of powers, and judicial restraint—exemplifies "Living Constitutionalism" at its worst and most dangerous.

Dangerous because Justice Douglas's ersatz "right to privacy" would, eight years later, be employed by the Supreme Court in *Roe* v. *Wade* to justify invalidating every state law affecting abortion. And in so doing, constitutionalize the murder of countless millions of the unborn.

232

A little history. A Texas statute, like those in a majority of the states at that time (the early 1970s), had outlawed abortion except to save the mother's life.

Jane Roe (a pseudonym)—unmarried, pregnant, and a pawn of pro-abortion zealots such as Planned Parenthood—sued in a federal court to declare the Texas anti-abortion statute unconstitutional.

Relying principally on *Griswold*'s "right of privacy" and the Fourteenth Amendment's now-established substantive due process "test", Roe claimed that the statute violated her rights of personal "privacy" and "liberty." She cited no other source, constitutional or otherwise, to justify her alleged right to an abortion—that is, her alleged right to destroy the live fetus she was carrying.

The Supreme Court's decision in *Roe* was, to be charitable, fragmented—even more than the *Griswold* decision had been. Of the nine Supreme Court justices in *Roe*, six wrote separate opinions. The majority opinion was written by Justice Harry Blackmun and concurred in by Chief Justice Warren Burger, Justices William O. Douglas, William J. Brennan, Potter Stewart, Thurgood Marshall, and Lewis Powell. Three of the concurring justices—Burger, Douglas, and Stewart—wrote their own individual opinions. While Justice William Rehnquist joined a dissent by Justice Byron White, Rehnquist wrote a separate dissenting opinion of his own. This was a sure sign—actually a confession—that the majority was on thin ice.

In his majority opinion, Justice Blackmun held the Texas anti-abortion statute unconstitutional.

Here's how he reached that momentous conclusion.

First, by canvassing a wide variety of sources, seeking to

ascertain what their attitudes were toward abortion—as if that had *anything* to do with whether there was a "right of privacy" lurking somewhere in the Constitution that would justify ripping a fetus from a woman's womb as a matter of convenience.

What sources?

Blackmun examined ancient views, which were inconclusive.

He claimed that the rigid anti-abortion stand of the Hippocratic Oath had been "unpopular" (with whom, and why?) at the time it was formulated.

He perused English common law, where to support the conclusion he was striving for, he hit pay dirt: even under early English statutes, abortion to save the mother's life was not considered a crime.

So what? The pending case was about whether the sovereign state of Texas had Tenth Amendment police power to enact an anti-abortion statute. If it did, was there *an explicit provision of the Constitution—an explicit constitutional right of Ms. Roe—that was violated by the statute?* English law rightly should have had nothing to do with the answer to those questions.

Blackmun liked British law because he didn't fare as well in his survey of American law: "By the end of the 1950s," he wrote, "a large majority of the jurisdictions [the states, in the United States] banned abortion, however and whenever performed, unless done to save or preserve the life of the mother."

Summarizing his survey of the past, Blackmun observed:

It is thus apparent that at [English] common law, at

234

the time of the adoption of our Constitution, and throughout the major portion of the 19th century, abortion was viewed with less disfavor than under most American statutes currently [1973] in effect. Phrasing it another way, a woman enjoyed a substantially broader right to terminate a pregnancy than she does in most States today. At least with respect to the early stage of pregnancy, and very possibly without such a limitation, the opportunity to make this choice was present in this country well into the 19th century. Even later, the law continued for some time to treat less punitively an abortion procured in early pregnancy.

These observations, of course, had nothing to do with the Tenth Amendment, federalism, separation of powers, the appropriate scope of judicial review, or the Bill of Rights— except to implicitly acknowledge that, until that time, legislation on the subject of abortion was exclusively the province of the *states*, whose governors, legislators, and courts apparently never realized that their laws somehow infringed a phantomlike "right of privacy."

Next, Blackmun turned his attention to medical views, past and prevailing at that time. Since the mid-nineteenth century, the American Medical Association had bitterly condemned abortion, only to ameliorate its harsh view in the mid-1960s. More pay dirt. In reviewing the American Public Health Association's pro-abortion position, Blackmun noted that just the year before, the American Bar Association had approved a Uniform Abortion Act prepared by the prestigious Conference of Commissioners on Uniform State Laws. Blackmun's potpourri of current views now included legal as well as medical authorities.

It was embarrassingly obvious what Blackmun was trying to cobble together from all this opinion gathering: *some kind of historical, cultural, social (but certainly not constitutional),* *justification for abortion.* If, in these respects, abortion had been treated even equivocally, the Court's task—coming up with a favorable abortion ruling—would be easier. Blackmun and his colleagues could write, as it were, on a clean slate. Ironically, but not surprisingly, what they wrote was, in turn, equivocal:

> We, therefore, conclude that the right of personal privacy includes the abortion decision, but that this right is *not unqualified* and must be considered against *important state interests* in regulation. (My emphasis.)

"Important state interests" again! And who, or what, is this "state"? Voters? Neighbors? Relatives? Politicians? Legislators? Judges? Bartenders? Batboys?

"State interests" this time regarding not marital sexual conduct (*Griswold*) or weak, dependent women (*Muller*), but the unborn, and in the wombs of the women who carry them— with the fetuses being the losers.

It is difficult to imagine any more naked altruist-collectivist-statist, let alone non-constitutional, ruling. Literal sacrifice to the norms of the "pro-choice" left, enforced by the strength of the government.

The Court had before it a case raising fundamental constitutional questions of federalism, separation of powers, the scope of judicial review, the Tenth Amendment, and the Bill of Rights.

Under those circumstances, Americans had the right to expect a United States Supreme Court decision that presented a solid array of legal-constitutional thought, reinforced with impeccable reasoning and irrefutable logic. We find in *Roe*

236

instead, as sole constitutional justification for its decision, the amorphous, Douglas-invented "right of personal privacy" unintelligibly and unintelligently imported in all its absurdity from *Griswold*.

Indeed, even Blackmun had to concede that Douglas's intellectually dishonest right of "privacy" was nowhere to be found in the Constitution.

So, following Douglas's earlier lead, Blackmun tried to weave a "privacy" "right" into the Bill of Rights by selecting threads where he could. Yet Blackmun's entire fifty-four-page opinion—which would invalidate anti-abortion laws nationwide and lead to literally uncountable deaths of the unborn—contained only a *single* paragraph devoted to the *constitutional* basis for the Court's conclusion:

> The Constitution does not explicitly mention any right of privacy. In a line of decisions, however, going back perhaps as far as . . . 1891 . . . the Court has recognized that a right of personal privacy, or a guarantee of certain areas or zones of privacy, does exist under the Constitution. In varying contexts, the Court or individual Justices have, indeed, found at least the roots of that right in the First Amendment . . . in the Fourth and Fifth Amendments . . . in the *penumbras* of the Bill of Rights . . . in the Ninth Amendment . . . or in the concept of liberty guaranteed by the first section of the Fourteenth Amendment are deemed "fundamental" or "implicit in the concept of ordered liberty" . . . are included in this guarantee of personal privacy. They also make it clear that the right has some extension to activities relating to marriage . . . procreation . . . contraception . . . family relationships . . . and child rearing and education . . . . (My emphasis.)

From a constitutional, let alone moral, perspective, this is sickening. Uncountable millions of the unborn were to die barbaric deaths because of roots, penumbras, ordered liberty . . . and be sacrificed on the altar of the Living Constitution's altruism, collectivism and statism.

The Court's nearly literal Solomonic decision scheduled the killing of the unborn this way: because the Court considered abortions within the first trimester to be as medically safe as, or even safer than, normal childbirth (this was 1973), abortions in the first three months of pregnancy "must be left to the medical judgment of the pregnant [woman and her] attending physician."

Because the Court invoked a state interest in the health of the pregnant woman (see *Muller* v. *Oregon*), abortions during "the stage subsequent to approximately the end of the first trimester" could be regulated "in ways that are reasonably related to maternal health" (e.g., licensed physicians, adequate facilities).

Because the Court asserted a state interest in potential life (which would be destroyed), "[f]or the stage subsequent to viability [approximately during the final trimester], the state . . . may, if it chooses, regulate, and even proscribe, abortion except where it is necessary, in appropriate medical judgment, for the preservation of the life or health of the mother." (Note the Court's presumptuous disregard of federalism, separation of powers and judicial restraint in virtually legislating for the fifty states.)

Few realized at the time that *Roe* v. *Wade* opened a Pandora's box when the Supreme Court cavalierly legitimized a "state interest" in pregnant women and their unborn children. Although in *Roe* anti-abortion laws were struck down, to the loud applause of the "pro-choice" zealots, they should not have rejoiced. Not only because of the barbaric consequences of the decision, but also because of its horrendous implications.

In 1973, some women were permitted to have abortions, sometimes.

But what about next time, if the "state interest" turns out to be a governmental Malthusian need to *compel* abortions?

A farfetched notion?

Science fiction?

Not if we accept the inescapable ultimate logic of *Roe* v. *Wade*—as seen from the perspective of a 1977 Supreme Court case.

The states, in the wake of *Roe* v. *Wade*, were obliged to revise not only their abortion laws but also a considerable number of related laws directly and indirectly affected by that decision. One example was Medicaid, which prior to *Roe* had funded certain *childbearing* expenses.

Connecticut Welfare Department regulations, which paid for *childbirth* expenses, limited state Medicaid benefits for first trimester abortions to those that were "medically necessary." In a 1977 case, *Maher* v. *Roe* (a different Roe), the Supreme Court was asked to decide "whether the Constitution requires a . . . State to pay for . . . [non-medically necessary] *abortions* when it pays for *childbirth*. (My emphasis.)

In other words, did Connecticut have a constitutional right to have a Medicaid funding policy that treated birth and abortion *differently*?

Before answering that question, the Court felt obliged to point out what *Roe* v. *Wade* had *not* held. According to the 1977 *Maher* v. *Roe* decision, "*Roe* did not declare an unqualified constitutional right to an abortion . . . . * * * [The decision] implies no limitation on the authority of a State to make a *value judgment favoring childbirth over abortion*, and to implement that judgment by the allocation of public [Medicaid] funds."

Got that?

Under, or despite, *Roe*, state governments can make "value judgments"—*which means passing laws*—in which statutes *limit* abortions.

All well and good. But pro-life people should not yet have applauded.

If the state can favor childbirth over abortion, it can favor abortion over childbirth, but in a much darker and more evil manner than it does today.

Absurd?

Following the 6–3 majority's statement in *Roe* that "[t]he State unquestionably has a 'strong and legitimate interest in encouraging normal childbirth' . . . an interest honored over the centuries," there appeared a footnote by the majority as astonishing as it was ominous:

> In addition to the direct interest in protecting the fetus, a State may have *legitimate demographic concerns about its rate of population growth.* Such concerns are basic to the future of the State and in some circumstances could constitute a substantial reason for *departure from a position of neutrality between abortion and childbirth.* (My emphasis.)

240

If government is not "neutral," by definition it necessarily tilts to one side or the other. And even if it tilts *for* childbirth and *against* abortion, under the rationales of *Muller*, *Griswold*, *Roe*, *Maher*, and other decisions too numerous to count, it can as quickly and easily tilt *against* childbirth and *for* abortion— not unlike democratic India, whose "demographic concerns about its rate of population growth" some years ago prompted it to depart "from a position of neutrality between abortion and childbirth" by instituting a program of *forced sterilization*. And let's not forget Communist China, whose perceived need for male infants has for decades resulted in state-ordered and state-sanctioned female infanticide.

This frightful story gets worse.

Three justices dissented in the *Maher* case, two of them the Court's leading liberals. One might have expected a ringing denunciation from Justices William J. Brennan and Thurgood Marshall of the majority's frightening assertion that, should population grow too large (or food become too scarce), society could forcibly rid itself of the unborn.

There was no denunciation.

Why?

Because in the end, most liberals and conservatives are, with regard to different issues, all altruists, collectivists, and statists, the only difference being what kind of government conduct they value or disvalue.

No one won in *Roe* v. *Wade*.

And no one won when procedural due process was converted into a substantive tool to be used against state legislation.

And no one won when virtually every provision of the Bill of Rights, through the Due Process Clause of the Fourteenth Amendment, was "incorporated" against the states.

We shall again see why in the next chapter when I discuss the First Amendment.

8.
The First Amendment

The First Amendment provides that "Congress shall make no law respecting an establishment of religion, or prohibiting the free exercise thereof. . . . "

There is an inherent tension between the Establishment Clause and the Free Exercise Clause.

Let's assume that Congress is considering a conscription law. All citizens between the ages of eighteen and twenty-nine will be drafted to serve the public interest, which will include engaging in combat. And then someone says, "Wait a second. I can't do that. I'm a Seventh-Day Adventist [or a Quaker], and my religion prevents me from killing people. I'm not going."

Hearing that objection, the sponsors of the bill realize that the prospective draftee is invoking the Free Exercise Clause of the First Amendment. They decide that some kind of an accommodation is necessary, so they insert an exemption into the bill: if someone adheres to a pacifist religion, he doesn't have to go.[84]

Is the exemption a prohibited "establishment"? Is government treating one religion different from other religions?

On the other hand, if there is no exemption, does the statute violate the pacifist's constitutional right to free exercise of his religion?

Before I get to the answer, let's establish (no pun intended) some context.

For reasons you'll soon see, the Supreme Court has long had difficulty with the First Amendment's Religion Clauses, less so with the Free Exercise Clause than with the Establishment Clause.

If a church is burning down, can a taxpayer-supported fire department respond, or would that be proscribed aid to religion? We'll see, after we look at the "tests" the Supreme Court has developed to resolve Establishment Clause cases.

First, the law has to be one of "general application," meaning that it must apply to everyone affected by it. The fire department is allocated two million dollars per year, and it's the department's job to put out all fires without reference to where, when or whom. The statute must be neutral on its face.

Second, it has to have a secular purpose, a non-religious purpose.

According to the Court, it has to have a "primary effect" which neither advances nor inhibits religion. In other words, the primary secular effect has to be neutral.

Finally, there cannot be "excessive entanglement" between government and religion.

It's obvious, is it not, that these so-called tests for Establishment Clause violations are highly subjective. One person's secular purpose is not necessarily someone else's. How people view primary effect, whether it advances or inhibits religion, is bound to foster disagreement. And what are the criteria for entanglement, let alone excessive entanglement?

The Establishment Clause cases are very ad hoc and very fact dependent, and in many of them the justices disagree with each other, although they may come out on the same side.

By now you probably won't be surprised if I tell you that in all the confusion about the Establishment Clause, there is one lucid voice—that of Justice Clarence Thomas.

To illustrate, I'll discuss a modern Establishment Clause case, one that I cover at length in *The Supreme Court Opinions of Clarence Thomas, 1991–2011*. The case is *Zelman* v. *Simmons-Harris*; it's an interesting case because it has three aspects: religion, race, and federalism.

Ohio had a school voucher program, meaning that parents of schoolchildren received vouchers from the state that they could use either to cover the costs of a private school or to reimburse homeschooling expenses.

The Ohio program affected religious schools because they, too, could participate in the voucher program. An Ohio parent could use the voucher at a Hebrew school or a parochial school in addition to any other private school.

Inevitably, the voucher program was challenged on Establishment Clause grounds.[85]

The Supreme Court ruled that there was no constitutional violation because the statute passed all the "tests." It was a neutral law on its face, having a secular purpose and a primary effect of not advancing or inhibiting religion, and it didn't excessively entangle government in religion.

A few years ago another Establishment Clause case reached the Supreme Court, *Van Orden* v. *Perry*, which caused a media frenzy in the United States. The question for the Supreme Court in *Van Orden* was "whether the Establishment Clause of the First Amendment allows the display of a monument inscribed with the 10 Commandments on Texas State Capitol grounds." The Court said the First Amendment protected the display. It didn't involve, let alone violate, the Establishment Clause.

Justice Thomas was with the majority but, not unusually, he went his own way in a concurring opinion that contains important insights about the Establishment Clause. First, Thomas said that the case would be easier "if the Court were willing to abandon the inconsistent guideposts it has adopted for addressing Establishment Clause challenges and return to the original meaning of the Clause. * * * The Framers understood an establishment 'necessarily to involve actual legal coercion.'"

> In no sense does Texas compel Van Orden to do anything. The only injury to him is that he takes offense at seeing the monument as he passes it on his way to the Texas Supreme Court Library. He need not stop to read it or even to look at it, let alone to express support for it or adopt the commandments as guides for his life. The mere presence of the monument along his path involves no coercion and thus does not violate the Establishment Clause."

Thomas was saying that the touchstone for the Framers was whether government was coercing people regarding religion. That's the test, not all the other criteria that the Court has created. However, Thomas didn't let it go at that.

He politely challenged all of the Supreme Court's previous Establishment Clause jurisprudence. The following is a fairly lengthy quotation, but it's an important nutshell criticism of prior Supreme Court Establishment Clause jurisprudence.

In The Supreme Court Opinions of Clarence Thomas, 1991–2011, I've written this:

> After weighing in on the constitutionality of the Ohio program, Thomas made a profound jurisprudential statement: "*as a matter of first principles, I question*

246

whether this [the Supreme Court's Establishment Clause] *test should be applied to the States.*"

Given that "incorporation" was at that time an entrenched dogma of Supreme Court jurisprudence and countless decisions rested on the doctrine, *with this one sentence Thomas was implicitly challenging the Due Process Clause premise underlying nearly a century of precedent involving the applicability to the states of virtually every provision of the federal Bill of Rights*—from the Establishment Clause of the First Amendment to the Cruel and Unusual Punishments Clause of the Eighth Amendment. (My emphasis.)

His words deserve to speak for themselves:

The Establishment Clause originally protected *States*, and by extension their citizens, from the imposition of an established religion by the Federal Government. Whether and how this Clause should constrain state action under the Fourteenth Amendment is a more difficult question.

Thomas continued:

Consequently, in the context of the Establishment Clause, it may well be that state action should be evaluated on different terms than similar action by the Federal Government. * * *

And here's what he says about originalism:

Returning to the original meaning would do more than simplify our task. It would also avoid the pitfalls present in the Court's current approach to such challenges. This court's precedent elevates the trivial to the proverbial "federal case," by making benign

247

signs and postings subject to challenge. Yet, even as it does so, the Court's president attempts to avoid declaring all religious symbols and words of longstanding tradition unconstitutional, by counterfactually declaring them of little religious significance. Even when the Court's cases recognize that such symbols have religious meaning, they adapt an unhappy compromise that fails fully to account for either the adherent's or the non-adherent's beliefs and provides no principled way to choose between them. Even worse, *the incoherence of the Court's decision in this area renders the Establishment Clause impenetrable and incapable of consistent application. All told, this court's jurisprudence leaves courts, governments, and believers and non-believers alike confused*—an observation that is hardly new. (My emphasis.)

In conclusion, Thomas continued his attack on existing Establishment Clause jurisprudence and indirectly demonstrated why originalist methodology is the only legitimate way to resolve constitutional questions.

The unintelligibility of this Court's precedent raises the further concern that, either in appearance or in fact, adjudication of Establishment Clause challenges turns on judicial predilections. * * * *The outcome of constitutional cases ought to rest on firmer grounds than the personal preferences of judges.* (My emphasis.)

To Justice Thomas, and to me, the solution to the problems created by Establishment Clause cases is self-evidently clear:

Much, if not all, of this would be avoided *if the Court would return to the views of the Framers and adopt coercion* as the *touchstone for our Establishment*

248

Clause inquiry. Every acknowledgment of religion would not give rise to an Establishment Clause claim. *Courts would not act as theological commissions*, judging the meaning of religious matters. Most important, our precedent would be capable of consistent and coherent application. While the Court correctly rejects the challenge to the Ten Commandments monument on the Texas Capitol grounds, *a more fundamental rethinking of our Establishment Clause jurisprudence remains in order.* (My emphasis.)

I now turn to the Free Exercise Clause, where the constitutional picture will be clearer, although one of the most interesting free exercise cases was decided by the Supreme Court over one hundred years ago.

Reynolds v. *United States* involved polygamy in the then-territory of Utah.

The Mormon Church, officially the Church of Jesus Christ of Latter-day Saints, was founded in the United States of America in 1830, and many of its adherents settled in Utah.

Congress had enacted a federal statute criminalizing polygamy. That meant the Free Exercise Clause of the First Amendment was involved directly. Not "due process" of the Fourteenth Amendment, because there was no *state* involvement.

The federal felony statute provided that "Every person having a husband or wife living who marries another whether married or single in the territory or other place over which the federal government has jurisdiction is guilty of bigamy and shall be punished by a fine of not more than $500 and by imprisonment for a term of not more than five years."

Set squarely against this federal anti-bigamy statute was the scriptural *duty* of male Mormons to practice polygamy. Even the Supreme Court of the United States, in the 1879 *Reynolds* case, acknowledged that

> this duty was enjoined, required by different books which Mormons believe to be of divine origin, that the members of the church believe that the practice of polygamy was directly enjoined upon the male members thereof by the Almighty God, that the failing or refusing to practice polygamy by such male members would be punished and that the penalty would be damnation in the life to come.[86]

It is easy for non-Mormons and non-believers to scoff at that religious requirement, but it was real to Mormons and impaled them on the horns of a dilemma: renounce and be damned, or render unto God and go to prison.

If he rendered unto Caesar that which was Caesar's (obeying the law), he affronted God (and he was damned). If he rendered unto God that which was God's (and practiced polygamy), Caesar was going to throw him into prison for five years and fine him $500. And if Reynolds did the five years and after his release continued to practice polygamy as his God demanded, he would probably go back to prison. A cruel, repetitive choice.

God won the first round. In accordance with the rituals and dictates of the Mormon religion, Reynolds took a second bride while married to his first wife.

Caesar was not amused. The federal government indicted Reynolds for violation of the anti-bigamy statute. Predictably, he defended on the ground that the First Amendment guaranteed him the right freely to exercise his religion. He was convicted in the territorial court, sentenced to prison, and eventually the case reached the Supreme Court of the United States.

The Supreme Court affirmed his conviction. That was bad enough. But the reasons given by the Court were worse.

The Court invoked English history, but that nation had been heavily Catholic, then had a national church, and had never had any kind of American-like free exercise of religion. Nor even a written constitution. Moreover, Reynolds was an American citizen, accused of violating American law, being judged by American courts, defending himself with the Free Exercise Clause of the First Amendment to the Constitution of the United States of America.

You wouldn't know that from what the Court wrote:

> Polygamy has always been odious among the northern and western nations of Europe, and until the establishment of the Mormon Church was almost exclusively a feature of the life of Asiatic and of African people.

Translation: "Our tribe doesn't engage in such uncivilized practices." Well, if the Supreme Court's conclusion couldn't legitimately rest on English history, and since it couldn't legitimately rest on abhorrence of savage practices, what was it based on? The altruist-collectivist-statist meter will tell us. The court observed that Congress was "free to reach [i.e., to criminalize] actions which were in violation of social duties."

Since there is no such thing as "society," just lots of other people who aren't you, the Court was saying that one's religious duty will be sacrificed to our tribe's moral standards, backed by the coercive power of the federal government

251

Lest anyone be uncertain about what the Supreme Court meant, here is more of what it said: "There never has been a time in any state of the union when polygamy has not been an offense against society." Against *whom*? Against the morally puritanical majority of Americans whose moral prejudices had caused Congress to enact the anti-polygamy law in the first place, the president to approve it, the prosecutors to enforce it, and the various courts to uphold its constitutionality.

"Society—the lots-of-other-people-but-not-the-Mormons—opposed polygamy, so society's values prevailed. No matter the cost to Mr. Reynolds.

Don't believe that the *Reynolds* case is an unenlightened aberration from the nineteenth century. Unenlightened, yes; aberration, no.

Let's look at what happened to Abraham Braunfeld and other Orthodox Jewish retail store owners in the City of Brotherly Love, Philadelphia. It's another example of Caesar trumping religious duties to God.

In the late 1950s, Braunfeld and other Jewish merchants ran up against Pennsylvania's "blue laws," which prohibited the retail sale of certain items on Sunday. But Braunfeld and the other Jewish merchants had a religious duty to close their stores on Saturday, their Sabbath.

Here was another conflict where American citizens found themselves on the horns of a "render to Caesar or to God" dilemma.

The blue laws were enforced, and eventually the cases reached the Supreme Court.

What happened?

Unlike *Reynolds*, which was a federal case and thus implicated the First Amendment, *Braunfeld* was a state case, so the defense had to be based on the substantively interpreted Due Process Clause of the Fourteenth Amendment.

Addressing the issue of free exercise of religion in *Braunfeld*, the Chief Justice of the United States, Living Constitutionalist Earl Warren himself, began his opinion with a well-established principle:

> "As pointed out in Reynolds, legislative power over mere opinion is forbidden but it may reach people's actions when they are found to be in violation of important *social duties* or *subversive of good order* even when the actions are demanded by one's religion." (My emphasis.)

After invoking other cases that weren't applicable, and even Thomas Jefferson, for the belief/action dichotomy, Warren wrote:

> The blue laws do not make unlawful any religious practice of [Braunfeld or the other Orthodox Jews]; the Sunday law simply regulates a secular activity and, as applied to [them], operates so as to make the practice of their religious beliefs more expensive. Furthermore, the law's effect does not inconvenience all members of the Orthodox Jewish faith but only those who believe it necessary to work on Sunday. And even these are not faced with as serious a choice as forsaking their religious practices or subjecting themselves to criminal prosecution. Fully recognizing that the alternatives open to [Braunfeld and the others]—retaining their present occupations and incurring economic disadvantage or engaging in some other commercial activity which does not call for

253

either Saturday or Sunday labor—may well result in some financial sacrifice in order to observe their religious beliefs, still the option is wholly different than when the legislation attempts to make a religious practice itself unlawful.

Reynolds, the Mormon, had been obliged to sacrifice his religious duty on the altar of society's belief that monogamy was the collective norm and that polygamy was immoral and socially unacceptable. To what, then, would Braunfeld's and his co-religionists' principles be sacrificed? Warren's answer:

> We cannot find a state without power to provide a weekly rest from all labor and, at the same time, to set aside one day of the week apart from the others as a day of rest, repose, recreation, and tranquility—a day when the hectic tempo of everyday existence ceases and a more pleasant atmosphere is created, a day which all members of the family and community have the opportunity to spend and enjoy together, a day in which people may visit friends and relatives who are not available during working days, a day when the weekly laborer may best regenerate himself. This is particularly true in this day and age of increasing state concern with public welfare legislation.

This saccharine quotation is from a *constitutional law* opinion by the Chief Justice of the United States. It is not from a legislature, whose business is weighing *policy* choices.

If you remember Mrs. Gotcher, Tiny Tim, and Mr. Muller from *Muller* v. *Oregon*, Warren's words, and what is behind them, should sound familiar. Recall that in the *Muller* case the Court agreed with the State of Oregon that Mrs. Gotcher's work was strenuous and that she was being exploited by Mr. Muller.

To his credit, Justice Brennan dissented, making it clear that the state should not be allowed to make any American choose between his religion and his livelihood. Justice Potter Stewart agreed with Brennan, actually characterizing the blue laws as requiring "a cruel choice," but to no avail.

There are two more points I shall make about the Free Exercise Clause, because they underscore the presence of the altruist-collectivist ethics, and the statist corollary, in religious affairs.

We know that modern free exercise law allows the government to intrude on even legitimate religious practices if there is present what is called a "compelling government interest" that is "narrowly tailored" to accomplish the legislative goal.

It takes four votes of the nine justices to grant a petition for a writ of certiorari, enabling a case to be reviewed by the Supreme Court.

Occasionally, if the Supreme Court denies review because there aren't four justices who want to take the case, one or more justices will openly disagree and explain why in writing.

Here's an example from the 1994 case of *Swanner* v. *Anchorage Equal Rights Commission.* A landlord owned some residential rental property in Anchorage, Alaska. He consistently refused to rent to couples that were unmarried because of a sincerely held religious belief that cohabitation was a sin. He did not want to be a facilitator.

The Anchorage Equal Rights Commission decided that the owner's renting policy violated various state laws prohibiting discrimination based on marital status.

The case went to the Alaska Supreme Court. It agreed with the lower court, ruling that the application of the law did not violate the owner's right to the free exercise of his religion (via the Due Process Clause of the Fourteenth Amendment, interpreted substantively) because the anti-discrimination laws served a "compelling state interest." The owner then filed a petition for a writ of certiorari in the Supreme Court seeking review of his case. Certiorari was denied.

Justice Thomas thought the Court should have granted the writ and decided the case. He explained his rationale thusly:

> If despite affirmative discrimination by Alaska on the basis of marital status [e.g., unmarried partner of a deceased does not share in estate, absent last will and testament] and a complete absence of any national policy against such discrimination, the State's asserted interest in this case is allowed to qualify as a "compelling interest"—that is, a "paramount" interest, an interest "of the highest order" [words used by the Alaska Supreme Court]—then I am at a loss to know what asserted governmental interests are not compelling. The decision of the Alaska Supreme Court drains the word *compelling* of any meaning and seriously undermines the protection for exercise of religion . . . .

To put the Alaska laws and its Supreme Court decision in the context of altruism-collectivism-statism, the rental property owner's religious beliefs were sacrificed to the state electorate's anti-discrimination (and anti-religion) values, backed by state force. And perhaps as many as eight justices of the Supreme Court of the United States were content to allow those religious beliefs to be trampled on.

The Religion Clauses share the First Amendment with speech guarantees: "Congress shall make no law . . . abridging the freedom of speech." For judges and practitioners alike, First

Amendment law is a vast subject with many identifiable subcategories.

If someone says Brad Pitt is a drug addict, that statement may constitute defamation, for which damages can be awarded. It's also punishment for speech.

If someone publishes a magazine containing the worst, most offensive kind of hardcore pornography, he will doubtless run afoul of both federal and state obscenity laws. That's also punishment for speech.

There's a doctrine called "fighting words," calculated to provoke a physical response from the person to whom those words are directed.

There are "hostile audience" situations where a speaker harangues a crowd, which then turns ugly, and the *speaker* is arrested for what ensues, not the troublemakers. That's more punishment for speech.

If someone says Michael J. Fox is a cripple, that may be considered hate speech because people with disabilities are in some situations considered a protected class.

If a political activist distributes anonymous leaflets on a street corner opposing a school tax, he could be punishable under a local ordinance.

In sum, speech *can* be punished, despite the First Amendment.

Under limited circumstances, such as in copyright cases and cases involving business secrets, speech can even be enjoined.

But of all the many categories of speech, there are two that prove Ayn Rand's altruism-collectivism-statism thesis better than any others. One is subversive advocacy. The other, political speech, is closely related.

257

Regarding subversive advocacy, I want to turn back the clock nearly a century to the World War I period.

Eugene V. Debs was twice a rabble-rousing Socialist candidate for President of the United States. He was indicted for ranting against the government in general and the draft in particular. Convicted, he went to prison. The Supreme Court affirmed his conviction. Debs was imprisoned for pure speech.

Whitney v. *California* was a case brought under the California Criminal Syndicalism Act. The charge was that Anita Whitney organized, assisted in organizing, and became a member of a group that would later advocate overthrow of the U.S. government. She met the same fate as Debs.

The *Debs* and *Whitney* cases and others, including the earlier *Schenck* case,[87] were merely prologue to the 1951 case of *Dennis* v. *United States.*

The *Dennis* case involved the Communist Party of the United States. Dennis and others were indicted for having conspired

> to organize as the Communist Party of the United
> States of America a society . . . of persons who . . .
> advocate the overthrow and destruction of . . . the
> United States by force and violence, and knowingly
> and willfully to advocate . . . the duty and necessity of
> overthrowing and destroying . . . the United States by
> force and violence.

Now, a slight digression. A conspiracy is (1) an *agreement* (which can be oral) to do an illegal act (2) coupled with an overt *act* (even a legal act) in furtherance of the agreement. Two people agree to rob a bank and realize they need a getaway car. One of them buys a Chevy. That's a consummated, prosecutable conspiracy.

The defendants made a free speech defense. In upholding their convictions, Supreme Court Chief Justice Fred Vinson stated categorically that

> Speech is not an absolute, above and beyond control by the legislature, when its judgment, subject its review here [of course!], is that certain kinds of speech are so undesirable as to warrant criminal sanction. *Nothing is more certain in modern society than the principle that there are no absolutes.* [I wonder if the Chief Justice was absolutely certain of that.] To those who would paralyze our Government in the face of impending threat by encasing it in a semantic straitjacket we must reply that *all concepts are relative* [certainly the concept of free speech]. (My emphasis.)

If, from the very first days of this nation, restraints on speech were not uncommon, if no less a patriot than Founding Father Thomas Jefferson believed that states could (and sometimes should!) censor speech and that a selective prosecution now and then of an unpopular speaker or editor was desirable, if during World War I anti-draft activists could be sent to jail for quoting the Ninth and Thirteenth Amendments, if American Communists could be sent to prison for merely agreeing to organize and advocate, if there are no absolutes and all concepts (such as liberty, freedom, and rights) are relative, *no one should be surprised that truly free speech has never existed in the United States.*

From time to time, free speech has been crushed by sacrificing those like Schenck, Debs, Whitney and Dennis, and their unpopular opinions, to the collective need of society for what it perceived as security against noxious ideas—all made possible by the government's monopoly on force and by its penal system backing that force.

As I said above, political speech is related to subversive advocacy.

So next, let's look at the seminal case involving political campaign finance laws, *Buckley* v. *Valeo*.

In 1974, over President Gerald Ford's veto, Congress imposed limits on political expenditures and contributions. Although the Supreme Court acknowledged that the limits "operate in an area of the most fundamental First Amendment activities," it upheld them for contributions but invalidated them for expenditures.

The Supreme Court's opinion in *Buckley* nakedly reveals just what a schizophrenic, cowardly compromise the decision was. It rested on this rationale: "The *expenditure* limitations . . . represent substantial merely than theoretical restraints on the quantity and diversity of political speech." (My emphasis.)

On the other hand, "[l]imitations upon the amount that any one person or group may *contribute* to a candidate or political committee entail only a marginal restriction on the contributor's ability to engage in free communication." (My emphasis.)

So "substantial" sacrifice of spenders' free speech is constitutionally unacceptable, but "marginal" sacrifice of contributors' free speech is constitutionally acceptable.

Apparently, the collective's interest in the former is less than in the latter. Again, we see the federal government putting its heavy thumb on the scale in favor of some at the expense of others.

For a few decades after *Buckley*, the Supreme Court picked its way through the minefield of political campaign finance laws, not really making any earth-shaking free speech rulings.

Along the way, in the *Nixon* v. *Shrink Missouri Government* case, Justice Thomas nailed the Court's ongoing indefensible contradictions:

> For nearly half a century, this Court has extended
> First Amendment protection to a multitude of forms
> of "speech," such as making false defamatory
> statements, filing lawsuits, dancing nude, exhibiting
> drive-in movies with nudity, burning flags, and
> wearing military uniforms. Not surprisingly, the
> [federal] Courts of Appeals have followed our lead
> and concluded that the First Amendment protects, for
> example, begging, shouting obscenities, erecting
> tables on a sidewalk, and refusing to wear a necktie.

Why has the Supreme Court's speech jurisprudence been in such a shambles for so long? If one understands Ayn Rand's "inner contradiction" and the role altruism-collectivism-statism has played in judicial decision making in speech and other areas involving individual rights and limited government, it is clear that too often the equation has been a balancing of whose interests were sacrificed to whom, on what basis, and why, with the government's enforcement power backstopping the collective's needs.[88]

9.
The Eighth Amendment

The Eighth Amendment provides that "[e]xcessive bail shall not be required, nor excessive fines imposed, nor cruel and unusual punishments inflicted." The amendment became effective in 1791, and one aspect in particular has in recent decades bedeviled the Supreme Court.

The amendment's genesis is found in the 1689 English Bill of Rights. The excessive-bail provision stemmed from the practice of some judges who, while granting bail, set it so high as to prevent a defendant's release on a writ of habeas corpus. The provision was a counterweight to the king jailing his enemies not for substantive offenses, but for nonpayment of the fines. I won't spend any time here on those clauses because there are not a great many decisions about them, and those that do exist are reasonably straightforward.

Although the Cruel and Unusual Punishments Clause textually speaks for itself, this clause has become problematic for the Supreme Court.

According to *The Heritage Guide to the Constitution,*

> Although the issue is disputed, the weight of scholarly opinion indicates that the ban on cruel and unusual punishment in the 1689 English Bill of Rights applied only to punishments not authorized by Parliament. The American colonial understanding, on the other hand, was that the ban applied to torturous punishments such as pillorying, disemboweling,

263

decapitation, and drawing and quartering. Inasmuch as such punishments were virtually absent in colonial America, Justice Joseph Story in his *Commentaries on the Constitution of the United States* believed that "[t]he provision would seem wholly unnecessary in a free government, since it is scarcely possible, that any department of such government should authorize, or justify such atrocious conduct."

This next point from the *Guide* is crucial to understanding what the Supreme Court has done with, and to, the Cruel and Unusual Punishments Clause:

Early Supreme Court interpretations subscribe to the view that *the clause only curbed torturous punishments* as defined at the time of the amendment's ratification. * * * The Court subsequently upheld execution by public shooting . . . and electrocution . . . . (My emphasis.)

In addition to the clause barring "torturous" punishments, according to the *Guide* another "possible meaning of the clause [was that it prohibited] *disproportionate* or *excessive* punishments." This notion was raised in a dissenting opinion in the 1892 case of *O'Neil* v. *Vermont*, but the Living Constitutionalists of that day were unable to command a majority of the Court. (My emphasis.)

Then, in the 1910 case of *Weems* v. *United States*, a Supreme Court majority adopted the *O'Neil* dissent.

The next major development in Eighth Amendment law, as the *Guide* observes, was that "[i]n *Trop* v. *Dulles* (1954), Chief Justice Earl Warren rejected reliance on the [Constitution's] original understanding as the appropriate standard in favor of the 'evolving standards of decency that mark the progress of a maturing society.' Since that time, the Supreme Court's views on the amendment have been confused, and the current [2005] Court appears divided and unable to agree on a common interpretive standard."

That's an understatement.

Thanks to the Living Constitutionalists' non-originalist "interpretation" of the Cruel and Unusual Punishments Clause, a powerful industry has developed that employs judges, lawyers, writers, publishers, foundations, lecturers, journalists, professors and grant writers, among others. All in service to the oxymoron of "prisoners' rights."

This constitutional scam began in 1976, sixty-six years after *Weems*.

The case was *Estelle* v. *Gamble*. A Texas prisoner, J. W. Gamble, hurt his back during a work assignment when a bale of cotton fell on him. Dissatisfied with the medical treatment he received, Gamble sued the warden and other prison officials under 42 United States Code, Section 1983 of the federal Civil Rights Act for alleged violation of his civil rights, to wit: his Eighth Amendment right to be free from "cruel and unusual punishments."

The Supreme Court, in an 8–1 decision, for the first time applied the Cruel and Unusual Punishments Clause not to *punishment*, but to *treatment*, and to medical treatment at that.

According to Associate Justice Thurgood Marshall's opinion,

> The [Eighth] Amendment embodies *"broad and idealistic concepts of dignity, civilized standards, humanity, and decency . . .,"* . . . against which we must evaluate penal measures. Thus, we have held

265

repugnant to the Eighth Amendment punishments which are incompatible with "*the evolving standards of decency that mark the progress of a maturing society,*" [Citing Warren's meaningless notion from] *Trop* v. *Dulles* . . . or which "involve the unnecessary and wanton infliction of pain" . . . .

These elementary principles establish the government's obligation to provide medical care for those whom it is punishing by incarceration. An inmate must rely on prison authorities to treat his medical needs; if the authorities fail to do so, those needs will not be met. In the worst cases, such a failure may actually produce physical "torture or a lingering death" . . . the evils of most immediate concern to the drafters of the [Eighth] Amendment. In less serious cases, denial of medical care may result in pain and suffering which no one suggests would serve any penological purpose. * * * The infliction of such unnecessary suffering is inconsistent with *contemporary standards of decency* as manifested in modern legislation codifying the common-law view that "it is but just that *the public be required to care for the prisoner*, who cannot by reason of the deprivation of his liberty, care for himself." My emphasis.)

Having ruled that the Cruel and Unusual *Punishments* Clause no longer applied solely to *punishments* but now also to the medical *treatment* of prisoners—who had already been *punished* by their sentences—the Court was obliged to formulate a test by which violation of "prisoners' rights" could be determined.

We therefore conclude that *deliberate indifference* to serious medical needs of prisoners constitutes the "unnecessary and wanton infliction of pain" . . . proscribed by the Eighth Amendment. This is true whether the indifference is manifested by prison doctors in their response to the prisoner's needs or by prison guards in intentionally denying or delaying access to medical care or intentionally interfering with the treatment once prescribed. Regardless of how evidenced, *deliberate indifference* to a prisoner's serious illness or injury states a cause of action under [Section] 1983 [of the Civil Rights Act]. (My emphasis.)

Thus was born to the Eighth Amendment's Cruel and Unusual Punishments Clause its bastard offspring, the "deliberate indifference" test: "We therefore conclude that *deliberate indifference to serious medical needs of prisoners constitutes the 'unnecessary and wanton infliction of pain' . . . proscribed by the Eighth Amendment.*" (My emphasis.)

Note the elements of this test, somehow divined from the plain words and original meaning of "cruel and unusual punishments." The clause now applies not to affirmative conduct, *punishment*, but to *inaction* (indifference). The clause now applies to *prisoners*, who have already been punished by being sentenced. The clause now applies not to the *presence* of *punishment*, but to the *absence* of *treatment*.

Estelle v. *Gamble* was a field day for the Living Constitutionalists, and the top of a very slippery slope.

The slide began in earnest sixteen years later, in 1992.

In *Hudson* v. *McMillian*, the Court divided its "deliberate indifference" test into two parts: a *subjective* element, "deliberate indifference" itself (a culpable state of mind), and an *objective* element, the "serious" medical need (brain

267

surgery, not removal of a hangnail). Hudson had been beaten by guards and "suffered minor bruises and swelling of his face, mouth, and lip. Blows also loosened Hudson's teeth and cracked his partial dental plate, rendering it unusable for several months."

Claiming that the beating violated his Eighth Amendment "civil right" to be free from "cruel and unusual punishments," Hudson sued.

In her opening paragraph for the Court's 7–2 majority, Justice Sandra Day O'Connor wrote:

> This case requires us to decide whether *the use of excessive physical force against a prisoner* may constitute cruel and unusual punishment when the inmate does not suffer serious injury. We answer that question in the affirmative.

Understand what O'Connor was saying: the Cruel and Unusual Punishments Clause can be violated by the use of excessive physical force against a prisoner *even if he does not suffer serious injury*. It's the amount of force applied, even if nothing comes of it.

O'Connor and her majority colleagues had traveled far indeed from real punishments such as disembowelment and decapitation.

The counterpoint argument to the "decision creep"[89] of the majority's ruling came from the lonely dissenting voice of Justice Clarence Thomas, articulating the originalist approach to the Eighth Amendment's Cruel and Unusual Punishments Clause—an approach which would, from then on, make his opinions the only defensible ones concerning the proper understanding of that clause. Anyone who wants to understand the current state of majority Supreme Court jurisprudence regarding the Cruel and Unusual Punishments Clause, and what is profoundly wrong with it, need only read Thomas's opinions about the clause.

> In my view, a use of force that causes only insignificant harm to a prisoner may be *immoral*, it may be *tortious* [an actionable civil wrong], it may be *criminal*, and it may even be *remediable under other provisions of the Federal Constitution*, but it is not cruel and unusual punishment.[90] (My emphasis.)

Nothing in American constitutional law could have been clearer than that. For one thing, even apart from the decisive history of the clause and its plain meaning, in *Trop*, *Estelle*, and *Hudson* the Court's majorities admitted they were stretching simply by their use of the terms "evolving standards." "Evolving" means "changing" or "developing." The justices were changing, developing—one could say rewriting—the constitutional law of cruel and unusual punishments, all in the name of *their* "evolving standards of decency," which was code for sacrificing the righteous justice owed to victims in order to coddle the criminals who had injured, often killed, them.

Speaking for the constitutionalists, Justice Thomas named what was really underpinning the majority's ruling:

> Today's expansion of the Cruel and Unusual Punishments Clause beyond all bounds of history and precedent is, I suspect, yet another manifestation of the pervasive view that the Federal Constitution must address all ills in our society. Abusive behavior by prison guards is deplorable conduct that properly evokes outrage and contempt. But that does not mean that it is invariably unconstitutional. The Eighth

Amendment is not, and should not be turned into, a National Code of Prison Regulation. To reject the notion that the infliction of concededly "minor" injuries can be considered either "cruel" or "unusual" "punishment" (much less cruel and unusual punishment) is not to say that it amounts to acceptable conduct. Rather, it is to recognize that primary responsibility for preventing and punishing such conduct rests not with the Federal Constitution, but with the laws and regulations of the various States.

The damage done by the Court's *Hudson* decision was compounded in the next term's case of *Helling* v. *McKinney*.[91]

A Nevada state prisoner, McKinney, sued his warden and other prison officials for violating his federal civil rights. According to Justice Byron White, author of the Court's majority opinion, McKinney's complaint

> alleged that [he] was assigned to a cell with another inmate who smoked five packs of cigarettes a day. * * * The complaint also stated that cigarettes were sold to inmates without properly informing them of the health hazards a nonsmoking inmate would encounter by sharing a room with an inmate who smoked . . . and that certain cigarettes burned continuously, releasing some type of chemical. . . . [McKinney] complained of certain health problems allegedly caused by exposure to cigarette smoke.

Which of the inmate's federal constitutional rights were allegedly violated?

Naturally, his right to be free from "cruel and unusual punishments," as guaranteed by the Eighth Amendment. And to be free not just from *immediate* harm but, as the Supreme

Court read the prisoner's complaint, free from harm to his *future* health.[92]

In light of Justice Thomas's dissent in *Hudson*, it would not have been difficult to predict on which side he would be in *McKinney* in his continuing effort to restore the original meaning of the Cruel and Unusual Punishments Clause.

He began his dissent by observing that in *Hudson* the Court had expanded the Eighth Amendment by ruling that the amendment is violated by force causing only a *minor* injury. Now, in *McKinney*, the Court was expanding the Cruel and Unusual Punishments prohibition to embrace merely *risk* of injury. Henceforth, under the Cruel and Unusual Punishments Clause, a prisoner could state a litigable claim simply by *alleging* that conduct by prison authorities caused a *mere risk of minor injury.*

Consistent with Thomas's approach to originalist statutory interpretation, he began with the words of the Eighth Amendment itself. In doing so, he cut to the heart of the Supreme Court's contemporary Eighth Amendment jurisprudence: The majority's "decision, like every other 'conditions of confinement' case since *Estelle* v. *Gamble* . . . rests on the premise that deprivations suffered by a prisoner constitute 'punishment' for Eighth Amendment purposes, even when the deprivations have not been inflicted as part of a *criminal* sentence."

In other words, if the Cruel and Unusual Punishments Clause barred only cruel and unusual *punishments*, because McKinney had not complained about *those punishments*—but instead only about second-hand smoke—he had no case.

Thomas then demonstrated that "[a]t the time the Eighth Amendment was ratified, the word 'punishment' referred to the

271

penalty imposed for the commission of a crime. * * * That is also the primary definition of the word today. As a legal term of art, 'punishment' has always meant a 'fine, penalty, or confinement inflicted upon a person by the authority of the law and the judgment and sentence of a court, for some crime or offense committed by him.'" He found no historical evidence to the contrary.

Indeed, the "cruell and unusuall Punishments"[93] provision of the English Declaration of Rights of 1689, the "antecedent to our constitutional text," was a response to *sentencing* abuses.

Nor, in the considerable discourse concerning the formation of the Constitution and creation of the Bill of Rights, was there anywhere even a hint that the concern over cruel and usual punishments included harsh prison conditions, or that the clause could be invoked on behalf of those who had already been punished by their sentences.

As a matter of fact, Thomas noted, the Founders had an example they could have emulated if they were concerned with harsh prison conditions. The 1792 State of Delaware constitution expressly provided that "Excessive bail shall not be required, nor excessive fines imposed, nor cruel or unusual punishments [94] inflicted." However, the wording of the Delaware constitution continued on to provide, as the Eighth Amendment does not: "*and in the construction of jails a proper regard shall be had to the health of prisoners.*" (My emphasis.) (From the perspective of constitutional analysis, this historical fact is devastatingly convincing. The Eighth Amendment was intended to apply only to *punishment*, which occurs only at *sentencing*.)

In making these points, and by a surgical analysis of *Estelle* and its antecedent cases, Thomas was challenging the premise upon which the Supreme Court's entire Eighth Amendment "conditions of confinement" / "prisoner's rights" jurisprudence had been built since *Estelle* was decided in 1976.

> Although the evidence is not overwhelming, I believe that the text and history of the Eighth Amendment, together with the decisions interpreting it, support the view that *judges or juries—not jailers—impose "punishment."* At a minimum, I believe that the original meaning of "punishment," the silence in the historical record, and the 185 years of uniform precedent shift the burden of persuasion to those who would apply the Eighth Amendment to prison conditions. (My emphasis.)

That burden, he argued, had not nearly been satisfied by the majority.

In closing his dissent, Thomas lamented where the Court's Eighth Amendment Cruel and Unusual Punishments Clause jurisprudence was heading. More important, he articulated a conflict that would affect his own role on the Court for years to come: *adherence to the principle of* stare decisis *in the face of wrongly decided cases that create "constitutional rights" out of the "Living Constitution's" thin air*:

> In *Hudson*, the Court extended *Estelle* to cases in which the prisoner had suffered only minor injuries; here, it extends *Estelle* to cases in which there has been no injury at all.[95] Because I seriously doubt that *Estelle* was correctly decided, I decline to join the Court's holding. *Stare decisis* may call for hesitation in overruling a dubious precedent, but it does not demand that such a precedent be *expanded* to its outer limits.[96] (My emphasis.)

The Supreme Court was pulling at the oars of the Cruel and Unusual Punishments Clause again in *Farmer* v. *Brennan*. In that case, a preoperative male transsexual who projected feminine characteristics made a "deliberate indifference" claim based on having been housed in the prison's general population, where he was assaulted and raped.

For the first time, the Court defined "deliberate indifference": "a prison official cannot be found liable under the Eighth Amendment for denying an inmate humane conditions of confinement unless the official knows of and disregards an excessive risk to inmate health or safety; the official must both be aware of facts from which the inference could be drawn that a substantial risk of serious harm exists, and he must also draw the inference." Because the Court believed that the record that had come to it from the trial court may not have adequately developed the facts, the case was remanded.

Justice Thomas concurred. His opinion reflects the concerns he had expressed earlier in *Hudson* and *Helling*. The Court was again "refin[ing] the 'National Code of Prison Regulation,' otherwise known as the Cruel and Unusual Punishments Clause," which is inappropriately applied to anything other than *judicial* punishment. What happened to Farmer—*and it was certainly wrong*—was not "punishment," and thus the prisoner, who may have had recourse under other laws, should have had *no* recourse under the Eighth Amendment.

Thomas did acknowledge, however, that "in approaching this case . . . we do not write on a clean slate. * * * Beginning with *Estelle* v. *Gamble* . . . the Court's prison condition jurisprudence has been guided, not by the text of the Constitution, but rather by 'evolving standards of decency that mark the progress of a maturing society.'" Although he "doubt[ed] that mode of constitutional decision making," in the name of *stare decisis* he concurred in the Court's judgment. But Justice Thomas "remain[ed] hopeful that the Court will reconsider *Estelle* in light of the constitutional text and history."

274

In *Farmer*, Thomas had remained steadfast in his Eighth Amendment jurisprudence: the Cruel and Unusual Punishments Clause applied only to punishments imposed by a criminal sentence, *Estelle* v. *Gamble* was wrongly decided, it should be "reconsidered," and in the meantime its reach should not be expanded—let alone should its applicability be measured by whether the prison authorities' conduct comported with "evolving standards of decency that mark the progress of a maturing society."[97]

The majority of the Supreme Court, however, has never accepted an originalist understanding of the Cruel and Usual Punishments Clause. As recently as 2010, Justice Thomas was still at the barricades, in a case entitled *Wilkins* v. *Gaddy*, summarizing the originalist understanding of the clause.

> . . . I continue to believe that *Hudson* was wrongly decided. [Citing] Erickson v. Pardus (2007) (dissenting opinion); Farmer v. Brennan . . . (1994) (opinion concurring in judgment); Helling v. McKinney (1993) (dissenting opinion); Hudson v. McMillian (1992) (dissenting opinion).

If anyone wants a front row seat to an explanation of the spectacle of how the Supreme Court has corrupted the Cruel and Unusual Punishments Clause—by sacrificing both crime victims, the historical and rational concept of punishment, and its constitutional embodiment to the collective queasiness about real punishment—he need only reread the indisputable words of Justice Thomas that I've quoted above.

Considerably more of his eloquence, again in counterpoint to the Supreme Court's conventional wisdom about a sensitive subject, is on display when it comes to the subject of race—a constitutional law subject where altruism-collectivism-statism is palpably evident.

275

10.
Equal Protection of the Law

The Fourteenth Amendment provides that no state shall "deny to any person within its jurisdiction the equal protection of the laws." But whose "rights" are to be protected? And at whose expense?

To begin answering these questions, it's necessary to understand the context of the Fourteenth Amendment—especially the actions and reactions that resulted in the amendment's enactment.

I'm going to explain the causal relationship between President Lincoln's Emancipation Proclamation, enactment of the three so-called Civil War Amendments, and the various Civil Rights Acts. You'll see that all of these were a clear progression toward the abolitionists' goal of ending not only slavery *per se* but all the "badges and incidents of slavery" as well.

I begin with President Abraham Lincoln's January 1, 1863 Emancipation Proclamation:

> I do order and declare that all persons held as slaves
> within said designated States and parts of States are,
> and henceforward shall be, free; and that the
> Executive Government of the United States, including
> the military and naval authorities thereof, will
> recognize and maintain the freedom of said persons.

As moral and necessary as the Emancipation Proclamation may have been, it was far from certain what binding constitutional effect it had. Lincoln could issue all the "proclamations" he wanted, but for any of them to be legal there had to be a constitutional basis.

Lincoln's rationale for his Proclamation was this: ". . . I, Abraham Lincoln, President of the United States, by virtue of the power in me vested as *Commander-in-Chief* of the Army and Navy of the United States in time of actual armed rebellion against the authority and government of the United States, and as a fit and necessary *war measure* for suppressing said rebellion . . . ." (My emphasis.)

At that time, there were Northern Democrats who doubted the Emancipation Proclamation's constitutionality and opposed the war if its purpose was to free slaves. For example, in Illinois, the Democratic Party controlled the state legislature, and "Copperheads" (a peace party that sought to end the war through negotiation) were dominant. Here's their view of the matter:

Resolution of the Illinois Legislature in Opposition to the Emancipation Proclamation, 1863.[98]

Resolved: That the emancipation proclamation of the President of the United States is as unwarranted in military as in civil law; a gigantic usurpation, at once converting the war, professedly commenced by the administration for the vindication of the authority of the constitution, into the crusade for the sudden, unconditional, and violent liberation of 3,000,000 negro slaves; a result which would not only be a total subversion of the Federal Union, but a revolution in the social organization of the Southern States, the immediate and remote, the present and far-reaching consequences of which to both races cannot be contemplated without the most dismal foreboding of horror and dismay. The proclamation invites servile

278

insurrection as an element in this emancipation crusade—a means of warfare, the inhumanity and diabolism of which are without example in civilized warfare, and which we denounce, and which the civilized world will denounce, as an uneffaceable disgrace to the American people.

Putting aside the hyperbole and translating this diatribe to mean that the Illinois Legislature thought the Emancipation Proclamation was unconstitutional, or non-constitutional, there was some merit to its point.

In classical mechanics, the third of Newton's laws of motion postulates that every action is accompanied by a reaction of equal magnitude but opposite direction. Although Lincoln's Emancipation Proclamation wasn't a mechanical phenomenon, it was a daring action that set in motion strong reactions.

A strong backlash reaction was the so-called Black Codes, slavery-lite, civil disabilities laws enacted by Southern states at the end of the Civil War which imposed strict limitations on the labor, property, contracts, movement, and other major aspects of the lives of former slaves. The restrictions were just a tad short of the slavery from which Negroes had just been emancipated.

The reaction to the Black Codes caused another action, ratification of the Thirteenth Amendment in December 1865: "Neither slavery nor involuntary servitude, except as a punishment for crime whereof the party shall have been duly convicted, shall exist within the United States, or any place subject to their jurisdiction."

But because the Thirteenth Amendment didn't expressly nullify the still-existing repressive Black Codes, the Civil Rights Act of 1866, designed to protect the freedmen from that discriminatory legislation, was passed in March of that year. It was vetoed by President Johnson, and then enacted over his veto the next month.

Civil Rights Act of 1866

Be it enacted, That all persons born in the United States and not subject to any foreign power . . . are hereby *declared to be citizens* of the United States; and such citizens, of every race and color, without regard to any previous condition of slavery or involuntary servitude, except as a punishment for crime whereof the party shall have been duly convicted, shall have the same right, in every State and Territory in the United States, to *make and enforce contracts, to sue, be parties, and give evidence, to inherit, purchase, lease, sell, hold, and convey real and personal property, and to full and equal benefit of all laws* and proceedings for the security of person and property, as is enjoyed by white citizens, and shall be subject to like punishment, pains, and penalties, and to none other, any law, statute, ordinance, regulation, or custom, to the contrary notwithstanding. (My emphasis.)

SEC. 2. And be it further enacted, That any person who, under color of any law, statute, ordinance, regulation, or custom, shall subject, or cause to be subjected, any inhabitant of any State or Territory to the deprivation of any right secured or protected by this act, or to different punishment, pains, or penalties on account of such person having at any time been held in a condition of slavery or involuntary servitude, except as a punishment for crime whereof the party shall have been duly convicted, or by reason of his color or race, than is prescribed for the punishment of

280

white persons, shall be deemed guilty of a misdemeanor, and, on conviction, shall be punished by fine not exceeding one thousand dollars, or imprisonment not exceeding one year, or both, in the discretion of the court.

As well intentioned as the Civil Rights Act of 1866 was, serious and widespread doubt existed about its constitutionality. The Act purported to grant so many rights to Negroes who only a few years earlier had been slaves that it touched some very raw nerves, and for that reason it was at risk for serious challenge. Many supporters of what the Act had tried to accomplish believed something more legally powerful was needed to secure the rights the Act purported to recognize.

That "something more legally powerful" became the Fourteenth Amendment. It was submitted to the state legislatures in June 1866, and rejected by most of the Southern states. But their restoration to the Union was made dependent on ratification, and by July 1868, the amendment had been ratified.[99]

> Section 1: All persons born or naturalized in the United States and subject to the jurisdiction thereof, are citizens of the United States and of the State wherein they reside. No State shall make or enforce any law which shall abridge the privileges or immunities of citizens of the United States; nor shall any State deprive any person of life, liberty, or property, without due process of law; nor deny to any person within its jurisdiction the *equal protection of the law*. (My emphasis.)

Section 5: "The Congress shall have power to enforce, by appropriate legislation, the provisions of this article.

But what about, specifically, the Negroes' right to vote? To resolve any doubt that the Thirteenth and Fourteenth Amendments protected that right, in February 1870 the Fifteenth Amendment was ratified:

> Section 1: The right of citizens of the United States to vote shall not be denied or abridged by the United States or any State on account of race, color, or previous condition of servitude.

> Section 2: The Congress shall have power to enforce this article by appropriate legislation.

Soon after ratification of this last of the three Civil War Amendments, Congress in 1871 enacted the so-called Ku Klux Klan Act whose purpose was to insure for Negroes the full benefits of the Thirteenth, Fourteenth, and Fifteenth Amendments.[100]

Against the background of these Amendments and Acts, I'll now examine the modern understanding and application of the Equal Protection Clause of the Fourteenth Amendment. Professors Nowak and Rotunda have observed, "In recent years the equal protection guarantee has become the single most important concept in the Constitution for the protection of individual rights." According to them,

> . . . the Supreme Court has formally adopted three standards of review in equal protection cases. The first standard is the "rational relationship" or "rational basis" test. . . . This test gives a strong presumption of constitutionality to the government action [of treating apparently similar persons differently]; the Court only invalidates the law if it has no rational relationship to any legitimate interest of government. The intermediate standard of review has been formally adopted for gender and illegitimacy cases. *

282

The Supreme Court appeared to use the intermediate standard in one case involving the denial of all public school education to children who could not prove that they were in this country lawfully, but the Court's opinion was not clear regarding the standard of review being used in that case.

When the government uses a classification based on race or national origin, the Supreme Court uses "strict scrutiny" and requires a classification to be necessary (narrowly tailored) to a compelling or overriding government interest.* * *

A law that uses a classification that burdens or impairs the ability of only one class of persons [e.g., Negroes] who wished to exercise a fundamental constitutional right [e.g., voting, travel, at least one appeal in a criminal case] will be examined under equal protection. * * * When the Court has used a formal test for the analysis for fundamental rights problems, it has most often stated that the law impairing the fundamental right must survive strict scrutiny and must be narrowly tailored to promote a compelling or overriding interest. [The same analysis is used if involved is a "suspect classification" (e.g., race, alienage, national origin).]

It's obviously much easier to state these analytical tests in the broad terms just quoted than it is to apply them to concrete facts.

Because I'm now going to discuss *racial* discrimination and segregation (a subset of discrimination), we'll be looking at the "suspect classification," not "fundamental right" category of Fourteenth Amendment Equal Protection Clause analysis.

Let's begin with the 1880 case of *Strauder* v. *West Virginia*, where a state statute flatly barred Negroes from jury service by providing that only white male citizens could serve. The Supreme Court rightly held the statute unconstitutional under the Equal Protection Clause of the Fourteenth Amendment.

The 1967 case of *Loving* v. *Virginia* involved a statute, common in fifteen other states, prohibiting and criminally punishing interracial marriages. Justice Potter Stewart, concurring in the Court's ruling that the statute was unconstitutional under the Equal Protection Clause, noted that "I have previously stated the belief that it is simply not possible for a state law to be valid under our constitution which makes the criminality of an act depend on the race of the actor." The correct reason, to support the right decision.

A more modern case illustrating the suspect classification analysis is *Adarand Constructors, Inc.* v. *Pena*. In that case the low bidder on a federal highway contract failed to be awarded the contract because *under federal law* the business was not controlled by "[s]ocially and economically disadvantaged individuals who were presumed to include black Americans, Hispanic Americans, Native Americans, Asian-Pacific Americans and other minorities or any other individual found to be disadvantaged by the small business administration."

What did the Supreme Court do? It correctly ruled that all racial classifications employed by any level of government had to be evaluated by the strict-scrutiny test. But in a failure to meet the issue head on, the Court remanded the case to the trial court because, the majority said, there was no trial record showing whether the federal statute was narrowly tailored to achieve a compelling interest. In other words, the trial court hadn't applied the test for this flagrantly suspect classification.

The Supreme Court majority consisted of Justice Sandra Day

O'Connor, who wrote the opinion, Chief Justice William Rehnquist, and Justices Anthony Kennedy, Antonin Scalia, and Clarence Thomas. Justices John Paul Stevens, David Souter, Ruth Bader Ginsburg, and Stephen Breyer dissented.

In Justice Thomas's partly concurring opinion, he implicitly recognized that when the government discriminates on the basis of race, altruism-collectivism-statism is often the driving force. [101]

> I agree with the majority's conclusion that strict scrutiny applies to *all* [emphasis in original] government classifications based on race. I write separately, however, to express my disagreement with the premise underlying Justice Stevens' and Justice Ginsburg's dissents: that *there is a racial paternalism exception to the principle of equal protection.* I believe that there is a "moral [and] constitutional equivalence" . . . between laws designed to *subjugate* a race and those that distribute benefits on the basis of race in order to foster some current notion of equality. *Government cannot make us equal; it can only recognize, respect, and protect us as equal before the law.*
>
> That these programs may have been motivated, in part, by good intentions cannot provide refuge from the principle that under our Constitution, *the government may not make distinctions on the basis of race.*
>
> As far as the Constitution is concerned, it is irrelevant whether a government's racial classifications are drawn by those who wish to *oppress* a race or by those who have a sincere desire to *help* those thought to be disadvantaged. There can be no doubt that *the*

285

paternalism that appears to lie at the heart of this [federal contract] *program is at war with the principle of inherent equality that underlies and infuses our Constitution. See Declaration of Independence* ("We hold these truths to be self-evident, that all men are created equal, that they are endowed by their Creator with certain unalienable Rights, that among these are Life, Liberty, and the pursuit of Happiness").

These programs not only raise grave constitutional questions, they also undermine *the moral basis of the equal protection principle*. Purchased at the price of immeasurable human suffering, the equal protection principle reflects our Nation's understanding that such classifications ultimately have a destructive impact on the individual and our society.

Unquestionably, "[i]nvidious discrimination is an engine of oppression." It is also true that "[r]emedial" racial preferences may reflect "a desire to foster equality in society." . . . But there can be no doubt that *racial paternalism and its unintended consequences can be as poisonous and pernicious as any other form of discrimination.*

So-called "benign" discrimination teaches many that because of chronic and apparently immutable handicaps, minorities cannot compete with them without their patronizing indulgence. Inevitably, such programs engender attitudes of superiority or, alternatively, provoke resentment among those who believe that they have been wronged by the government's use of race. These programs stamp minorities with a badge of inferiority and may cause them to develop dependencies or to adopt an attitude that they are "entitled" to preferences. * * *

286

In my mind, government-sponsored racial discrimination based on benign prejudice is just as noxious as discrimination inspired by malicious prejudice.[102] In each instance, it is racial discrimination, plain and simple. (My emphasis throughout.)

Thomas's reference to the "moral basis" of the Equal Protection Clause implicitly recognizes the point he had made elsewhere, that "every racial classification helps . . . some races and hurts others." The "racial classification" is made by the government and enforced with its monopoly of force. Those who are "hurt" have their rights sacrificed by the collective to the needs of those "helped." To paraphrase Justice Thomas, when a statist government sacrifices the rights of some (i.e., Adarand Constructors, Inc.) to the collective needs of others (i.e., "black Americans, Hispanic Americans, Native Americans, Asian-Pacific Americans and other minorities or any other individual found to be disadvantaged by the small business administration") the moral basis of the Equal Protection Clause is violated.

Thomas's reference to stamping minorities "with a badge of inferiority" is hardly limited to federally engineered construction contracts. Perhaps the worst example is in the context of affirmative action, which also racially discriminates against those not in the protected class, and for the same reasons.

In the affirmative action case of *Grutter* v. *Bollinger*, the question for the Court, in Justice O'Connor's words, was "Whether the use of race as a factor in student admissions by the University of Michigan law school is unlawful." Ruling for herself and the four liberals, Stevens, Souter, Ginsburg, and Breyer, O'Connor ruled that the school had a "compelling interest" in the creation and maintenance of a diverse student body and that because the compelling interest was "narrowly tailored," the school could constitutionally use race as an admissions factor.

I want to be very clear that what is currently euphemistically called "affirmative action," usually in the name of "diversity," is in reality raw, unconstitutional racism in its intention and in its impact on non-minorities, who are usually white male Americans. As Justice Thomas wrote:

> The absence of any articulated legal principle supporting the majority's principal holding suggests another rationale. I believe what lies beneath the Court's decision today are the benighted notions that one can tell when racial discrimination *benefits* (rather than *hurts*) minority groups . . . and that racial discrimination is necessary to remedy general *societal* ills. This Court's precedents supposedly settled both issues, but clearly the majority still cannot commit to the principle that racial classifications are *per se harmful* and that almost no amount of *benefit* in the eye of the beholder can justify such classifications. (My emphasis.)

There is a simple point here. When the government uses its monopoly power for racially discriminatory purposes, there are no winners. Those discriminated against have their interests—e.g., award of a legitimately bid contract, merit admission to a law school—sacrificed to the collective's perception of its or someone else's needs, with the "beneficiaries" also losing. The latter may get the contract to build a road, or be admitted to Michigan Law School, but they are worse off for becoming complicit in theft and trading a short-term good for a long-term undermining of what could later protect them: *the moral and constitutional force of an honestly interpreted and applied Equal Protection Clause.*

288

As I mentioned earlier, racial segregation is a subset of racial discrimination. This brings us to *Brown* v. *Board of Education* (I)[103] in 1954. The question for the Supreme Court in that case was whether states could constitutionally segregate public schools on the basis of race. It was a revisiting of the nineteenth century case of *Plessey* v. *Ferguson*, where the "separate but equal" doctrine was born. The answer in *Brown* (I) was "no," but to the extent the opinion written by Chief Justice Earl Warren was steeped in sociology rather than a straightforward "strict scrutiny" / "compelling interest" analysis, the decision is weaker than it could, and should, have been.

But the Court reached the correct conclusion.

The next year, *Brown* (I) was followed by *Brown* (II), the decision that minted the phrase "with all deliberate speed." The principle of unconstitutional racial segregation had been established in *Brown* (I), but the question of what was supposed to happen next was still unanswered. Racial segregation, especially in the South, was a deeply entrenched system reaching into politics, law, economics, finance, culture—indeed every aspect of society. Although *Brown* (I) was limited to public education, the principle it established would inevitably, and probably sooner than later, be felt across that entire societal spectrum.

But first, how to handle the schools? Said the Court in *Brown* (II): "School authorities have the primary responsibility for elucidating, assessing and solving these problems. Courts will have to consider whether the action of school authorities constitutes good faith implementation of the governing constitutional principles." So the cases were remanded to the original trial courts, which were told to use equitable principles to grant relief.

289

This was the beginning of federal judicial control of local schools. The federal district courts were instructed to order that the parties be admitted "with all deliberate speed," and, by implication, all other public school students similarly situated, on a non-segregated basis.

Following *Brown* (II), for a long time the Supreme Court kept its hands off, allowing local federal district courts to deal with the implementation problem, which was substantial. Just as with the Black Codes, most of the Southern states tried to erect one roadblock after another to implementation. There were so-called transfer plans, which allowed students to go from one school to another, but increased the likelihood of *de facto* racial segregation. Some states closed their public schools. Others created "freedom of choice" plans, allowing students to select what school they wanted to attend. Under certain circumstances it became difficult to move from one school to another. And on and on it went, with implementation of *Brown* (I) seemingly ever further away.

In 1968, after growing impatience with the widespread implementation delays, the Supreme Court decided *Green* v. *County School Board*, ruling that "[t]he burden on a school board today is to come forward with a plan that promises realistically to work, and promises realistically to work now."

But some thought that the *Green* decision underscored the profoundly important distinction between *eliminating segregation* and *requiring integration*. This is a crucial distinction. Racial segregation can result from benign factors such as housing and similar patterns, in which case there is no violation of the Equal Protection Clause. On the other hand, if racial segregation is the product of government action, it's unconstitutional and must be eliminated. But does it follow that elimination is enough, or must schools then be *forcibly integrated*?

The 1995 case of *Missouri* v. *Jenkins* provided the answer.

In 1985, a Missouri federal district court issued a remedial order to eliminate all vestiges of state-imposed public school segregation in Kansas City. What did the judge want? Why, among other things that would supposedly eliminate government segregation, curriculum improvements and library upgrades. Also, the district judge had the power to order the local school district to increase the tax rate to cover the costs of complying with his remedial order.

As a result of the remedial order, over the following years, hundreds of millions of dollars were spent to comply. By 1995, when the *Jenkins* case had returned to the Supreme Court (it had been there in 1990), the cost of the 1985 remediation order for the Kansas City Municipal School District was $2 million *annually*, some $20 million *in toto*.

By then, the federal district judge had made two other orders. One imposed salary increases for all but three of the district's approximately 5,000 employees, teachers, and staff. The other created a "magnet" school district designed to attract non-minority students into largely minority schools.

Remember that a *federal* judge did this to a *state* municipality and school district. So much for federalism.

The question for the Supreme Court was whether the judge had exceeded his constitutional power. Chief Justice Rehnquist, for a 5–4 majority, said that the judge had.

The stronger argument for the majority position, however, came from a concurring opinion by Justice Thomas. "It never ceases to amaze me," he wrote, "that the courts are so willing to assume that anything that is predominantly black must be inferior. Instead of focusing on remedying the harm done to those black schoolchildren by segregation, the District Court here sought to convert the Kansas City, Missouri, School District (KCMSD) into a 'magnet district' that would reverse the 'white flight' caused by *desegregation*." (Emphasis in original.)

What came next in Thomas's concurring opinion has to be characterized as astonishing, by any standard. The second black Supreme Court justice in history (and the only one among the nine justices at that time), in words that revealed his moral stature, took aim at the sacrosanct 1954 *Brown* (I) desegregation decision. Not at its result, but at its methodology. What Thomas wrote about the Constitution, about race, about racial segregation in *Jenkins* is more apt, let alone more eloquent, even than the unanimous Supreme Court opinion authored by then–Chief Justice Earl Warren in *Brown* (I).

Said Justice Thomas:

> Two threads in our jurisprudence have produced this unfortunate situation, in which a District Court has taken it upon itself to experiment with the education of the KCMSD's black youth. First, the court has read our cases to support the theory that black students suffer an unspecified psychological harm from segregation that retards their mental and educational development. This approach not only relies upon questionable social science research rather than constitutional principle, but it also rests on an assumption of black inferiority. Second, we have permitted the federal courts to exercise virtually unlimited equitable powers to remedy this alleged constitutional violation.
>
> The exercise of this authority has trampled upon principles of federalism and the separation of powers

and has freed courts to pursue other agendas unrelated
to the narrow purpose of precisely remedying a
constitutional harm.

He then cut to the core of the case:

> The District Court inferred a continuing constitutional
> violation from two primary facts: the existence of de
> jure ["by law"] segregation in the KCMSD prior to
> 1954, and the existence of de facto segregation today.
> The District Court found that in 1954, the KCMSD
> operated 16 segregated schools for black students, and
> that in 1974, 39 schools in the district were more than
> 90% black. Desegregation efforts reduced this figure
> somewhat, but the District Court stressed that 24
> schools remained "racially isolated," that is, more
> than 90% black, in 1983–1984. For the District Court,
> it followed that the KCMSD had not dismantled the
> dual system entirely. The District Court also
> concluded that because of the KCMSD's failure to
> "become integrated on a system-wide basis," the dual
> system still exerted "lingering effects" upon KCMSD
> black students, whose "general attitude of inferiority"
> produced "low achievement . . . which ultimately
> limits employment opportunities and causes poverty."

In other words, Thomas was saying that the *Jenkins* trial court
had inferred that there was a violation *now* because there had
been a violation *then*. *De jure* then, *de facto* now.

The problem was that there was no *causality*, no link between
then and now. There was nothing to show that what had
occurred in 1954 (and earlier) was the connecting cause of
what was happening now. As Thomas said,

> It should now be clear that the existence of one-race

293

schools is not by itself an indication that the State is practicing segregation. * * * That certain schools are overwhelmingly black in a district that is now more than two-thirds black is hardly a sure sign of intentional state action. * * * District Courts must not confuse the consequences of [pre-1954] de jure segregation with the results of larger social forces or private decisions. * * *

When a District Court holds the State liable for discrimination almost 30 years after the last official state action, it must do more than show that there are schools with high black populations or low test scores. Here, the district judge did not make clear how the high black enrollments in certain schools were fairly traceable to the State of Missouri's actions. I do not doubt that Missouri maintained the despicable system of segregation until 1954.

But *I question the District Court's conclusion that because the State had enforced segregation until 1954, its actions, or lack thereof, proximately caused the "racial isolation" of the predominantly black schools in 1984.* In fact, where, as here, the finding of liability comes so late in the day, I would think it *incumbent upon the District Court to explain how more recent social or demographic phenomena did not cause the "vestiges."* This the District Court did not do. (My emphasis.)

And then Justice Thomas returned to *Brown* (I), and he took it head on. "It is clear that the District Court misunderstood the meaning of *Brown* I. *Brown* I did not say that "racially isolated" schools were inherently inferior; the harm that it identified was tied purely to de jure segregation. Indeed, *Brown I itself did not need to rely upon any psychological or*

294

social-science research in order to announce the simple, yet fundamental, truth that the government cannot discriminate among its citizens on the basis of race." (My emphasis.)

Brown (I), Thomas was saying, shouldn't have rested on pseudo-scientific Swedish and other social science, but instead on a straightforward application of the Equal Protection Clause of the Fourteenth Amendment. "Psychological injury or benefit is irrelevant to the question whether state actors have engaged in intentional discrimination, the critical inquiry for ascertaining violations of the equal protection clause." And there was no evidence KCMSD had done that.

But he wasn't finished. "The time has come for us to put the genie back in the bottle." Thomas was talking about the decades-long virtual blank check the Supreme Court had given the federal district courts to craft so-called remedies for the consequences of official racial discrimination, while at the same time not permitting constitutional principles such as federalism to stand in the way of our drive to reform the schools.

No better example existed of what he was talking about than the massive expenditure that the district court had ordered. Thomas blamed earlier Supreme Court decisions for the judicial overreaching we see before us today, and he acknowledged that it was, perhaps, "the price we now pay for our approval of such extraordinary remedies in the past." And not just in the realm of public education, because "judges have directed or managed the reconstruction of entire institutions and bureaucracies with little regard for the inherent limitations on their authority."

Because the Founders intended no such extravagant remedial powers and because such powers cut against the core principle of federalism, Thomas rejected them. He knew what those

295

remedial powers were really being used for: ". . . the federal courts should also avoid using racial equality as a pretext for solving social problems that do not violate the constitution." In the end, he said, "The desire to reform a school district, or any other institution, cannot so captivate the judiciary that it forgets its constitutionally mandated role. Usurpation of the traditionally local control over education not only takes the judiciary beyond its proper sphere, it also deprives the States and their elected officials of their constitutional powers. At some point, *we must recognize that the judiciary is not omniscient, and that all problems do not require a remedy of constitutional proportions*." (My emphasis.)

Indeed, Justice Thomas had written a fitting epitaph for too many decisions of the Supreme Court, from the days of John Marshall to the present.

Conclusion

I began this book with the proposition that underlying every political, social, and economic system are necessarily ethical principles, and that Ayn Rand had identified America's "inner contradiction" as the altruist-collectivist ethics augmented by their political corollary, statism.

If these ethics have been at the root of America's legal and political system from the beginning—and the motivating force for many Supreme Court decisions—the inescapably crucial question is, where does America go from here?

There are two possibilities, each representing a different philosophy and thus a different direction for the United States of America.

The first direction is exemplified by the following political party platform. Many of its planks raise no eyebrows today and, indeed, many have become law in the days since President Franklin Delano Roosevelt's "New Deal."

> We ask that the government undertake the obligation above all of providing citizens with adequate opportunity for employment and earning a living.
>
> *The activities of the individual must not be allowed to clash with the interests of the community, but must take place within its confines and be for the good of all.*

Therefore,

We demand an end to the power of the financial interests.

We demand profit sharing in big business.

We demand a broad extension of care for the aged.

We demand the greatest possible consideration of small business and the purchases of the national, state, and municipal governments.

In order to make possible to every capable and industrious citizen, the attainment of higher education and thus the achievement of a post of leadership, the government must provide an all-round enlargement of our entire system of public education.

We demand the education at government expense of gifted children of poor parents.

The government must undertake the improvement of public health—by protecting mother and child, by prohibiting child labor . . . by the greatest possible support for all clubs concerned with the physical education of youth.

We combat the materialistic spirit within and without us, and are convinced that a permanent recovery of our people can only proceed from within on *the foundation of the common good before the individual good*. (My emphasis.)

This political party platform reeks with the very same altruist-collectivist-statist doctrines that we've seen permeate

298

American constitutional adjudication. It was the work of those who knew very well the meaning and the implications of subordinating the individual to society's wishes via the use of government force. Indeed, the platform's architects constructed an entire regime on the foundation of these doctrines.

This political party platform was adopted on February 24, 1920, in Munich, Germany, by the National Socialist Party of Germany, the Nazis.

I said there are two possibilities. Here is the other one.

> The concept of individual rights is so prodigious a feat of political thinking that few men grasp it fully—and two hundred years have not been enough for other countries to understand it. But this is the concept to which we owe our lives—the concept which made it possible for us to bring into reality everything of value that any of us did or will achieve or experience. . . .[104]

The choice is unambiguous.

And ours to make.

Notes

1. In the context of this book, by "republican institutions" I mean the political and legal structure established by the Constitution of the United States of America, to wit:

> A representative federal republic comprising a national government possessing strictly limited, delegated powers, and constituent states and the people possessing residual powers not delegated nor specifically withheld;

> The powers of that federal government being checked by the principles of federalism, separation of powers, and limited judicial review;

> A federal Bill of Rights (and certain of the later amendments applicable to the states) protecting individuals from the power of the federal and state governments; and

> A textually explicit, non-judicial process for amending the Constitution.

2. Suffice it for my present purposes to understand that the principle of individual rights holds that each person is sovereign, that no one has the right to violate that sovereignty by initiating physical force (and, some say, by committing fraud), and that the only basis for relations between individuals is mutual voluntary consent. This principle is exemplified by the Declaration of Independence, the guarantees explicit and

301

implicit in the limited government established by the Constitution and recognized by the Bill of Rights and substantive amendments to the Constitution

3. By "limited government" I mean the political, legal and constitutional structure established by the Declaration of Independence and the Constitution of the United States of America.

4. Much of the substance of this book derives from that series of lectures and from my essays and books

5. I will not discuss most of the Fourth, Fifth, and Sixth Amendment provisions because they deal primarily with criminal law: search and seizure, self-incrimination, double jeopardy, right to trial by jury, and so forth.

6. The United States of America is blessed with a written Constitution and Bill of Rights which, in principle, are devoted to the protection of individual rights and the concept of limited government. Interpretation and implementation of the Constitution and Bill of Rights results in what is called "constitutional law," a term often bandied about with considerable imprecision.

Lest there be any doubt throughout this book about what I mean by that term, here is my working definition of "constitutional law" (derived mostly from the late Professor Edward S. Corwin's definition):

    a. A body of principles,
    b. derived from the interpretation or application,
    c. by a high court [e.g., the Supreme Court of the United States],
    d. of a written constitutional document,

e. in the course of disposing of cases,
f. in which the validity of some act of governmental power,
g. national, state or local,
h. has been challenged,
i. in relation to the constitutional document.

In other words, generally speaking, "constitutional law" results from comparing government action against what the people of the United States have authorized it to do, and against rights retained by the people.

7. Ayn Rand, "Man's Rights," *The Virtue of Selfishness* (The New American Library, 1965), p. 127. Internal quotation marks added.

8. According to *Webster's New World Dictionary of the American Language, second College Edition*, a "society" is nothing more than "a group of persons . . . ." Meaning, other people.

9 *Webster's New World Dictionary of the American Language, second College Edition.*

10 Ayn Rand, "Faith and Force: The Destroyers of the Modern World," *Philosophy: Who Needs It*, p. 74.

11 *Ibid.*

12 Ayn Rand, "Racism," *The Virtue of Selfishness*, p. 175.

13 Ayn Rand, "The Only Path to Tomorrow," *Reader's Digest*, Jan. 1944, p. 8.

14 Dictionary.com.

15 Some historians, political scientists, and others have contended that the "Iroquois Constitution" was a precursor to the United States Constitution. Nothing could be further from the truth. The Iroquois constitution was nothing more than an arrangement between a loose confederation of Indians, bearing not the slightest resemblance to our later Constitution with its explicit recognition of individual rights, limited government, federalism, separation of powers, an independent judiciary— all steeped in political philosophy with its roots in the Enlightenment.

16 See the Third Amendment to the Constitution of the United States of America.

17 Georgia did not send a delegation.

18 Congress recommended that another be held in May 1775.

19 See Henry Wadsworth Longfellow's "Paul Revere's Ride," which begins:

> Listen, my children, and you shall hear
> Of the midnight ride of Paul Revere,
> On the eighteenth of April, in 'Seventy-five;
> Hardly a man is now alive
> Who remembers that famous day and year.

20 There were those, Ayn Rand among them, who would consider the reference to a "creator" as reflecting a mystical view of ethics. We will see that Jefferson's reference did create considerable constitutional problems for the Supreme Court.

21 "Letter to Spencer Roane," September 6, 1819, *The Words of Thomas Jefferson*, Paul Leicester Ford, ed.

22 A series of three asterisks (***) indicates that for editorial

reasons the author has removed at least one sentence; ellipses (…) indicate that less than one sentence has been removed.

23 I have added the text in the next paragraph that appears in brackets.

24 Monongahela Navigation Co. v. United States, 148 U.S. 312 (1893).

25 The first quotation is by Justice Chase, the second by Justice Iredell.

26 The word "mandamus" is from the Latin, literally meaning "We command." According to *Black's Law Dictionary*, "[t]his is the name of a writ . . . which issues from a court of superior jurisdiction [e.g., the Supreme Court of the United States], and is directed to a private or municipal corporation, or any of its officers, or to an executive, administrative or judicial officer, or to an inferior court [e.g., the United States District Court for the District of Colorado] commanding the performance of a particular act therein specified [e.g., impanel a jury in a criminal trial], and belonging to his or their public, official, or ministerial duty, or directing the restoration of the complainant to rights or privileges of which he has been illegally deprived." A less wordy definition from *Black's Law Dictionary* is "A writ issuing from a court of competent jurisdiction, commanding an inferior tribunal, board, corporation, or person to perform a purely ministerial duty imposed by law." For example, a Superintendent of Motor Vehicles refused to issue a driver's license to an applicant who had satisfied every condition for its issuance. Because the Superintendent had no discretion—issuance was "mandatory" upon satisfaction of the requirements—a court could (and would) issue a Writ of Mandamus compelling the Superintendent to "perform a purely ministerial duty imposed by law."

27 Though not entirely relevant here, it is worth mentioning that the Judiciary Act of 1789 vested the federal courts with vast jurisdiction over civil and criminal cases, a jurisdiction which during the following years would grow even larger through federal legislation and judicial decisions.

28 *Black's Law Dictionary* (fifth ed.) defines "original jurisdiction" as "[j]urisdiction in the first instance. Jurisdiction to take cognizance of a cause [claim] at its inception, try it, and pass judgment upon the law and facts. Distinguished from *appellate* jurisdiction   [hearing appeals from lower courts]."

29 Hughes had one of the most high-level public careers in American history. He was governor of New York, Associate Justice of the Supreme Court of the United States, secretary of state, judge on the International Court of Justice, Chief Justice of the United States, and Republican presidential candidate in 1916 against Woodrow Wilson.

30 They had sized up the situation correctly; after the election of 1800, federalists would never again elect a president.

31 *The Writings of Thomas Jefferson* (Med. Ed., 1905) X, p. 302.

32 Nowak, John H. and Rotunda, Ronald D. *Constitutional Law (7th Ed.)*, 5. In ruling as he did, Marshall avoided a direct confrontation with the Republican Administration because he didn't have to order them to deliver Marbury's commission, or do anything else.

The late Yale University law professor Fred Rodell summed up Marshall's achievement this way: "John Marshall, by fastening on a petty point of proper legal procedure in an essentially insignificant case, by attacking a harmless bit of a statute that had been enacted not by Republicans but by Federalists, by

306

handing his political opponents, with magnificent opportunism, a strictly Pyrrhic victory (Marbury never got his commission), established the supremacy of the judiciary over the rest of the federal government." (Rodell, Fred, *Nine Men: A Political History of the Supreme Court From 1790 to 1955.*) Marshall accomplished all this in a single case, and he never had to deal with the constitutionality of the Republicans' Repeal Act or face down Jefferson, Madison, or the Republicans.

33 While *Marbury* v. *Madison* was the first Supreme Court decision to declare an *Act of Congress* unconstitutional, the Court's first decision declaring an action of the *president* to be unconstitutional was in the case of *Little* v. *Barreme* in 1804, the so-called *Flying Fish* case. President John Adams had issued an order in 1799, during our brief war with France, that authorized the Navy to seize ships bound for French ports. Adams's order, however, was inconsistent with an earlier Act of Congress declaring that the government lacked such authorization. After a Navy captain seized a Danish vessel (the *Flying Fish*) pursuant to Adams's order, the ship owners sued the captain in an American maritime court for trespass. Marshall rejected the captain's argument that he couldn't be sued because he was following presidential orders. The Supreme Court noted that commanders "act at their own peril" when they obey invalid orders—and the president's order was invalid because it was beyond his powers in light of the earlier congressional act.

34 I use the word "interpretation" because it is the one commonly used to describe what the Supreme Court, and lower courts as well, do when ascertaining the meaning of words in the Constitution and federal statutes. However, I do so reluctantly because interpretation in popular usage has the soft connotation of being subjective. For example, I "interpret" a given word one way, and you can "interpret" it differently.

As we shall see, proper constitutional "interpretative" methodology does not allow for subjective meanings.

35 The Supreme Court has never ruled on whether this residence requirement contemplates continuous presence in the United States, or whether cumulative presence satisfies Article II, section 1. There is evidence to support either interpretation.

36 See, for example, The Supreme Court Opinions of Clarence Thomas, 1991–2011 (2d edition) by Henry Mark Holzer.

37 Speech by Associate Justice William J. Brennan Jr. to the Text and Teaching Symposium, Georgetown University, October 12, 1985, Washington, D.C., reprinted in *The Great Debate: Interpreting Our Written Constitution*, published by the Federalist Society as Occasional Paper No. 2 (1986). Although Brennan neglected to name those whose "needs" were to predominate, throughout his long career on the Supreme Court his opinions starkly revealed who were to be the beneficiaries of his, and society's, largesse.

38 Opinion Journal, *Wall Street Journal*, October 19, 2005.

39 "The powers not delegated to the United States by the Constitution, nor prohibited by it to the States, are reserved to the States respectively, or to the people."

40 Article I, section 1, Constitution of the United States of America.

41 Article II, section 1, Constitution of the United States of America.

42 Article II, section 2, Constitution of the United States of America.

43 Article III, section 1, Constitution of the United States of America.

44 Wood, Gordon S., *The Creation of the American Republic, 1776–1787*, p. 151. The author, writing in 1969, added in a footnote that "[t]he literature on separation of powers is enormous."

45 Wood, Gordon S., p. 152.

46 The principle of separation of powers should not be confused with what is often referred to as "checks and balances." An example of the latter is the requirement that some presidential appointees must be confirmed by the Senate. Another is that the president may trump the federal criminal justice system by granting commutations and pardons.

47 As noted above, Articles I, II and II expressly delegate separate legislative, executive and judicial power. The president delivers the State of the Union message to Congress, and proposes legislation. Congress has the power to enact it, or not. The president has the power to approve legislation, or not, and Congress has the power to override a veto. The House of Representatives, by a mere majority, has the power to withhold appropriations. The impeachment power, as we saw in the case of President William Jefferson Clinton, is divided: half of the House of Representatives is needed to impeach, and two-thirds of the Senate is required to convict. The Constitution contains other examples as well.

48 Powell was a Democrat.

49 Fifth edition

50 The intent and wording of the statute included heterosexual married couples.

51 That's the federalism part. While not literally a horizontal-

separation-of-power situation as well, the Supreme *Court* was deciding the constitutionality of a state *legislative/executive* enactment.

52 Note Harlan's having lumped together adultery (at least one party married), homosexuality (same gender) and fornication (consensual, presumably adult) on the one hand, and incest (sibling and other familial) on the other. The first three and the fourth are quite different.

53 Federalism can sometimes take odd twists and turns. A little-known example relates to Thomas Jefferson's position on *which level* of the American government possessed the power to violate freedom of speech.

The year was 1798.

The federalists, in an attempt to stifle dissent, passed the infamous Alien and Sedition Acts. We needn't spend time on the Alien Act, even though it gave the president power to remove aliens from the country, because it was not seriously enforced. The Sedition Act, however, was. The Act prohibited publication of false, scandalous, and malicious writing against the government, Congress or the president with intent to defame or bring them into contempt or disrepute!

John Adams was president, the federalists were in power, and they used the Sedition Act against members of the Republican Party because they were criticizing the Adams administration. Some journalists actually went to jail.

The prosecutions were flagrant (and unconstitutional) violations of the First Amendment. Recall Hamilton's position regarding the bill of rights controversy: "Why for instance, should it be said, that liberty of the press shall not be restrained, when no power is given in the constitution by which restrictions may be imposed?"

In response to the Sedition Act and its enforcement, the Republicans even more vigorously attacked the incumbent government. Writing under pseudonyms, Madison and Jefferson penned resolutions for the Virginia and Kentucky legislatures, arguing that the Alien and Sedition Acts be repealed at the next session of Congress.

In the Kentucky resolution, Jefferson relied on a classic "states' rights" position— actually a misnomer because states don't have rights, only powers; individuals have rights. Jefferson's objection to the Sedition Act wasn't so much that freedom of speech and liberty of the press were being trampled on. What bothered the primary author of the Declaration of Independence was that the trampling was being done by *federal* boots. Almost as an aside did he mention the First Amendment. The entire tenor of his remarks makes clear that he viewed the Acts as nothing more than a matter of "sealing the rights of the states" rather than expressing concern for the journalists who were being sent to jail.

In one of Jefferson's letters to Abigail Adams, he explained that his condemnation of the Sedition Act didn't come from his belief in the right to unrestrained comment in political affairs. Rather, "[t]he First Amendment reflected a limitation upon Federal power leaving *the right to enforce restrictions on speech* to the *states.*" (My emphasis.)

Compounding his secular apostasy, Jefferson held that some "well-placed prosecutions" of journalists might not be such a bad thing. In regard to the Alien and Sedition Acts, Jefferson's was a perverse kind of federalism, where the argument is over *which level* of the United States government, federal or state,

311

has the power to violate the Constitution—a phenomenon which, as we shall see later, has repeated itself throughout American constitutional history.

54 *The Works of Alexander Hamilton*, ed. by J. C. Hamilton, Vol. IV, p. 104 ff. Emphasis in original.

55 *The Writings of Thomas Jefferson*, ed. by H. E. Bergh, Vol. III, p. 145 ff. Emphasis in original.

56 Note that Marshall incorrectly quotes the Commerce Clause, substituting twice the word "or" for the Constitution's "and."

57 Because the Fourteenth Amendment did not reach *federal* action, in a companion case to *Brown* involving racial segregation in District of Columbia public schools, the Supreme Court ruled that the Due Process Clause of the Fifth Amendment, which applied to the federal government, possessed "equal protection content."

58 Hearings before the Senate Committee on Commerce on S. 1732, 88th Cong. 1st Sess., parts 1 and 2.

59 See Gerald Gunther, *Constitutional Cases and Materials*, 10th ed., p. 203. It's worth noting that neither the senators nor Professor Gunther objected to the "public accommodations" provision of the proposed Civil Rights Act as such. It was fine with them that private businesses operating locally could be required by the federal Congress to relinquish their racially motivated choices. As we've seen, the opposition was limited not to the *principle* at stake, but rather to the *constitutional* basis for the prohibition of private choice, preferring not the Commerce Clause but rather the Fourteenth Amendment (which could not have applied because of its state-action requirement).

60 Justice William O. Douglas concurred in *Katzenbach* v. *McClung*, confessing that for him there were no limits of any kind on the scope of the Commerce Clause—not since Congress, according to Douglas, possesses the "power to regulate commerce in the interests of *human rights*" (my emphasis). How far that power could extend is limited only by one's imagination, and by every real and supposed moral and other wrong afflicting our nation.

That said, there are two cases that provide some hope that today's barely conservative Supreme Court (Roberts, Scalia, Thomas, Alito and sometimes Kennedy) will impose limits on, if not cut back, the century-old metastasis of the Commerce Clause.

The first case involved the federal Gun-free School Zone Act of 1990. It prohibited possession of guns within 1,000 feet of schools (subject to some exceptions). In the Supreme Court, *United States* v. *Lopez* presented the question of whether the legislation, which by definition had only a local impact, was a legitimate exercise of a power by Congress under the Commerce Clause.

By a vote of 6–3, the Court ruled that it wasn't. In other words, it was unconstitutional. Justice Thomas's concurring opinion best explains why: "[t]he Court today properly concludes the Commerce Clause does not grant Congress the authority to prohibit gun possession within 1,000 feet of a school." However, he took the occasion "to observe that [the Court's] case law has drifted far from the original understanding of the Commerce Clause." His goal in writing separately, he said, was "simply to show how far we have departed from the original understanding and to demonstrate that the result we reach today is by no means 'radical' [as Justice Stevens's dissent asserted] . . . ."

313

Five years later, in *United States* v. *Morrison*, the Supreme Court held unconstitutional under the Commerce Clause a provision of the federal Violence Against Women Act that provided a civil remedy for victims of *intra*state rape. Once again Justice Thomas wrote a concurring opinion.

Although he agreed that in *Morrison* the majority had correctly applied *Lopez*, he objected to the perpetuation of a "substantial effects" test by which to measure Congress's power under the Commerce Clause: How much does the congressionally regulated activity affect Interstate Commerce? "[T]he very notion," he wrote, "is inconsistent with the original understanding of Congress' powers and with this Court's early Commerce Clause cases. By continuing to apply this rootless and malleable standard, however circumscribed, the Court has encouraged the Federal Government to persist in its view that the Commerce Clause has virtually no limits. *Until this Court replaces its Commerce Clause jurisprudence with a standard more consistent with the original understanding, we will continue to see Congress appropriating state . . . powers under the guise of regulating commerce.*" (My emphasis.)

This book is to be published on the Internet before the Supreme Court argument on the constitutionality of "Obamacare."

As to the mandate that American citizens purchase health insurance, I have said from the time the idea first surfaced that it's unconstitutional, certainly under *Lopez* and *Morrison*, let alone under an originalist decisional methodology.

Constitutional law aside, the mandate that Americans purchase medical insurance is not only an exercise in raw statism, it is yet another sacrifice of the interests of those who choose not to spend their money on medical insurance they don't want, to the

314

needs of others who, in lacking that insurance by choice, will have those who are insured pick up the bill.

Whatever other grounds are offered to sustain the individual mandate, it cannot be imposed under the Commerce Clause.

61 All legal challenges to conscription after 1918 were of a more limited nature, designed to test or clarify particular provisions, such as the religious exemption clause and the law's alleged "inequality" for exempting women—except one case unsuccessfully brought by me challenging the draft law under the Ninth Amendment.

62 These two cases are not the only examples of the altruist-collectivist ethics at work when the government exercises its war powers. Those ethics were invoked also as a justification for government to control economic affairs. I have noted in Chapter 2 President Truman's seizure of private steel mills during the Korean War, and the Court's disapproval only on the ground that he acted unilaterally. Had Congress agreed, the war power would have sufficed for the seizure of private property. It would not have been the first time. Nor the last.

In 1947, a federal law was enacted establishing certain forms of rent control in major United States cities. In the case of *Woods* v. *Miller,* the Supreme Court upheld the statute's constitutionality, pursuant to an Article I, section 8 power delegated to Congress. What power? The war power, of course. After all, there was a war, soldiers fought in it, when they returned home there was a scarcity of housing, *ergo* the war/war power was held to justify a federal rent control law.

63 Note that the Founders did not end the President's inaugural oath with the words "So help me God."

64 The Constitution also delegated to the president the power to request opinions (e.g., the Bank Controversy), to grant

reprieves and pardons (e.g., Bill Clinton and fugitive financier Mark Rich), to appoint specified public officials (e.g., "wise latina" Associate Justice of the Supreme Court Sonia Sotomayor) and to "take Care that the Laws be faithfully executed" (e.g., Barack Obama's refusal to enforce the federal Controlled Substance Act, thus allowing states like California and Colorado to ignore the Act's prohibition on growing, selling, purchasing, and using marijuana).

65 It should be noted that in *Curtiss-Wright,* the President was acting with the express approval of Congress. Justice Sutherland's approval of a broad presidential power over foreign relations would necessarily be tempered if a president acted in opposition to the will of Congress, as we saw earlier in the case of *Youngstown Sheet & Tube* v. *Sawyer* when President Truman seized the steel mills during the Korean War.

66 *The Heritage Guide to the Constitution*, p. 293.

67 "NICHEVO! The most common word in the Russian language is Nichevo. It just means 'Don't worry; let things take their course.'" *The New York Times Magazine*, March 17, 1918, p. 89.

68 The vote was 5–3 because Chief Justice John Roberts recused himself. He had ruled for the government while sitting on the United States Court of Appeals for the District of Columbia Circuit.

69 Justice Scalia dissented, emphasizing the jurisdictional issue. He noted that Justice Stevens could not find even one case "in the history of Anglo-American law (before today) in which a jurisdiction-stripping provision was denied immediate effect in pending cases, absent an explicit statutory reservation.

By contrast, the cases granting such immediate effect are legion . . . ."

Adverting to fundamental originalist principles, Scalia wrote that "[w]orst of all is the Court's reliance on the legislative history of the [Detainee Treatment Act] to buttress its implausible reading of §1005(e)(1). We have repeatedly held that such reliance is impermissible where, as here, the statutory language is unambiguous. * * * As always—but especially in the context of strident, partisan legislative conflict of the sort that characterized enactment of this legislation—the language of the statute that was actually passed by both Houses of Congress and signed by the President is our only authoritative and only reliable guidepost." In other words, the statute establishing jurisdiction was clear on its face, and that was that.

70 In some cases, the judge rather than a jury can be the decider of facts.

71 While the Tenth Circuit's decision was only on the ripeness issue, the balance of the Court's opinion dealt with the underlying constitutional free speech issue, even though it was not then before the court. The Court of Appeals remanded the case to the district court. But in the two-judge majority opinion they signaled very strongly their belief that the campaign finance law was unconstitutional, sending a clear signal to the trial judge that he had better declare it so because they didn't want to see the case back in their court again. Indeed, in their reversal they specified that their remand to the trial judge was "for proceedings not inconsistent with this opinion." The trial judge got the message, and on the remand did hold the statute unconstitutional.

72 The congressman was Bill Richardson, who later became

governor of New Mexico.

73 One of those real cases was another litigation of mine. The Federal Humane Slaughter Act was passed in 1957 and provides for the humane slaughter of livestock animals. When the legislation was pending, objections were made by Jewish groups that the proposed statute unconstitutionally interfered with their free exercise of religion because of the theological requirements of ritual slaughter. Hence, an exception was inserted into the bill exempting religious slaughter.

I was asked to challenge the exemption on constitutional grounds (that, in violation of the Establishment Clause of the First Amendment, the federal government preferred a religious practice over secular legal requirements).

I knew the government would argue that my plaintiffs lacked standing to sue. In those days, the standing requirement was that a plaintiff needed a distinct and palpable injury, and a fairly traceable causal connection between the injury and the conduct that was being challenged. Could he show a substantial likelihood that he would get relief if he won?

Who would that be? Who, arguably, had standing?

Because this was test-case litigation, the plaintiffs had to reflect a broad spectrum of parties arguably injured by the statute's religious exemption. Accordingly, I had plaintiffs who were Jews, non-Jews, vegetarians, vegans, meat eaters, atheists, agnostics, Christians. I even sued on behalf of "all livestock animals now and hereafter awaiting slaughter in the United States." As I recall, there were eleven individual plaintiffs, the animals, and several organizations and *ad hoc* committees. I pleaded all of these in the complaint, making the necessary standing allegations. Predictably, the government sought to dismiss the complaint on the ground that nobody had standing to sue.

In the end, the three-judge trial court finally threw in the towel on standing, ruling that *someone* among all my plaintiffs must have standing. Ultimately, the Supreme Court ruled that the statute was not unconstitutional. However, we would not have gotten even that substantive result had we not first surmounted the problem of standing to sue.

At about the same time, a group of standing cases arose in the lower federal courts arising from the Vietnam War, and in none of them did the courts recognize the plaintiffs' standing to sue.

A former congresswoman, Elizabeth Holtzman, sued the Secretary of Defense to enjoin the bombing of Cambodia. She was held both to lack standing (she wasn't being bombed) and to be presenting a political question.

In another case, *Harrington* v. *Schlesinger*, four congressmen sued the Secretary of Defense, claiming that the continued expenditure of funds anywhere in Indochina violated various federal laws. The federal court ruled they had only a generalized grievance, indistinguishable from those of all other citizens.

A few years later, Harrington was at it again, this time suing George H. W. Bush as Director of the CIA. This time, Harrington complained about allegedly illegal Central Intelligence Agency activities and appropriations. The United States Court of Appeals for the District of Columbia Circuit noted that Harrington's real quarrel was with his colleagues in the House of Representatives. No standing to sue, because ruling otherwise would "lead inevitably to the intrusion of the courts into the proper affairs of the coequal branches of government." So we see again that the standing-to-sue doctrine has its roots in separation of powers.

Senator Robert Dole, in *Dole* v. *Carter*, sued President Jimmy Carter, charging that Carter's agreement to return the religiously important crown of St. Stephen to Hungary was actually a treaty subject to Senate approval. The Supreme Court ruled that Dole had brought a non-justiciable political question. He also lacked standing to sue.

74 The final limitation on the exercise of judicial power—the seventh referred to above— is the doctrine of "adequate and independent state grounds," firmly derived from Article III.

Let's assume that somebody brings a case in a federal court and they have two claims. One is a federal constitutional claim; the other, a claim that there's a violation of state law.

If the case is disposed of on the state ground, and the ruling is independent of the federal ground, the Supreme Court will decline to review it. As Justice Robert Jackson explained, "[t]his court has always adhered to the principle that it will not review judgments of state courts that rest on adequate and independent state grounds. The reason is found in the partitioning of power between the state and federal judicial systems [federalism] and in the limitations of our own jurisdiction. Our only power over state judgments is to correct them to the extent that they incorrectly adjudge federal rights."

75 The case was argued in the Supreme Court on October 24, 1963. I remember the oral argument well because my wife and I were involved in the case to be argued on that day's calendar immediately following *Durfee* v. *Duke*.

76 A discussion of what constitutes jurisdiction is well beyond the scope of this book.

77 In 1863, Congress enacted a statute providing that during "the present rebellion" President Lincoln could suspend habeas corpus if he believed it was necessary. Recall that in the Guantanamo cases, neither the Military Commissions Act nor the Detainee Treatment Act, passed by Congress and signed by the President, was considered by the Supreme Court good enough reason to supplant the relief available to these enemy combatants through habeas corpus.

It would have been much better, when the President was delegated all that power immediately after 9/11 to fight the War on Terror, if Congress had given him the power to suspend habeas corpus within very narrow, carefully defined situations not affecting American citizens. If Congress had, the Guantanamo cases would likely have been decided differently.

78 The last paragraph of Article I Section 9 provides that "[n]o Title of Nobility shall be granted by the United States . . . ." As of now, the Supreme Court has not taken any case involving Duke Ellington, Count Basie, Lady Gaga, Queen Latifah, Barron Hilton, Earl Hines or the entertainer formerly known as Prince—let alone King Kong.

79 Article 1, Section 10 is replete with what states are prohibited from doing. For example, they can't enter into treaties, alliances, or confederations, which keeps them out of the federal domain of foreign affairs. They can't issue bills of credit or "make any Thing but gold and silver Coin a Tender in Payment of debts . . . .," to keep them out of the national monetary system.

80 When I quote Justice Thomas so often, I do so because he is the Supreme Court's leading originalist, and is very clear and correct on important subjects of constitutional law, especially individual rights and limited government.

81 A "starcher" was the term used in those days by the laundry industry for the employee whose job it was to apply starch to dress shirts. In the early 1900s, rarely were hand laundries firmly instructed, "No starch."

82 Ebenezer Scrooge did give the Gotcher family only a lump of coal. But, for the reason discussed in the text, despite Mrs. Gotcher's hard work (she eventually became head starcher), Tiny Tim did not get his sled for Christmas. The rest of Tiny Tim's sad story is well known.

83 This is the same rationale that underlay the monstrous program that would come a quarter century later in Nazi Germany.

On March 20, 2000, Joshua Hammer, an experienced journalist, wrote an article for *Newsweek International* entitled "Hitler's Children" subtitled "They were the offspring of a Nazi program to create a racially pure 'Master Race.'"

He wrote of a woman named Helga Kahrau:

> Her parents barely knew one another. An ardent Nazi, her mother met Helga's father, a German Army officer, in Berlin at a party celebrating Hitler's conquest of France in June 1940. They had a one-night stand, and nine months later Mathilde gave birth in a "Lebensborn," or "Source of Life," home outside Munich. The home was one of several set up by Heinrich Himmler's dreaded SS to care for *unmarried*

pregnant women whose racial characteristics, blond hair, blue eyes, no Jewish ancestry, fit the Nazis' Aryan ideal. At birth, Helga was anointed as one of the Fuhrer's elect, part of a generation of "racially pure" children who would populate the German Empire as it ruled a conquered Europe for the life of the 1,000-year Reich. (My emphasis.)

84 Under some draft acts and regulations, depending on one's religious requirements, a prospective draftee was either deferred (his service merely postponed, perhaps forever) or exempted (so he would never have to serve).

85 I want to reiterate that when a state case refers to a provision of the Bill of Rights (e.g., the "Establishment Clause" in *Zelman*), neither the litigants, the courts, nor I am speaking literally. *The Bill of Rights does not apply to the states.* It is the Fourteenth Amendment that applies to the states. References in state cases to the "First Amendment" or any other amendments is merely shorthand for the Due Process Clause of the Fourteenth Amendment.

86 To whatever extent the Mormon religion requires or countenances male practitioners of that faith marrying, or outside of marriage having sexual relations with, underage girls, that conduct should be condemned as immoral and prosecuted as a serious crime. Statutory rape is statutory rape, no matter if its motive is religious. Whatever sympathy one might have for Mormon religious practices should be reserved for consenting adults exercising a religious duty imposed under threat of eternal damnation, a duty one would think was protected by the express language of the First Amendment.

87 I dedicated an earlier book—*Speaking Freely: The Case Against Speech Codes*—to "Jacob Abrams, Joseph

Beauharnais, Walter Chaplinsky, F. J. Chrestensen, Eugene V. Debs, Ralph Ginzberg, Benjamin Gitlow, Charles T. Schenck, Charlotte Anita Whitney, and the too many others who offended merely by speaking words the authorities did not wish to hear. It matters not that some of those words may have been odious. Because the speakers were in America, they had a right to speak."

88 There have been several important political speech/ campaign finance law cases since *Shrink Missouri Government*, but they don't add anything to the subject and theme of this book. Suffice it to say that both the state and federal governments are knee deep in regulating political speech in general and electoral speech in particular—and for the same reasons we've seen so far throughout this book. Almost always there is more at work with legislatures and courts than simply speech considerations. Indeed, what happens in speech cases, as in all others, is ultimately determined by ethical considerations, even if most of the players involved are not consciously aware of that.

89 "Decision creep" is my name for judicial decisions that keep extending the principles of those which preceded it.

90 So much for the liberals who, when the *Hudson* decision came down, lambasted Thomas wrongly—and viciously—for being indifferent to physical abuse of a prisoner.

91 Some of the following discussion of the Cruel and Unusual Punishments Clause is taken *verbatim* from pages 119–122, including Notes, of *The Supreme Court Opinions of Clarence Thomas, 1991–2011*, published in 2012 by McFarland & Company, Inc. of Jefferson, North Carolina.

92 The Supreme Court remanded the case to the federal district

court, "to provide an opportunity for McKinney to prove his allegations, which will require him to prove both the subjective ['deliberate indifference'] and objective [actual injury] elements necessary to prove an Eighth Amendment violation." In addition, on remand "the prisoner must show that the risk of which he complains is not one that today's society chooses to tolerate."

93 Thomas quoted the historically correct spelling.

94 The Eighth Amendment language is "cruel *and* unusual" punishments.

95 Footnote omitted.

96 This is an important insight into responsible jurisprudence. Even though Thomas believed the *Estelle* precedent to be wrong, he also believed that the principle of *stare decisis* exists as an important limitation on judicial activism, cautioning hesitancy in overruling prior cases. However, as his dissent makes clear, he draws the line at *extending* a wrongly decided precedent.

97 In *Overton* v. *Bazzetta*, for the reasons he gave in *Hudson*, Justice Thomas reiterated that the Eighth Amendment's Cruel and Unusual Punishments Clause was limited to a criminal case's *sentence*: "[R]egulations pertaining to visitations are not punishment within the meaning of the Eighth Amendment.

98 Illinois State Register, January 7, 1863.

99 Later, New Jersey and Oregon actually rescinded their ratifications.

100 There was another Civil Rights Act in 1875 that included

anti-discrimination provisions for public accommodations (inns, hotels, theaters, railroads and their "ladies" cars). It was held unconstitutional in the 1883 *Civil Rights Cases*. This was private, not government, racial discrimination.

101 No justice, not even Justice John Marshall Harlan in *Plessy* v. *Ferguson*, and certainly not Chief Justice Earl Warren in *Brown* v. *Board of Education* (I), has written more cogently and passionately about modern Supreme Court decisions on the subject of race. Some of the following discussion is taken *verbatim* from pages 149–156, including Notes, of *The Supreme Court Opinions of Clarence Thomas, 1991–2011*, published in 2012 by McFarland & Company, Inc. of Jefferson, North Carolina.

102 Here, Justice Thomas inserted a footnote: "It should be obvious that *every racial classification helps, in a narrow sense, some races and hurts others.* As to the races benefitted, the classification could surely be called "benign." Accordingly, whether a law relying upon racial taxonomy is "benign" or "malign" . . . either turns on "whose ox is gored" . . . or on distinctions found only in the eye of the beholder." (My emphasis.)

103 *Brown* (I), the "desegregation decision," is differentiated from *Brown* (II), which was the 'implementation" decision.

104 Ayn Rand, "A Nation's Unity," *The Ayn Rand Letter*, Vol. II, No. 2, p. 3, October 9, 1972.

The American Constitution and Ayn Rand's "Inner Contradiction"
**and other titles by
Professor Holzer
are also available as
Kindle e-books on Amazon**

http://amzn.to/AmericanConstitution-Rands-Contradiction

Professor Holzer's website is www.henrymarkholzer.com;

He blogs at www.henrymarkholzer.blogspot.com; and can be

contacted by e-mail at hank@henrymarkholzer.com.